EXTREMITIES

EXTREMITIES

Trauma, Testimony,
and Community

Edited by Nancy K. Miller
and Jason Tougaw

UNIVERSITY OF ILLINOIS PRESS
URBANA AND CHICAGO

♾ This book is printed on acid-free paper.
Library of Congress Cataloging-in-Publication Data
Extremities : trauma, testimony, and community /
edited by Nancy K. Miller and Jason Tougaw.
p.   cm.
Includes bibliographical references and index.
ISBN 0-252-02743-4 (cloth : alk. paper)
ISBN 0-252-07054-2 (paper : alk. paper)
1. Victims—Biography—History and criticism.
2. Autobiography.
3. Psychic trauma.
4. Suffering.
HV6250.25.E9   2002
809'.93592—dc21   2001005921

Contents

EXTREMITIES

Introduction: Extremities

Nancy K. Miller and Jason Tougaw

> **extremity 1:** something that is extreme: as **a** (1): an outlying or terminal part, section or point: the farthest or most remote part, section, or point: the most advanced part: the farthest extent: the farthest projection: the very end (2): a limb (as of the body) or other appendage: an arm or leg; *usu:* a hand or foot **b** (1): a condition of extreme urgency or necessity: a highly crucial state of affairs: a time of extreme danger or critical need: extreme adversity (2): a moment marked by imminent destruction or dissolution **c** (1): an extremely intense degree (2): a culminating point (3): *archaic* extreme severity or rigor **d** *obs* an instance or act of extravagant behavior **e** the fullest possible extent: utmost limit: utmost degree **f** (1): a very severe, violent, drastic, or desperate act or measure (2): a single remaining source of help or plan of action: sole recourse: final resort **2:** the quality or state of being extreme—**in extremities:** at the end of one's resources: in a most crucial or dangerous condition or position: at the point of death—**to the last extremity:** to the point of death: to the death.
>
> —excerpted from *Webster's Third New International Dictionary* (unabridged), 1968.

"The old century," historian Eric Hobsbawm remarks in *The Age of Extremes,* "has not ended well" (17). Looking back from the fragile perspective of the new millennium, it would be hard not to feel staggered by the inventory of catastrophic human suffering Hobsbawm has drawn. Consciously or unconsciously, we live in the wake of the atrocities brought by war and genocide, in the long shadow cast by their prolonged aftermath.

If every age has its symptoms, ours appears to be the age of trauma. Naming a wide spectrum of responses to psychic and physical events often with little in common beyond the label, trauma has become a portmanteau that covers a multitude of disparate injuries. Stories that would seem to belong to different orders of experience enjoy troubling intimacies. But whatever their origin, the effects of historical trauma have a tenacious hold on the popular imagination.

The term "trauma" describes the experience of both victims—those who have suffered directly—and those who suffer with them, or through them, or for them, if only by reading about trauma. Literary works, in particular the memoir, recently and in great number have turned to narratives that record for public consumption the personal strain on the body and the mind produced by certain kinds of extreme suffering, from the annihilatory technologies of the Holocaust to the devastation of AIDS. We've become accustomed in American culture to stories of pain, even addicted to them; and as readers (or viewers), we follow, fascinated (though as many profess disgust), the vogue of violent emotion and shocking events.

In a culture of trauma, accounts of extreme situations sell books. Narratives of illness, sexual abuse, torture, or the death of loved ones have come to rival the classic, heroic adventure as a test of limits that offers the reader the suspicious thrill of borrowed emotion. The private zones of the body have migrated into public domains and the limits of tellable experience have expanded, almost dissolving the border of the conventional markers that separated the private self from the public citizen. What does it mean, Ross Chambers asks in this volume, "to be haunted by a collective memory . . . of painful events that few, if any, living members of the culture may have directly perpetrated or suffered from in their own persons?" As the boundaries break down, our ideas about the workings of historical memory and events necessarily change, even if we don't fully understand the implications of these new biographical models and modes of identification.

The urge to break the silence and ignore taboos about the life (and increasingly, death) of the body that drives many of these stories shows no sign of remission. The successful, sometimes ingenious, and often crude, marketing of vicarious suffering owes something but not everything to the triumph of the memoir (and biography)—the emotional appeal of the true story. But the remarkable renewal of autobiographical writing in the late twentieth century is not solely a feature of wide-scale narcissism or the idioms of identity politics. The culture of first-person writing needs to be understood in relation to a desire for common grounds—if not an identity-bound shared experience, then one that is shareable through identification, though this too will vary in degrees of proximity. The memoir and all forms of personal testimony not only expand the boundaries of identity construction and the contours of the self but also lay claim to potential territories of community. In complex and often unexpected ways, the singular "me" evolves into a plural "us" and writing that bears witness to the extreme experiences of solitary individuals can sometimes begin to repair the tears in the collective social fabric.

Most retrospective views of twentieth-century history assign the Holocaust a privileged place as the paradigmatic event of unspeakable human suffering, of lives lost in extremity over the course of what Hobsbawm calls the "Short Twentieth Century," 1914–91 (3). The Holocaust has also become, especially in recent years, the focus of a great deal of contemporary thinking and writing about the nature of extreme experience. Despite the troubled debates over the ethics of representing the Holocaust at all, the rich library of Holocaust texts, the archive of historical documents, and the monuments memorializing the crisis of inhumanity that fractured the century have generated both aesthetic appreciation (alternately dismay) and critical analysis.

The commercial success of movies like *Schindler's List* and *Life Is Beautiful* made it possible for large audiences to take pleasure in—or at least be comfortably moved by—the Holocaust as spectacle. This phenomenon has continued with the box-office triumph of Mel Brooks's musical comedy *The Producers,* featuring "Springtime for Hitler," the song and dance number already notorious from Brooks's 1968 movie version. In the same entertainment season (springtime 2001), Anne Frank's story, produced by the Walt Disney company, was shown on network television. The postmodern disconnect of a Disney version of the Holocaust conjures the scene in Art Spiegelman's *Maus* where Vladek Spiegelman imagines that his Holocaust survivor story, drawn by his son the cartoonist, could make Art as famous as Walt Disney (I, 133). Such is the unpredictable legacy of history reworked by contemporary culture. As we write this introduction in 2001, the "famous joke" referred to by one of the characters in Philip Roth's 1993 *Operation Shylock*—"'There's no business like *Shoah* business'" (133)—is still a propos. Indeed, the unprecedented success of Holocaust suffering marketed for mass consumption and popular entertainment seems to know no limits.

For postwar generations Anne Frank's *Diary of a Young Girl* has represented the so-called triumph of the human spirit in extremity, the universalizing symbol of Jewish Holocaust experience. This girl who feared she would never grow up to become a woman left behind a text that became an international best-seller, subjected to successive editions as well as theatrical and film adaptations. (In the wake of a recent television mini-series, Amazon.com offered an interactive CD-ROM visit to the Anne Frank House.) Victor Klemperer's recently published diaries, *I Will Bear Witness,* offer a less comfortable (and infinitely longer) record of a European life despoiled by Nazi domination. This two-volume account of Klemperer's years (1933–45) spent in progressive degradation in Dresden documents the devastating effects of life under critical conditions from the point of view of a mature man, a Jew who had been baptized a Protestant (I, viii). In the passage below, Klemperer describes the stakes of writing and hiding the diary, whose pages his Aryan wife periodically secreted for safekeeping:

> This afternoon Eva is going to Pirna to fetch some money. I shall give her the diary pages of the last few weeks to take with her. After the house search I found several books, which had been taken off the shelf, lying on the desk. If one of them had been the Greek dictionary, if the manuscript pages had fallen out and had thus aroused suspicion, it would undoubtedly have meant my death. One is murdered for lesser misdemeanors. [. . .] So these parts will go today. But I shall go on writing. That is *my* heroism. I will bear witness, precise witness! (II, 61)

Unlike Anne Frank, Victor Klemperer survived and so did his diaries, though they were discovered and published only after his death. But in each case, the author's literary ambitions were posthumously fulfilled, the gift for writing recognized. Both diaries serve as reminders not just of past history but of the cost more generally of living in history; the entries chart for us the small acts of daily bravery that constitute a single human being's resistance to political violence. Anne Frank's diary, Melissa Müller claims, is "the most widely read document about the Nazi crimes" (ix). *I Will Bear Witness* has only begun its journey.

If the Holocaust supplies the paradigm of modern, incommensurable suffering, many of the ethical and aesthetic, moral and formal dilemmas involved in bearing witness to the horrors of the Holocaust reappear and are reconfigured in different national and political contexts. This is not to suggest that other kinds of disaster should be compared in literal ways to the Holocaust as a limit event. Rather, as the essays collected here show, the Holocaust has produced a discourse—a set of terms and debates about the nature of trauma, testimony, witness, and community—that has affected other domains of meditation on the forms the representation of extreme human suffering seems to engender and require.

In a study of W. E. B. Du Bois's trip to the Warsaw Ghetto in 1949, Michael Rothberg argues for a more dialogic approach to the question of the relationship between studies of the Holocaust and those of other traumatic events that have shaped and continue to shape Western history, without "collapsing the Nazi genocide into the banal litany of modern catastrophes." As he shows, a kind of double vision, analogous to Du Bois's famous "double consciousness," makes it possible to see the Holocaust in its atrocious specificity. The paradox is only apparent. "Pursuing the question of race and violence in a comparative framework," Rothberg suggests, "would allow Holocaust studies to benefit from a relaxation of the border patrol that too often surrounds and isolates discussion of the *Shoah*" (186). By the same token, to bring analyses of Holocaust-related material into other studies of extreme experience across a broad range of historically located contexts, as we have done in this book, also helps clarify the unique texture of each situation.

If, moreover, the Holocaust in our time stands not only *for* memory but for what is owed *to* memory, then that lesson should lead us to a more intense awareness of what implicates us in the lives of others. It is far easier, even seductive, to memorialize past injustice, to weep over human crimes of another era, than to take responsibility for what's before our eyes. "When I began thinking about this text," Annie Ernaux observes in her personal narrative *Shame,* "the market square in Sarajevo suffered a mortar attack that killed several dozen people and wounded hundreds of others. In the written press some journalists wrote, 'we are overcome by shame.' For them, shame was something they could feel one day and not the next, something that applied to one situation (Bosnia) and not another (Rwanda). No one remembers the blood shed on the market place in Sarajevo" (110). The shame of our modernity is due in part to the ease with which world horror seems to vanish before our very eyes.

It's often difficult to stay focused on what should demand attention or action, to resist turning the page. *Against Forgetting: Twentieth-Century Poetry of Witness,* Carolyn Forché's stunning anthology that begins with "The Armenian Genocide (1909–1918)" and ends with "Revolutions and the Struggle for Democracy in China (1991)," offers a map of the world meant to counter a collective amnesia about the history we live through, often without paying the daily reports of its horrors too much mind. The poems Forché has assembled, she writes, all "bear the trace of extremity within them" (30). The poets did not all survive, but their works "remain with us as poetic witness to the dark times in which they lived" (29). We often prefer to read about "dark times," rather than doing anything about them. And yet reading is not without its own burdens. In "Consuming Trauma," Patricia Yaeger scans the morning newspaper and wonders: "I'm horror-struck reading an article about Mexico, or Dakar, or Des Moines, or Dubuque and then I glance at a body clothed by Lord and Taylor and feel reprieve (or anger, or desire, or bare nausea)."

Dominick LaCapra has coined the expression "empathic unsettlement" to describe the desired response of the "secondary witness"—historians like himself or literary critics like Yaeger, ordinary readers and viewers (thinking of movies like *Shoah* and *Schindler's List*)—who may and perhaps should empathize with the victims of atrocity, but without taking on, even in imagination, in "a kind of virtual experience," their identity ("Trauma" 722). The "secondary witness," he argued earlier, in an essay about Claude Lanzmann's film *Shoah,* "should reactivate and transmit not trauma but an unsettlement . . . that manifests empathy (but not full identification) with the victim" (267). The challenge to those who read and write about trauma is to acknowledge its power and domains and also to let it rest: one should "neither confuse one's own voice or position with the victim's nor seek facile uplift, harmonization, or closure" ("Trauma" 723). Trauma has its historical specificity that must be respected. This cautionary formulation entails another: "not everyone traumatized by events is a victim" (723), LaCapra remarks, referring to the perpetrators of crimes against humanity. In an analogous argument about the importance of keeping distinctions when discerning the nature of traumatic experience, Juliet Mitchell in *Mad Men and Medusas* makes the following, sure to be controversial, claim: "although the Holocaust is one of the most grotesque events known to mankind, this does not automatically qualify it as traumatic in itself. . . . Too often cruelty and trauma are made to be synonymous" (299).

Whatever theory of trauma one embraces, there's no escaping the promiscuous application of the diagnostic, which tends to universalize suffering with little attention paid to the singularity of the experience: "In an everyday context," Mitchell writes, "we tend to look at a range of difficult or tragic occurrences from an observer's point of view and label them 'traumatic.' Instead, I want to define trauma from the perspective of the person who experiences it" (298).

By definition, memoir, autobiographical fiction, poetry, and personal criticism devoted to life lived in extremities all tell a story about trauma from the perspective of the person who experiences it. They share what Mitchell calls "some lowest common denominator" (298). But should some experiences count for more on the scale of suffering, when evaluated according to a measurement that places surviving the Holocaust in a universe of its own? In this book we've decided to run the risk of juxtaposition, without, however, seeking to make literal comparisons. A memoir about the camps like Ruth Klüger's, or Sandra Gilbert's prose elegy about her husband's sudden death; Kathryn Harrison's literary confession of father/daughter incest or Annie Ernaux's unveiling of a family's disgraceful bodies; Eve Sedgwick's autobiographical advice columns in *MAMM* or the testimony in memoir form of men dying of AIDS; photographs of female-to-male transsexuals or the testimony of massacre survivors; all share the burden of narrating the extreme, of giving shape to what once seemed overwhelming, incomprehensible, and formless. These traumatic records all bear witness to whatever experience has broken "through the subject's protective shield" (Mitchell 291). We've chosen to retain the word "trauma" despite its potential overuse because it enfolds the diverse accounts of broken boundaries that are the subject of this book.

The task of reading the reports of extreme events that constellate the history of the twentieth century requires an adjustment of our skills as readers. These essays are concerned primarily with literary and visual representations of traumatic experience in a variety of forms, an experience that "in its sheer extremity," as Ruth Leys characterizes it, constitutes an "affront to common norms and expectations" (298). Thus, faced with the literary effects of what Rothberg has called "traumatic realism," the disorientation that attends the reader's arrival in a universe that violates all expectations, we are forced to reexamine the troubling conjuncture of the extreme and the everyday. An "epistemological and a social category," as Rothberg defines it in his present essay, this concept offers a new way of looking at the stakes of Holocaust representation, at how testimonial writing—about the Holocaust but also other occasions of atrocity—holds together on the page what the mind tends to keep apart. But if Rothberg elucidates the textual operations of what might appear to be a linguistic or mimetic predicament, he also insists on the work representation performs on—or perhaps in—the reader as a kind of pedagogy. The "traumatic realist project" produces something like a document whose origin belongs to the past (and those who died in it) but whose effects belong both to the present and the future—to the living readers whose post-traumatic responsibilities are both retrospective and prospective.

In the case of Ruth Klüger's memoir or Victor Klemperer's diaries the reader might imagine she has gained direct access to those extreme death-bearing sites and everyday scenes of violence. But that would be to miss the gap that always separates language from reference as does the space between a train and the platform, to invoke a haunting Holocaust image. Like the traveler, the reader on the heels of the writer's experience must always be wary of the space that makes the journeying possible in the first place—lest we stumble, which of course we must.

At the same time, moreover, despite the record of witness there are those who believe that the Shoah defies representation. "Whoever assumes the charge of bearing witness in their name," declares Giorgio Agamben in *Remnants of Auschwitz* of the survivors who escaped the ranks of the dead, "knows that he or she must bear witness in the name of the impossibility of bearing witness" (34). As Art Spiegelman's therapist in *Maus* sorrowfully maintains: "Anyway, the victims who died can never tell *their* side of the story, so maybe it's better not to have any more stories" (II, 45). And yet the stories keep coming and keep getting read. Why should this be so? As Arendt concludes in *Eichmann in Jerusalem,* about the will of totalitarian domination to have its victims disappear without a trace: "The holes of oblivion do not exist. . . . One man will always be left alive to tell the story" (232–33).

The problem of transmission does not diminish for those who survive the survivors—and their stories. The challenge entailed in finding a form in which to represent extreme experience involves a related yet distinct set of issues for the children of survivors and those of their generation within whom the story, however it is told, lives on. Marianne Hirsch has named this phenomenon "postmemory": "identification with the victim or witness of trauma, modulated by an admission of an unbridgeable distance separating the participant from the one born after." Through mediated acts of identification, the subjects of postmemory can revisit the past in relation to a previous generation (Art Spiegelman and his father and mother, to choose a well-known example); postmemory also entails reaching across genetic and familial ties to the experience of others to whom one is not related by blood, but whose story in life or art has the power to pierce the membrane of self-definition.

Writers and artists of the post-Holocaust generation have come to embody, as they refigure, an experience not theirs and yet a part of a historical legacy that touches them deeply. Like the mark under the breast of the mother of Toni Morrison's character Sethe in *Beloved,* the tattoo on the arm of a camp survivor functions as the sign of traumatic experience retained on the skin and in the body. Morrison's novel tells a story of intergenerational transmission, demonstrating the daughter's responsibility in the recognition of another's suffering. How should a daughter acknowledge the effect of her mother's trauma? Hirsch's "empathic aesthetics" give a feminist inflection to LaCapra's notion of "empathic unsettlement"—a protocol of looking and feeling that keeps remembrance open and porous but also bounded and closed to further penetration.

Trauma, one could say, never happens only once. "The story of trauma," Cathy Caruth has argued in her reading of traumatic temporality, should be understood as "the narrative of a belated experience," and in that sense also can be followed through "its endless impact on a life" (7). A phenomenon of delayed response, trauma often unfolds intergenerationally; its aftermath lives on in the family—but no less pervasively in the culture at large. The story can deeply affect those who have not stood directly in the path of historical trauma, who do not share bloodlines with its victims. The question of how a poet transmits the memory of the Holocaust takes a famously troubling turn when like Plath she imagines herself to be the daughter of a Nazi father. Sylvia Plath's poems "Daddy," "Lady Lazarus," and "Getting There," and, as we'll see, Binjamin Wilkomirksi's narrative, *Fragments,* provide striking examples of how in particular the collective trauma of the Shoah crosses national and genetic borders and continues to permeate post-Holocaust culture.

Do you have to be Jewish, Plath's poetry might be seen to ask, do you need a biographical connection to the Holocaust, to feel close to the victims, to imagine their journeys to suffering and oblivion, to figure in language and through poetic devices the suicide of prisoners and survivors? These literary works, each symptomatic of its particular historical moment, raise in acute form the question of what the proper relation between any individual and the legacy of the Shoah might be. Plath's critics were outraged by the poet's use of Holocaust material to express personal suffering: "how dare she presume to imagine herself as one of the victims?" To make heard the stories of the imagined dead, Plath deploys the rhetorical trope of prosopopoeia. The figure reveals the uses and abuses of empathy. On the one hand, simulating the voices of those who are absent may be interpreted as a productive act of empathy. Prosopopoeia, Susan Gubar argues in this volume, provides a "haunting surrogate" to the fate to which a post-Holocaust writer might have been destined. On the other, Plath's poetry also offers "a critique of the lure of empathy," seen as a "ruse . . . of identification."

Even more acutely than Plath's poetry, Binjamin Wilkomirski's "memoir" forces sticky ethical questions. Wilkomirski's bestseller *Fragments* was praised to the skies for being uncannily authentic before being denounced as a fraud. Anyone who read the book before the imposture of its author was exposed in 1998 will remember the shock that came from the harrowing description of a child's nightmare in a concentration camp. Now the shock comes from the fact of Holocaust appropriation. "Being an extreme case," Susan Suleiman observes, "*Fragments* poses certain questions starkly: . . . To whom does the memory of the Holocaust belong?" (554). The scandal of this affair points to the extreme difficulty of adjudicating the ownership of collective memory faced with the extraordinary malleability of empathy in contemporary culture. Rather than bar non-Jews or non-survivors from access to this memory as though it were copyright, as readers (not to say citizens) we have the task of sorting out the feelings of uneasiness some experience when ownership appears threatened. When shock leads to total dismissal, the legacy of the Holocaust as a more broadly human, mind- and body-shattering catastrophe, one could argue, is also threatened.

Meditating on the Wilkomirski/Dössekker border crossing, Ross Chambers examines the process by which an individual may come to "confuse the collective historical consciousness concerning outrageous events with painful personal memories; and to confuse them to the point of being *inhabited* (i.e., haunted) by the events *as though* he or she had actually lived through them." As Gubar demonstrates in the case of Plath's poetry, empathy in representations of extreme experience operates from two interrelated positions: the writer's relation to the material she wishes to convey and the reader's response. In *Fragments,* whose narrative obeys the formal properties of asyndeton (a rhetorical figure that operates through the omission of certain logical connections), readers supply the missing pieces. Asyndeton, Chambers argues, is "a privileged figure of Holocaust witnessing" because readers must make a connection to what's described by finding a place of pain in themselves to which they may relate a suffering they probably have not experienced; remembering *with* the other in this bodily (and yet rhetorical) way is an intense form of "reader involvement." Like postmemory, this involvement entails a double movement of recognition: what joins one to the victim and what separates. Faced with the gaps and incompletion of testimony, readers fill in the blanks from their own storehouses of memory and "phantom pain." Through this traffic of affective connection between writer and reader, individual attachment may serve to balance an overwhelming sense of collective loss that is not restricted to the Holocaust; it also characterizes, Chambers suggests, AIDS testimonial writing. At the same time, however, whatever the attachment between writer and reader, there remains in every act of witness a place of opacity, what Agamben calls a "lacuna," that cannot be illuminated or put into language (39). In the same way, prosopopoeia may conjure the dead but no figure of speech can ever bring back the missing bodies or their words.

"*Why has testimony,*" Shoshana Felman asks, "*become at once so central and so omnipresent in our recent cultural accounts of ourselves?*" (Felman and Laub 6). If every century has been marked by extreme experience, it has become almost compulsory in ours to document the disaster. It's as though we "feel a need to record everything," Geoffrey Hartman observes, "even as the event is occurring" (*Longest Shadow* 106). Whatever the temporal relation to the event (on the spot or after the fact); whatever the medium (video, film, memoir, fictional or critical confession, public testimony or legal deposition); and whatever the degrees of emotional involvement; we bear witness individually for ourselves, our own sake, but always in relation to others (again, both individually and in the name of a community). In that process, the act of testimony also becomes a speech act and draws meaning from its effects on the listener. Acts of witness bind teller and listener through what Wendy Chun in "Unbearable Witness" calls a "contract of listening" (this contract is not unlike the one binding writer and reader in autobiographical acts although these are not formally, as we'll see, the same activity). "For the testimonial process to take place," explains Dori Laub, "there needs to be a bonding, the intimate and total presence of an *other*—in the position of one who hears. Testimonies are not monologues; they cannot take place in solitude. The witnesses are talking *to somebody*: to somebody they have been waiting for for a long time" (Felman and Laub 70–71). Testimony attempts to bridge the gap between suffering individuals and ultimately communities of listeners, whose empathic response can be palliative, if not curative.

Practicing analyst and active participant in the Video Archive for Holocaust Testimonies at Yale, Laub is in many ways the ideal listener—trained in the art of attentiveness, and self-conscious about his role. In the world at large, however, ideal listeners and settings seldom appear. And even Laub's model is vulnerable to the power of defenses entailed in receiving the story. "A sense of outrage," "a flood of awe and fear," "foreclosure through facts," and "hyperemotionality" (72–73) all can interfere with the testimonial act. The transmission of a witness's story is therefore doubly complicated, first by the witness's own degree of temporal, spatial, and emotional distance from what is being documented, and second, by the listener's reactions.

Inevitably, the nature of testimonial dynamics varies as it engages with the emotional logic of different historical situations, even while displaying many of the characteristics of those delineated by Laub: the fraught interaction of witness and listener; the quest for words commensurate with experience; the creation of metaphors to compensate for the failure of language faced with the exorbitance of the literal; the exposure of private suffering to establish modes of negotiation between the intimate and public; all of which—ideally—result in the formation of "an affective community" (Hartman, Interview 220) that can encompass both witnesses and listeners.

Sometimes listeners can be too powerful. Even testimony that garners a vast and sympathetic audience, like that of Zivia Lubetkin, a young Polish Zionist who witnessed the 1943 Warsaw Ghetto uprising, can be received in such a way that the experience of the testifier gets lost in the process. Orly Lubin retells Lubetkin's story, arguing that she sacrificed herself to the Zionist cause by reshaping her words and her delivery to make them palatable for interlocutors struggling to unite a ravaged diaspora and build a nation. Zionist leaders literally rehearsed the degradation out of her speech and the tears out of her delivery, until her account became satisfactorily coherent and uplifting. What remains of Lubetkin's performance are thirty-five seconds of film that itself bears witness to the transformation of flesh into symbol. A woman's body became heroic, raised to the national scale. By definition testimony, in particular the genre of *testimonio,* always unites individual and collective in the testifying body. Zivia Lubetkin, Lubin argues, "had no interest in the 'I'—neither in its uniqueness, nor in its relations with the others." As a result, however willingly, Lubetkin was biographically effaced between the past she endured and the future envisioned by the Zionist movement.

If testimony about traumatic experience always has a double function, both producing social discourse and initiating individual recovery, these two effects do not necessarily coincide. In Lubetkin's case, the building of an ideological discourse took precedence over personal healing. In these foundational moments of nationhood, Zionists were not ready to highlight the trauma of individual shock, of one person's lived experience. Rather they sought to integrate personal experience within its fragile borders, reshaping narrative within its demands for a heroic history, and seek-

ing to overcome the recent catastrophes to the Jewish peoples. Subsequently, in keeping with "the upbeat and universalist postwar mood," the Warsaw Ghetto uprising, Peter Novick argues in *The Holocaust in American Life,*
was made into "the central symbol of the Holocaust" (114-15).

Testimony records a movement from individual experience to the
collective archive, from personal trauma to public memory. But when
testimony located on a national stage is riven by conflicting aims among
those bearing witness, such a transformation is impeded. This is evident
in the debates between feminists and postfeminists that ensued after the
1989 massacre at Montreal's École Polytechnique. Even though the killer, Marc Lepine, explicitly targeted female students—killing six of them—
citing hatred for feminists as his motivation, the political resonance of the
violence was obscured by the divided response to the horror. The drive to
testify, Chun shows, was frustrated by a persistent dissension between
survivors who identified themselves as feminist and those who did not;
while some sought healing in the effects of public speech, others demanded privacy. The debate initiated a battle over how to interpret the events
and how to recover from the trauma they produced, a battle never resolved. In Chun's view, the goal of testimony is not "to cure either the
speaker or the listener but rather to respond and listen so that survival is
possible." For some individual healing may indeed have resulted from
speaking out, but that healing was not recorded in any collective response.
In effect, the social discord that emerged in response to the massacre in
the first place resolved itself on the side of a collective agreement to restore
the status quo.

In memoir form or public debate, questions of testimony can fracture
communities of fellow-sufferers along ideological lines, divide as well as
bridge. When a memoir records a trauma occurring in the present, as AIDS
memoirs do, readers are fragmented into those who feel at risk and those
who disavow it, separating themselves from the writer of the testimony.
In AIDS memoirs, Jason Tougaw shows, what connects reader and writer
is the risk for infection—so that listening involves tolerating an elaborate
exegesis of AIDS symptoms, both bodily and social. AIDS memoirs written
from within the epicenter of the pandemic during the period (roughly
1985-95) when AIDS was, however wrongly, still primarily associated with
gay men, asked readers to confront their own anxieties. Reading about HIV
re-enacts the disconcerting chain of transmission charted by the virus itself. The trauma that compels the testimony creates a community of readers through their shared vulnerability. When trauma continues in the

present, readers find themselves implicated beyond the page. Listening may be necessary for survival, but reading AIDS memoirs means avowing what healthy readers would prefer to disavow: the threat of the virus.

Writing about illness in a public forum creates the possibility of community. The intimate tone of "Off My Chest" (beginning with its title), Eve Kosofsky Sedgwick's witty advice column in *MAMM* magazine, implies a shared, if not collective, struggle, through her own experience of living with the disease of breast cancer. Sedgwick offers concrete, subjective, empathic, and opinionated advice for women overwhelmed by the practical politics of breast cancer treatment. The column's publication in *MAMM* (importantly, the sister-publication of *POZ*, a magazine for the HIV community), whose explicit aim is to establish a breast cancer community, means that ideally the readership will include healthcare professionals, therapists and social workers, and family members of women with breast cancer. Sedgwick speaks with the authority of the patient and the commitment of a longtime feminist critic willing to risk exposure and the language of commonality: "But listen, here's the bottom line. . . . The only certainties are that you will have feelings, and that over time even the strongest of them will change and change again. . . . That's what being alive means."

We've been making an argument about the role testimony plays in the construction of community and collective identity; we've also been emphasizing the public spaces in which private anguish is brought into the public record and into public memory. Weighing the merits of "writing wrong," seeking the widest context for her story, Sandra Gilbert concludes that "anyone who has suffered the shock of what is experienced as a wrongful death has had to engage with what it is impossible to tell yet somehow essential to speak, if only stammeringly." To tell the story is to attempt, as Gilbert describes the process here, "to relieve the pain of reliving the pain," to write the "untellable grief." Traumatic experience, in this sense, is silenced pain that demands a voicing—and a hearing. But is everything good to tell?

Writing wrong is an attempt to right wrongs, to refuse to keep private, solitary suffering locked away, to put one's story into the public domain, to take it out of the bosom of the family it has wounded and place it in a discourse that makes the story shareable with others. "'You must not tell anyone,' my mother said, 'what I am about to tell you'" is the first line of Maxine Hong Kingston's *The Woman Warrior* (3). "'*You better not never tell nobody but God. It'd kill your mammy*'" is the injunction for a daughter not to tell that hangs as an epigraph in italics over Alice Walker's epistolary novel, *The Color Purple* (11). These two immensely successful texts (non-fiction and fiction) by twentieth-century women writers who refuse to remain silent record the stakes of revelation, make public narratives of what was meant to remain shrouded in privacy. Both literary works, King-Kok Cheung shows, bear witness to a dare: "to listen to their own pains, to report the ravages, and, finally, to persist in finding strengths from sources that have caused inestimable anguish" (172). The family, feminist theorists have shown, as an apparently safe scene of private life, can be dangerous to girls and women. The desire to report the crime, to tell all, and in particular to violate the conspiracies of silence and shame that constrain girls' voices, also resides at the heart of Kathryn Harrison's notorious memoir *The Kiss* and Annie Ernaux's *Shame.*

Contemporary chronicles of the self refuse the limits of decorum rather than restrict the project of uncovery. The confessional memoir makes the private public—secrets, fantasies, taboos. Freud believed that the secret lives of the mind offend if revealed unmediated: "The day-dreamer carefully conceals his phantasies from other people because he feels he has reasons for being ashamed of them. I should add now that even if he were to communicate them to us he could give us no pleasure by his disclosures" (443). "Creative Writers and Day-Dreaming" has an anachronistic feel in a therapized culture obsessed with circulating its shameful secrets (pace Foucault). But of course in this essay Freud was making a distinction between everyday fantasies and creative works—it's above all the aesthetic that makes the fantasies of others palatable or seductive.

In the testimonies of extreme experience that attend to the crises of the body and the mind, the relation between ethics and aesthetics comes under pressure, strained and subject to debate. With confessional writing, especially the memoir form that deals with sexuality and bodily distress within the family, that relation is sometimes stressed to a breaking point for both writer and reader. The question of where to draw the line in taste and genre poses shifting dilemmas for critics, who intervene in the debate and shape reception. What's tricky for readers are the moments when within what Leigh Gilmore calls the "less inflected dimensions of everyday life" feelings of "harm and pleasure" get combined: when the home turns dangerous and the familial erotic (31).

Though the comparison may seem odd, the reception history of *Fragments* has much in common with that of *The Kiss.* Laura Frost observes that *The Kiss* disturbed reviewers because it raised "questions of referentiality and authorial presence." On the epistemological front, readers doubted Harrison's story and excoriated its teller. Harrison's perceived equivocation and generic manipulation produced "revulsion and horror." Critics objected to Harrison's airing of family secrets, to the ease with which she sanctioned the ultimate violation of kinship in a narrative that collapsed distinctions between the realm of the extreme and the everyday—above all, banalizing the taboo. But this was to confound form and content. Critics appear to have been trumped by the paradox of confessional memoir, a genre that exposes secrets only to re-conceal them through aestheticization. Apparently intent on frustrating the transmission of this story of father-daughter incest, reviewers resorted to questions about genre and form. Still, if critics went to great lengths to dismiss Harrison, readers kept buying books.

If any recent memoir tested the limits of familial dsyphoria, *The Kiss* capped those of Harrison's American precursors of the genre (despite the fact that the genre of the book was subject to debate). In the French novelist and memoirist Annie Ernaux's bestselling narrative *Shame,* scenes of domestic trauma haunt the daughter and produce a form of writing that takes the reader to the edge of abjection. Ernaux stages her affront to expectations within the body of the text, throwing down a gauntlet to readers: "I have always wanted to write the sort of book that I find it impossible to talk about afterward, the sort of book that makes it impossible for me to withstand the gaze of others" (109). In a way, the challenge of a writing that seeks to penetrate the nature of shame and to override its inhibitions on the page participates in the project of "traumatic realism" that we invoked earlier, a writing project that like *The Kiss* (despite the vastly different subject matter) forces the reader to confront the uncomfortable contiguity of the extreme and the everyday—precisely *in* the everyday. And again, for women, the family in its dailiness is often the site of trauma, of domestic violence and bodily shame. The first sentence of *Shame* boldly bypasses the injunction to remain silent: "My father tried to kill my mother one Sunday in June, in the early afternoon" (13). Perhaps in a kind of fin de siècle exhaustion with *politesse,* first-person memorialization in the 1990s produces an unsettlement that aggresses and alienates the reader, sometimes causing an anxious withdrawal, sometimes nervous excitement.

Wayne Koestenbaum's "Aryan Boy," a fragmented remembrance, begins with a small piece of family history. The son's story of a disturbing memory unfolds outside the tent of traumatic conventions. On the contrary, the boy imagines the possibility that his father was laughing as he reminisced. "At some overnight nature retreat, long ago, outside of Berlin, my father woke to discover someone pissing on his head. It was the Aryan boy in the upper bunk. While my father told me this story, I was bathing, under his supervision; a plastic cup floated beside me in the soapy water." The anecdote, one of the few his father had told about his childhood in Nazi Germany, moves through a series of episodes in which a boy's body, the legacy of the Holocaust, masculinity, the entanglements of penises and pissing continue to reverberate until they come together in a final melding of aesthetics and ethics—relief at not liking *Triumph of the Will,* of not finding "the Aryan boy attractive as he leaned over and let pour onto my head his golden arc." Like Harrison's and Ernaux's memoirs, Koestenbaum's radically brief narrative—a boy's memory of a father's story of humiliation—is a story in large part about bodies; and its structure stages the embarrassments of a hesitant sexuality at home (and not at home). The segments and their headings—"The Reproduction Story," "One Problem with This Discourse," and so on—function as captions to the verbal snapshots of the family album. At the same time, they embody the episodic structure of memory (traumatic and commonplace) and remind the reader how artful life writing necessarily must be.

In "A Palinode on Photography and the Transsexual Real," Jay Prosser elaborates a form to fit a body that both is and isn't what it appears to be. Prosser makes a critical confession—one that is not set to reveal something new but to correct, to modify the shape of an earlier revelation about the meaning of gender—and genitals. Writing "as a" transsexual about transsexuality means charting space in public discourse for a subject position that confuses, repels, and fascinates readers. The confusion and the fascination originate from the same source. As a critic coming to grips with an argument he had made about what photographs can tell us about the referent they seem to capture, Prosser (like Chambers and Rothberg in different contexts) works through the Lacanian notion of the real as that which cannot fail to elude us: "transsexuality," he writes, "resonates for our moment because the process of surgical reassignment seems to offer a literalization of the traumatic loss of the real and our attempt to regain the real *through* trauma." Transsexuality operates both as literal cutting of the body, a contemporary trauma indebted to the technology of modernity, and as the metaphor for trauma as a crisis in and of knowledge. The relation between the crossing body and the real is like the unbridgeable one between interlocutors that testimony seeks to erase.

There is an uncanny (which is also to say willfully canny) match be-

tween the form of the palinode—a recanting—and the fate of the transsexual body. You can't ever fully erase the previous message—of argument
or gender. The trauma in this instance has to do both with getting it right
(the right body) and having been wrong (the imperfect argument). You
can never take it all back, just as Prosser finds himself unable to say of
Loren Cameron's nude self-portrait, "But he has no penis!" At the extreme
limits of representation (and this is perhaps the conundrum at the heart
of gender) there is a point where what can't be put into words is what we
just can't stop talking about, without quite ever getting there.

Contemporary writers push the envelope, the experiment, of identity—in the most literal sense of the word—to see what message it bears; in
some cases, the medium *is* the message, as John Updike suggests in an
essay about his psoriasis, "At War with My Skin": "It pains me to write
these pages. They are humiliating—'scab-picking,' to use a term sometimes levelled at modern autobiographical writers" (44). Updike points
not only to the inevitable slippage between literal and metaphorical domains of selfhood, between, say, scab and soul, but also the desire to overcome the vulgarity of picking in public. Scabs are the benign version of
scars, the traces of wounds trying to heal on the surface of the skin. Skin
holds memory and, as we've seen in the cases of tattoos and marks, mute
signs of old humiliations. Picking scabs keeps the wounds open. Life writers are willing to tolerate the mess of embarrassment because they also
expect their scabs and scars to remind readers of theirs. In hoping for par-
ity, they can wish for clemency.

Perhaps as readers of contemporary life-writing, shoppers for shocks to
our systems and values, literary critics and teachers of literature, look to
meet if not match the wounds of others. We demonstrate a willingness to
be bruised, to have our indifference challenged. Reading for the extreme
is a way to consider the politics of empathy and acknowledge the limits of
our civic engagement. So perhaps we should ask ourselves what's going on
when we read a literature that takes us, however indirect the route, to the
limit of norms and expectations, to the edge, sometimes, of what appears
to be the tolerable. We need to worry more about why we like to buy and
read these narratives of life in extreme conditions that serve as a scary mirror in which we contemplate not ours but another's face.

We inhabit an academic world, on Patricia Yaeger's reading, that cher-
ishes what we've called the literature of affront, a world of critics "busy consuming trauma—eating, swallowing, perusing, consuming, exchanging,
circulating, creating professional connections—through its stories about
the dead." As teachers and students it's uncomfortable to dwell upon our

contractual obligations both toward the dead and toward the living, whose pain is represented in material that often causes powerful reactions of discomfort or shame, or even, an ambiguous pleasure in picture of suffering.

Extremities is an attempt to acknowledge the moral murkiness of the enterprise, to bear witness to the power of a culture whose cogito, according to Geoffrey Hartman, appears to be "I bleed, therefore I am" (in Ezrahi, 295). In *Extremities* we have wanted to evoke a circular meditation that moves from Patricia Yaeger's opening salvo about the dangers we incur by being overly confident that our theories can accommodate all the contingencies our reading practices may encounter; from collective atrocity, through public testimony, through the family, to the lonely gesture of telling "the story of storylessness" that shattered one woman's life. We've looked at art and national testimony, poetry and barbed wire, photographs of surgically reconfigured bodies and broken limbs, the soil of urine and a father's kisses. Stories that challenge the limits of representation and transmission resonate because they chronicle experience that has yet to be incorporated within the popular imagination. The Holocaust, we've suggested, dominates our critical horizon because its chroniclers have been so vigilant in forging indelible marks, in creating monuments to it in public memory. More recently, a flood of writers has followed suit, carving out new discursive territory to document a range of extreme experiences earlier generations of writers had consigned to silence—the anatomy of illness, the horror at the heart of the family. The common thread connecting these stories about fatal illness, premature death, incest, family trauma, and sexual fantasy that have been addressed in this book is that they call attention to the working of extreme experience in our own lives, in some cases close to home, in others most remote. If through listening or reading, readers find only approximations of the damaged consciousness that makes itself felt in art and writing, the words and images may nonetheless compel us to listen and respond. Recounting the extreme, we believe, sometimes has the power to form a community entangled together through the act of listening.

Solidarity, Richard Rorty has suggested, requires the "imaginative ability to see strange people as fellow sufferers"; requires, we might add, a recognition of our own linguistic and psychological limits. We can begin to take political responsibility, he argues, by "increasing our sensitivity to the particular details of the pain and humiliation of other, unfamiliar sorts of people" (xvi). But as we've seen, a reader's involvement with the painful details of another's story entails both the pleasures of the imagination and the defenses of personal boundaries—and these reactions shape the exercise of identification across the borders of the unfamiliar. Accounts of extreme experience set in motion an ambivalent desire to look, to grapple with real suffering, and at the same time to look away—to put the book down, including this one. The essays in *Extremities* try to come to terms with the pulls of those mixed emotions. Their authors articulate the necessity of an ethical response to the experiences of those fellow sufferers who might not (and often do not) resemble us. The forging of community is both an arduous and utopian project, beyond the realm of a single essay or book; but any reader can take a first step toward collective self-consciousness by negotiating pathways of responsiveness and responsibility between what is both strange and familiar, distant and all too close.

• • •

We complete the editing of this manuscript in the aftermath of the World Trade Center's destruction: September 11, 2001. This tragic overture to the twenty-first century has changed the context of this book, jarred our perspective. We are only beginning to take the measure of the new testimonies to loss, the new contexts of traumatic experience that this event has produced. Glued to television screens, as if mesmerized by the recirculation of the images, the repetition of eye-witness accounts, we attempt to fathom the unfathomable: We talk about our disbelief as a way of learning to believe. As rescue efforts, criminal investigations, and political strategies develop, the horror becomes narrative. For better or worse, a story is taking shape—visual, fragmentary, for now open-ended.

NOTE

We thank Rebecca Hogan and Joseph Hogan for editing the special issue of *a/b: Auto/Biography Studies*, "Extremities: Memoirs at the Fin de Siècle," and for their generosity in allowing us to republish some of those essays here. We are also grateful to Gloria Fisk, Susan Gubar, Marianne Hirsch, and Michael Rothberg for their judicious editorial responses to this collection.

WORKS CITED

Agamben, Giorgio. *Remnants of Auschwitz: The Witness and the Archive*. Trans. Daniel Heller-Roazen. New York: Zone Books, 1999.

Arendt, Hannah. *Eichmann in Jerusalem: A Report on the Banality of Evil*. New York: Viking, 1963.

Caruth, Cathy. *Unclaimed Experience: Trauma, Narrative, and History*. Baltimore: Johns Hopkins University Press, 1996.

Cheung, King-Kok. "'Don't Tell': Imposed Silences in *The Color Purple* and *The Woman Warrior.*" *PMLA* 103.2 (1988): 162–74.

Ernaux, Annie. *Shame.* Trans. Tanya Leslie. New York: Seven Stories Press, 1998.

Ezrahi, Sidra. "After Such Knowledge, What Laughter?" *Yale Journal of Criticism* 14.1 (2001): 287–313.

Felman, Shoshana, and Dori Laub. *Testimony: Crises of Witnessing in Literature, Psychoanalysis, and History.* New York: Routledge, 1992.

Forché, Carolyn, ed. *Against Forgetting: Twentieth-Century Poetry of Witness.* New York: Norton, 1993.

Freud, Sigmund. "Creative Writers and Day-Dreaming." *The Freud Reader.* Ed. Peter Gay. New York: Norton, 1989.

Gilmore, Leigh. *The Limits of Autobiography: Trauma and Testimony.* Ithaca: Cornell University Press, 2001.

Hartman, Geoffrey H. *The Longest Shadow: In the Aftermath of the Holocaust.* Bloomington: Indiana University Press, 1996.

———. Interview by Jennifer Ballengee. "Witnessing Video Testimony." *Yale Journal of Criticism* 14.1 (2001): 217–32.

Hobsbawm, Eric. *The Age of Extremes: A History of the World, 1914–1991.* New York: Vintage, 1996.

Kingston, Maxine Hong. *The Woman Warrior: Memoirs of a Girlhood Among Ghosts.* New York: Vintage, 1989.

Klemperer, Victor. *I Will Bear Witness: A Diary of the Nazi Years, 1933–1941.* Trans. Martin Chalmers. New York: Random House, 1999.

———. *I Will Bear Witness: A Diary of the Nazi Years, 1942–1945.* Trans. Martin Chalmers. New York: Random House, 1999.

LaCapra, Dominick. "Lanzmann's *Shoah:* 'Here There Is No Why.'" *Critical Inquiry* 23 (Winter 1997): 231–69.

———. "Trauma, Absence, Loss." *Critical Inquiry* 25 (Summer 1999): 696–727.

Leys, Ruth. *Trauma: A Genealogy.* Chicago: University of Chicago Press, 2001.

Mitchell, Juliet. *Mad Men and Medusas: Reclaiming Hysteria.* New York: Basic Books, 2000.

Müller, Melissa. *Anne Frank.* Trans. Rita and Robert Kimber. New York: Holt, 1999.

Novick, Peter. *The Holocaust in American Life.* New York: Houghton Mifflin, 1999.

Rorty, Richard. *Contingency, Irony, and Solidarity.* Cambridge: Cambridge University Press, 1989.

Roth, Philip. *Operation Shylock.* New York: Vintage, 1993.

Rothberg, Michael. "W. E. B. Du Bois in Warsaw: Holocaust Memory and the Color Line, 1949–1952." *Yale Journal of Criticism* 14.1 (Spring 2001): 169–90.

Spiegelman, Art. *Maus I: A Survivor's Tale: My Father Bleeds History.* New York: Pantheon, 1986.

———. *Maus II: A Survivor's Tale: And Here My Troubles Began.* New York: Pantheon, 1991.

Suleiman, Susan. "Problems of Memory and Factuality in Recent Holocaust Memoirs: Wilkomirski/Wiesel." *Poetics Today* 21.3 (Fall 2000): 543–59.

Updike, John. *Self-Consciousness: Memoirs.* New York: Viking Penguin, 1990.

Walker, Alice. *The Color Purple.* New York: Pocket Books, 1983.

PART ONE

Trauma, Culture, Theory

ONE

Consuming Trauma; or,
The Pleasures of Merely Circulating

Patricia Yaeger

Wallace Stevens begins his poem "The Pleasures of Merely Circulating" with delicious nonsense:

> The garden flew round with the angel,
> The angel flew round with the clouds
> And the clouds flew round and the clouds flew round
> And the clouds flew round with the clouds.

I want to exit from these giddy circles and come down to earth, asking the reader to join me on a journey less certain of its pleasures. Come down, then; let's run the length of this field, sallying back and forth between two ill-matched citations: the first an inviting statement of purpose from a new academic journal, the second an oddly moving, oddly spectral statement from Derrida:

> *Journal x* is not committed to any particular set of answers or even approaches to the question of pleasure, only the question itself. . . . Our immediate editorial goal is a good deal more modest, indirect, and open-ended: to serve as a sort of ongoing research archive into what Zizek might call "enjoyment as an intellectual factor" by publishing scholarly and personal essays that themselves give pleasure. (Kamps and Watson 2)

First of all, mourning. We will be speaking of nothing else. It consists always in attempting to ontologize remains, to make them present, in the
first place by *identifying* the bodily remains and by *localizing* the dead (all
ontologization, all semanticization . . . finds itself caught up in this work
of mourning but, as such, it does not yet think it; we are posing here the
question of the specter, to the specter). (Derrida 9)

L'Allegro, Il Penseroso; gang of pleasure, gang of pain; Team Jouissance,
Team Specter. . . . running over and through this field, I really want to run
around it: to run, if nowhere else, amok. But for me there is no other way.
If I am to write this essay, I have to navigate the work of mourning in order to arrive at pleasure's archive—sliding between opposing manifestos,
hoping to create a small universe in which I can suture two inverse incli-
nations—namely, our irrepressible longing for pleasure and our traffic in
specters: our omnivorous conversations with the implacable dead.

As I start to write this an announcement comes in from Pretoria. Five
of the murderers of Steven Biko have confessed under the auspices of a
general amnesty. A few days later, the *New York Times* article on Biko's
death features a strange double picture from a museum exhibit in Pretoria. At its outer reaches the camera has recorded a grand, upflung portrait
of Biko's head—suggesting a persona already classicized, at a distance,
monumental, heroic. A didactic body, yes, but also, in its way, a body for
pleasure—evoking identification with the spirit of a deeply ethical man.
Beneath this picture the museum has flung another replica of Biko's person (this time solid, tactile, plastic, inert) depicting a body face-down,
bound, contorted, bleeding, opened: a terrifying representation of a person battered and left to die on the floor of a South African jail.[1]

Between the heroic picture and its obscene plastic double, this exhibit attempts to instantiate two different versions of mourning. First, it offers a body that is easy to introject, to sublimate into a system of great,
representative men. But beneath this sublime portraiture we meet something more tenuous: a body harder to swallow. Instead of Biko's greatness
we are reminded of the power of his political adversaries and his own loss
of agency: of flesh that is open to brutality, inertia, decay; of a world un-
approachable through grief but openly melancholy over the body's vulnerability and its unfinished projects—a space with too much ancestry.
In presenting a butchered body that refuses to be consumed (tipping the
viewer back and forth between heroism and the desuetude or disquiet of
unusable grief), this double picture attempts, as Derrida says, to "ontolo-

gize remains," to give them density, spatiality, to *identify* bodily remains "by *localizing* the dead."

How do we speak to the dead? Or speak about them? What weight should they have in our texts? Last week I waved the picture of Biko's bodies at my students—trying to drive home the contrast between the semiotics of the epic body and the relentless grotesque—trying to say, "Look, body politics is not just a topic in this course but a set of tropes we constantly deploy." And yet my voice breaks when I talk about the body that inhabits the bottom half of the frame, and I think—I don't like my dead to be this local. It upsets the balance, calls out too many ghosts. But every time I get rid of one ghost, another takes its place. This time I am shopping. I see a placard in the back window of a large van. "A drunk driver killed my son. I am MADD." Once again the unexpected ontologizing of remains, the relentless localizing. I want to walk away, and yet my own flesh surprises me with its vehemence—an anger directed not at the drunk driver, but at the narrator, the driver of this car. I think, "Why is she saying this to me?" before I construct the proper empathic response. Of course this woman has as much right to hurl invectives, to call out the ghost, as anyone.

What do we owe to the dead? For IRA nationalists (those who became political prisoners during the 1970s and supported the Hunger Strike of 1981), the dying demanded a special brand of silence; they aroused a painful new consciousness about the irrelevance of everyday speech. "When a guy was on hunger strike in the wing, the noise level went down. Everybody was conscious all the time that there was someone next to you dying. When the food came around you had to be conscious about not shouting, 'What do you think of the meat today?' Your complaints were relegated to something meaningless. You couldn't go to the door and shout, 'There's something with this grub'" (Feldman 248). It seems all too clear what one owes to the dying, but with the dead, the case seems utterly different and perhaps more diffuse:

> The night Bobby Sands died was just . . . you never heard a sound for hours. Nobody spoke and nobody would go near the door. The way we knew he was dead, a screw came down and there was a grill at the end of the wing, and with his baton he started banging the grill slowly, Dong!—dong!—dong!—like a church bell. It was just a hollow sound. From that point on whenever someone died the screws would ring the grill and another one would walk up the wing slowly pulling a trolley behind him, saying, "Bring

out your dead. How many dead do youse have for us today?" It was like the plague. (Feldman 249)

Once we enter this hollow space and try to imagine Sands's slow and deliberate death, the thematizing question—what do we owe to the dead?—seems impertinent and much too obtuse. And yet deferring this question seems equally counterproductive. We need to take note of the ease with which Bobby Sands's heartbeat, his voice, can be displaced by a screw, a prison guard, banging the grill slowly. As the guard cries out in his mocking voice, the empty space left by a man's death becomes frighteningly co-optable, available to others; it demands renewed efforts at counterspeech. And yet—how do we narrate or speak for the dead? What allows this speech to grant them proper weight, substance, dignity? If this weight is too heavy, can we go on writing? Do we want to? If the weight is too light, can we do justice to the injustices endured by the specter?

In interviews with members of the IRA prison collective recorded in Allen Feldman's *Formations of Violence: The Narrative of the Body and Political Terror in Northern Ireland,* we learn that for those who bore witness to Sands's death, "a new sense of urgency . . . set in all around. It meant that you were *scriobhing* [writing] all day. . . . it gave everybody a sense of doing something" (247). It is the question of writing, of finding proper tropes, that obsesses Sands's fellow prisoners:

> The Hunger Strike completed the textualization of the prisoner's body. As Bobby Sands and subsequent hunger strikers lay dying, the rest of the Blanketmen engaged in the intensified production of political texts that were smuggled out of the prison. These texts constituted a literature of conversion, letters to international organizations, political groups, unions, governments, and prominent individuals which publicized the Hunger Strike and asked support for the protest. Certain prisoners writing with pen refills on cigarette papers were able to produce 200 letters a day. It was a remarkable literary production which seemed to flow directly from the dying body of the hunger strike. (250)

The ventriloquism we lend to the dead, the tropes we clothe them in, can have the power to re-dress their bodies, to speak volumes.

Differently positioned (not only *not* incarcerated, but at relative leisure to pursue polymorphous political passions), liberal academics also reproduce for themselves and their students stories of trauma, structural violence, systematic injustice, slaughter, inequality. These painful stories—

about deterritorialization, decolonization, people pushed past the margins, bodies brutalized, children victimized, populations dying, in exile—suggest a world of subsemantic history that demands the weight of political speech. At the same time (or, within the same heterodox space but under another name), we inhabit an academic world that is busy consuming trauma—eating, swallowing, perusing, consuming, exchanging, circulating, creating professional connections—through its stories about the dead. We are obsessed with stories that must be passed on, that must not be passed over. But aren't we also drawn to these stories from within an elite culture driven by its own economies: by the pains and pleasures of needing to publish, by salaries and promotions that are themselves driven by acts of publication, by the pleasures of merely circulating?

From within this complex matrix of pleasure and pain, I want to come back to my earlier question. Given the danger of commodification and the pleasures of academic melancholy—of those exquisite acts of mourning that create a conceptual profit—what are our responsibilities when we write about the dead? In describing the fate of Bobby Sands, or the bodies of "cunts" (designated male victims of political violence) and "stiffs" (dead bodies that deliver a "message" of feminization to the other side) that have transformed Belfast's political geography, does Allen Feldman meet these responsibilities, does he take the right tone? Do I? How are we allowed to taste the deads' bodies, to put their lives in our mouths? How do we identify the proper tone, the proper images—for holding, for awakening, someone else's bodily remains?

It was an article published in *Journal x* that first conjured this question—pushing my own body toward extremity. Barry Gildea's "Estranged Fruit: Making and Unmaking in Mississippi's Jails" begins with portraits of black men who have died in Mississippi's jails; it focuses on the death of Andre Jones, the son of local NAACP activists, who was brought to the Simpson County Jail on August 22, 1992, on multiple charges that included carrying a concealed weapon and possessing a stolen vehicle. He was eighteen. Less than twenty-four hours later Jones was found hanging in his cell—dangling from the shoelace of his own Nike sneaker.

I want to take up the status of griefwork, of the work of mourning, within the context of Andre Jones's death and this death's circulation in academic writing. What happens when we "textualize" bodies, when we write about other people's deaths (or other people's cultures) as something one "reads"? Gildea sees jails as "sites for complex and plural readings, especially where contested hangings occur. The incidental death category marks the first opportunity to explore a more imaginative or creative interpretation of the jail hanging as a mythic and literary act of incidental annihilation through intentional civil disobedience" (124). What does it mean to convert someone's death while in custody into a "literary act"? If Jones's death was, in fact, a suicide, how should we respond to the suggestion that his failure to leave a suicide note must be "read" as an act of resistance? (That is, what constitutes proper evidence for drawing such a conclusion? Who is doing the "writing" here—and why?) Or how do we evaluate this conclusion: "By resisting the urge to determine and dictate the meaning of his death, Jones has ensured that he will be heard. He imposes no meaning, but still 'imprisons' you within a text, a world of his own (un)making, a world which soon becomes peopled with the texts of other hanging bodies" (116). In what sense can a hanging body be "a text"? What happens when "imprisons" becomes a floating signifier that slips away from its referent so easily? No longer a description of the physical crisis experienced by black men in custody, it becomes a loosely held metaphor describing the psychological status of an elite group of readers.

This transferability suggests a too-easy equivalence between epistemological prisons and actual ones, between the dead and the living. What are the dangers inherent in figuring—or dis-figuring—the specter? How far should we go in invoking the ghost, how far in consuming its traumas? If circulating the suffering of others has become the meat and potatoes of our profession, if this circulation evokes a lost history but also runs the danger of commodification, how should we proceed? In producing figures that are either too vacuous or too lurid, too theatrical or too theoretical, can one reproduce trauma or loss in the wrong way? To put this somewhat differently—how do we control our own acts of *écriture,* of seeming to read bodies, when we may really be reading, then reinscribing our own figurations?

To answer these questions, my argument needs to extend beyond its other-directed critique. To stay honest, I will have to turn back on my own mode of troping the death of Steven Biko, my own act of invoking the specter. (Was this a too-opportunistic, too-lurid way of inviting the audience into this essay? And who decides?) But I also want to focus on two urgent questions. First, what is the role of the critic's own writing in producing someone else's death as "text"? Second, what resources should elites bring to bear in ventriloquizing the world on behalf of non-elites—how conscious should we be about usurping others' worlds with our words? These are questions with subtexts: in asking whether there are proper and improper styles for eliciting the stories of the dead, we need to reexamine the appropriations of anthropology's powerful methods within the burgeoning field of cultural studies. And in asking whether we can participate in critique without overriding local mourning, we need to reexamine the thematics of loss that so preoccupies a post-marxist academy. For if the abiding question of this essay is What do we owe to the dead? this has to be nuanced once again. The question is not only what is *our* stake in their narratives, but what is *their* stake in ours?

With these questions in mind, let us turn again to "Estranged Fruit: Making and Unmaking in Mississippi's Jails," for this is an essay that speaks about the recently dead—about a young black man, and then another black man, of white men and women—found hanging. The deaths of these black men in custody have been interpreted by their own African American communities as lynchings, but labeled officially as suicides. Gildea repeats the official verdict, arguing that these deaths are suicides, that they "indicate a strong commitment to live or die by a *nomos* other than that of the state of Mississippi: namely, the dignity, honesty, and sovereignty of a pure form of American individualism. Inmate suicide is a singular act of subversion, both a renunciation and an enunciation of violence" (139). The fine line between ventriloquism and de-personification (what I will later describe as the de-anthropomorphism of the persons of black men who have died while in custody) gets breached again and again—perhaps because the author of "Estranged Fruit" is so eager to close the door on the possibility that these men were murdered; or perhaps because in the specter's presence "appropriate" acts of personification are hard to control. In any event, he argues that the quick availability of southern narratives of lynching for describing deaths while in custody may cause left-leaning critics to overlook the despairing sense of agency that drives some men and women to kill themselves while in jail.

This desire to construct a scene of agency rather than victimization is complexly motivated. Gildea insists that the "theory" that Jones and his compatriots were lynched "has abstracted the villains, so that all of white Mississippi is implicated as a mob" (120). Indeed? What are the author's own transference points, the nodes of racial crisis or white writing that motivate such observations? What anxieties might the narrative of a black man's "heroic" suicide attempt to ward off? What are the problems in transferential thinking that remain sublimated or subliminal within the current methods of cultural studies? Clearly, this argument about heroic suicides in custody suffers from numerous epistemological glitches, including its misapplication of a romantic version of unified selfhood (the invocation of "a pure form of American individualism"), its description of the possibility of a purely instrumental response to prison trauma (in ecstatic tones reminiscent of Byron's "The Prisoner of Chillon"), and its ends-dominated interpretation of events (the notion that we're allowed to write history backwards, from results we can see to intentions we can only intuit). But however strong my sense of epistemological recoil at the model of history that constructs Gildea's conclusions, my first response, in reality, was not this academic.

What disturbed me even more than this essay's argument is the question of how the dead are narrated—how their bodies are glossed. The pivotal, mediating figure who introduces this essay is Andre Jones—a black man found hanging by his own shoelace. The section introducing his story begins with a subtitle—"Starting on a Shoe String"—a string of words that makes Jones's body the subject of cleverly nuanced academic play. What is gained by this painful irreverence, a pun that works over and through a dead man's body with the cavalier bitterness of a good Gershwin song? I think, what am I able to demand of the author of this or any essay, as she or he holds open the bodies of others for my gaze? I think, language is difficult, and objects never go into their concepts without leaving something behind, without leaving a remainder. But in this essay I find something more than a remainder—I find too many remains. There are too many bodies here and too little care for them.

However bitterly or acerbically it is meant, the pun "starting on a shoestring" functions to lighten the burden of writing about the dead. In taking a body already disfigured by violence and making a "figure" out of it— a trope, a pun, a sleight-of-word—the author relocalizes Jones's death within the entrepreneurial space of academic play. Elsewhere this disfiguration seems even more dangerous:

> For Andre Jones, jail hanging may have been a somatic form of cultural criticism attesting to the incontestable reality of the pain and torture of Mississippi jails. But as Scarry would predict, the "language" of this hanging event is not entirely clear. . . .
>
> Scarry's work emphasizes the importance of reading the body as a text, a valuable approach to the story of Jones's death. The posture of Andre Jones emphasizes the body in a way that cancels the contents of the world: the suspension of a body from the shower bar, dangling like fruit, fleshy, pulpy, a liquefying solid. The human involved is reduced from a sentient being into a mere body, matter, the object of gravity's pull. In the case of Jones, a single shoestring unmakes the made, for in his world shoes were

both a possession of status and a position of plight, as in "I wouldn't want to be in your shoes." His hanging synthesizes each connotation so that the plight of pain becomes objectified and he becomes, like the shoe, something that dangles from a string. Andre Jones the sentient being disappears and is represented by a black Nike hightop sneaker, the kind young urban blacks sometimes kill for. Because of shoes, some urban teenagers kill others; by means of shoes, do some jailed urban teenagers kill themselves? Andre Jones did not kill for shoes but instead died by means of them, his Mississippi-made body transformed into both a shoe and a field of crisis. Unfortunately for Mississippi, however, the hanging of Andre Jones has the appearance of bearing the antecedent state insignia of lynching. (115)

These paragraphs ride on the same somatic techniques that the Pretoria museum exhibit uses to vivify Steven Biko's death—they swerve between a heroicizing classicism and the prurient anarchy of the grotesque. The author begins with a small gesture of heroism. If Jones has killed himself, this act becomes a form of "somatic cultural criticism": that is, in death his body is wedded to theory; it becomes a visceral act of cultural critique (it is "like" a cultural critic's acts of cultural criticism). Almost immediately Gildea retracts this violent yoking of unlike subjectivities, and his text moves dialectically to acknowledge that the remains of this death are bodily, not linguistic, so that any act of "reading" must come to a halt, at least until "theory" can come to the rescue. To cope with the subject's silence, the critic must borrow figures that permit the reading of this body as text: "a valuable approach." (But valuable for whom? Who profits when someone's else's body is turned into a set of tropes to be perused as an academic commodity? Even silence can become a surplus value the reader can reap.)

Here two different modes of problematic thinking become visible. First, this paragraph appropriates figures from Billie Holiday's performance of "Strange Fruit," a bitter song about the effects of lynching and mob violence in the postbellum South. In the first verse of this song, death is almost made bearable—it is lightened—by displacing the traumas endured by once-living men onto an aestheticized object from the natural world:

Southern trees bear strange fruit,
Blood on the leaves and red at the root.
Black bodies swinging in the southern breeze,
Strange fruit hanging from the poplar trees.

But while "men" and "fruit" are too easily linked, the song points to the distance between living metaphors and dead bodies. That is, the fact of displacement (the way that the personification of "fruit" is so eerily mapped onto the de-anthropomorphized bodies of black men) makes a political statement. It suggests that these bodies have already endured such displacement long before their death. In the pre–civil rights South, African Americans—whether dead or alive—were barred from crossing the symbolic threshold into personification; from the perspective of the dominant culture they were forced to hover in the uncivil space between human and inhuman worlds. As Hortense Spillers describes the lives of black women during this period:

> Slavery did not transform the black female into an embodiment of carnality at all, as the myth of the black woman would tend to convince us. She became instead the principal point of passage between the human and non-human world. Her issue became the focus of a cunning difference . . . the route by which the dominant male decided the distinction between humanity and "other". . . [decided that] black is vestibular to culture. In other words, the black person mirrored for the society around her what a human being was not. (76)

Holiday's singing defines the hanging bodies of black men as another point of impossible passage. That something as heavy as a body can be made so light, irrelevant, and metaphoric is the first ironic point of this song. The second is that this lightness is only possible because African American men had already been de-anthropomorphized by white society. Thus Holiday's allusion to the lynched bodies of black men as "strange fruit" resounds so caustically because these men have died several deaths. As metaphors, the song's spectral bodies offer a doubly mimetic space— the frightening specter of "emphasis added" to injury. This song not only calls out to the traumas endured by black men but opens a space for exploring the dehumanization (the lost personhood or personification) suffered by the African American community at large. The re-imaging and de-animation of black bodies as "fruit for the crows to pluck" offers a commentary not only on the practice of lynching, but on a white metaphysic that makes blackness vestibular to humanity.

In Gildea's "reading" of Andre Jones's body, the metaphors are complicit in rather than critical of these older acts of dehumanization. His essay ignores what "Strange Fruit" knows too well: that the dangers implicit in the rhetoricization of a black man's body can have material effects—that the de-personification of African Americans is an ongoing, repetitive stratagem within American history. The argument that, in creating his own hanging death, Andre Jones "objectifies" himself on his own shoestring seems too self-serving. In "Estranged Fruit" men are made into metaphors so they can be harvested by the critic.

Rhetoric is often complicit in evacuating dead men's and women's worlds; it can cancel the brutal facticity of the body's local fate for the appropriative potentials of metaphor. At the same time, some form of troping, of de- or re-anthropomorphizing—is inevitable whenever we speak of the dead. What does it mean to turn bodies into rhetoric?

THE WEIGHT OF THE DEAD

The Communist Manifesto begins with a ghost: *"Ein Gespenst geht um in Europa*—a specter is haunting Europe." But in *Specters of Marx* Derrida stalks the ghost of Marx himself. He not only wants to conjure the lost ghosts of communism, but Marx's own obsession with specters: "Men make their own history [*ihre eigene Geschichte*] but they do not make it just as they please [*aus freien Stücken*]; they do not make it under circumstances chosen by themselves, but under circumstances directly encountered, given and transmitted from the past [*überlieferten Umständen*]. The tradition of all the dead generations [*aller toten Geschlecter*] weighs [*lastet*] like a nightmare on the brain of the living" (quoted in Derrida 108). In calling out to the specter we encounter a new kind of nightmare—not the gothic terror of being haunted by the dead, but the greater terror *of not being haunted,* of ceasing to feel the weight of past generations in one's bones. That is, the words we use to hold the dead, to call out to them, are too porous, too leaky. Even the English version of Marx's phrase "the tradition of all the dead generations weighs like a nightmare on the brain of the living" has more heft in the German. In Marx's original text, the specter weighs, or "'lastet wie ein Alp,' that is, weighs like one of those ghosts that give nightmares; the French translation reads simply 'pèse d'un poids très lourd,' weighs very heavily; as often happens in translations, the ghost drops off into oblivion or, in the best of cases, it is dissolved into approximate figures" (Derrida 108).

The problem haunting my essay is precisely the danger of this dissolution of the dead into "approximate figures." Take, for example, my attempt to invoke the ghost in the paragraph on Steven Biko that begins this essay. I want to instantiate a physical dignity for the dead, to invoke the terrors of imprisonment and choicelessness (the nightmare weight that descends upon Biko) as well as the forces of history that Biko, in his political actions, sought to lift. I want some portion of this weight to descend on the reader's body—to create a burdensome space for thinking about the relationship between representational melancholy and political praxis.

But as soon as I open this scene, something else starts to happen; I remobilize the specter for a different set of rhetorical ends. Planning to talk later in this essay about what happens to black men in prisons, I ask the invocation of "Biko" to set the scene. His body lends itself to the project of making this essay into a well-working object, an echo chamber for my most urgent ideas. In the midst of such considerations, where are we, how close to the ghost? And what happens to the work, the figuration of mourning? I write a sentence, then strike it out: "I wanted to name my son after Steven Biko, but couldn't, didn't—a martyr's name. But aren't half the names in the white man's canon martyr's names—just buried under centuries of over-use?" It sounds too personal, it breaks the tone, draws too much attention to my own psychic investments in this project when I want to draw out something more serious. But one of my criticisms of Gildea's essay is precisely the question of transference. In making a body into a text, what investments does the cultural critic bring to her work, and when should they become visible?

Meanwhile, I'm looking over my shoulder and thinking about audience: How well is my interpretation taking hold? Am I doing better than other interpretations? But before resolving this problem my efforts to invoke the specter are taken over by the sheer delight of thinking, by the spectacular lure of analysis. Invoking the ghost, I become half-acrobatic, take pleasure in associative vertiginousness and move farther from the lure of the specter. That is, the very act of thinking about the spectral object makes it even more spectral. Adorno defines the problems the thinking subject encounters in each act of definition or analysis in his *Negative Dialectics*:

> The spell cast by the subject becomes equally a spell cast over the subject. Both spells are driven by the Hegelian fury of disappearance. The subject is spent and impoverished in its categorial performance; to be able to define and articulate what it confronts . . . the subject must dilute itself to the point of mere universality, for the sake of the objective validity of those definitions. It must cut loose from itself as much as from the cognitive object, so that this object will be reduced to its concept, according to plan.

The objectifying subject contracts into a point of abstract reason, and finally into logical noncontradictoriness. (139)

This is a ponderous passage containing a crucial idea. First Adorno marks the impoverishment of the subject, of the "texting" person. In seeking definitions or articulations with "objective validity" the subject cuts herself loose from the cognitive object. This object, in turn, is cut loose from everything except for its "concept"—its de-materialized idea. In writing or thinking we experience a need to turn things into concepts so that they can be spoken about. But this very need casts a spell that breeds disappearance: both subject and object are diluted and spent when they are described under a common denominator. Both object and subject "contract": the simultaneous disappearance of two different contexts. This is the very problem that the double bodied exhibit in the Pretoria museum is trying—so awkwardly—to make intelligible. Neither of these bodies allows Biko to haunt us sufficiently; each flirts with the problem of disappearance.

I seem to have come to a binary impasse: Either (1) the ghost speaks, or (2) we must endure—that is, become complicit in—its silence, in the attenuation of the dead within the oblivion of approximate figures (figures designed to communicate, but always encountering the emptiness of the concept, the flatness of theory, the excess of lurid projections, or the instrumentality of the body made spectacle). But there is a third possibility, one narrated by Homer in *The Odyssey*, in the scenes where Odysseus journeys to Hades to talk with the dead. Abandoning Circe for Ithaca, Odysseus is faced with another detour; he requires "the strengthless heads of the perished dead" to learn "how to make your way home on the sea where the fish swarm" (X, 540). Faced with this journey,

the inward heart in me was broken,
and I sat down on the bed and cried, nor did the heart in me
wish to go on living any longer, nor to look on the sunlight.
But when I had glutted myself with rolling about and weeping,
then at last I spoke aloud. (X, 496–99)

Odysseus must find a form of speech not overburdened with grief, with figures of glut or excess. In fact, his strategy for getting the dead to speak will involve a similar self-regulation. Approaching Hades, Odysseus digs a pit and pours libations for the dead: "first / honey mixed with milk, then a second pouring of sweet wine" (X, 519–20). Finally this pit is filled with the blood of the living:

Now when, with sacrifices and prayers, I had so entreated
the hordes of the dead, I took the sheep and cut their throats
over the pit, and the dark-clouding blood ran in, and the souls
of the perished dead gathered to the place, up out of Erebos, brides, and
     young unmarried men, and long-suffering elders,
virgins, tender and with the sorrows of young hearts upon them,
and many fighting men killed in battle, stabbed with brazen
spears, still carrying their bloody armor upon them.
These came swarming around my pit from every direction
with inhuman clamor, and green fear took hold of me. (XI, 34–43)

This "dark-clouding" blood becomes the locus of a bizarre plenitude; it provides three different conundrums for thinking about the "approximate figures" of the dead.

First, why is this blood necessary? It would seem that the dead can speak only when they partake of the things of this world. If the images clothing the dead are important, it is because these figures are the gateway to their availability. At the same time, the dress we bestow upon the phantom is inevitably our own. That is, the trace of the specter's speech resides neither in the dead's wished-for presence nor in their oblivion, but in their inevitable hybridity. They must be fed on the lifeblood, the figures of the present, if they are to speak.

And here we come to a second conundrum. Odysseus offers this sacrifice so that the dead can become substantial. But when the phantoms begin to swarm, Odysseus instructs his men to draw their swords. Initially, only a handful among the restless "hordes of the dead" are allowed to drink, the rest are withheld figuration. Here we face the question of both posthumous harm and equal access to figuration—how do we choose *who* can speak, how do we account for the missing persons of the dead? The gatekeeping function or archival censorship of historical narrative is the source of Benjamin's by-now famous call for a materialist, interventionist history: one that reestablishes a possible voice for "those who are lying prostrate"; that refuses the victors' ghosts. "To articulate the past historically does not mean to recognize it 'the way it really was' (Ranke). It means to seize hold of a memory as it flashes up at a moment of danger. . . . Only that historian will have the gift of fanning the spark of hope in the past who is firmly convinced that *even the dead* will not be safe from the enemy if he wins. And this enemy has not ceased to be victorious" (255). For Benjamin "the way it really was" is always an invention of the victor's culture. We find an example in *Z Magazine* in the parodic portrait of an anchorman reading the evening news: "This just in, a Pakistani jet crashed into a Libyan cruise ship killing all 5000 passengers instantly." In the next frame he looks irritated: "I don't get it . . . where's the story?" A hand juts into the frame with an update and suddenly the anchorman reads with renewed emphasis: *"There were three Americans on board! Oh the Humanity!"* For the phantom to speak, it must participate in the *telos* of Odysseus's journey, in his country-seeking quest.

Given this telos, is it surprising that among those originally withheld figuration and left in the margins is Odysseus's mother? When Odysseus sees her, "I broke into tears at the sight of her and my heart pitied her, / but even so, for all my thronging sorrow, I would not / let her draw near the blood until I had questioned Teiresias" (XI, 87–89). When his mother speaks, Odysseus wants nothing more than to hold her:

> Mother, why will you not wait for me, when I am trying
> to hold you, so that even in Hades with our arms embracing
> we can both take the satisfaction of dismal mourning?
> Or are you nothing but an image? (210–14)

Why does Odysseus, who at first refuses to talk to his mother, now long for her embrace? In addition to the question of gatekeeping, Homer opens a space for meditating upon the image as a way of both "holding" and "holding off" the material presence of the dead.[2]

Michel de Certeau suggests that we are always at the margins of Hades, always surrounded by meditative spaces that hold open (and speak for) the dead. "There is no place that is not haunted by many different spirits hidden there in silence, spirits one can 'invoke' or not. Haunted places are the only ones people can live in" (108). But in a letter that questions these enchantments my friend Richard Godden demurs:

> Concerning your account of place as haunted with the residues of wasted work: the problem is that ghosts are the evacuees of memory and that to obtain substance they must be shed by the actions (and thoughts) of those who live. Unless the specter materializes through lived institutions, he / she / it will forget their paths, leave no track and evaporate. I have always been simultaneously impressed and skeptical over Volosinov's claim that "no word forgets its path"—would that this were so. Surely the linguist meant "no word should be permitted to forget its path."

In search of such memories, what forgiveness, what reprieve? In recognizing that every space is haunted, we are still at one remove from the enormity of transgenerational haunting. It is only when someone bears witness or gives the specter its due (its space of political and institutional articulation) that the empty images of the dead can be held up and held open. Given the importance of writing from within the complexity of our own killing fields, is "textualization" really so bad as a strategy? Isn't the task of abstraction a valiant attempt to answer Benjamin's plea for a politically responsible history—one that reaches out deliberately, blindly, to respond to a moment of danger?

DOING ANTHROPOLOGY WITH A DEAD SUBJECT

1. How do we account for—and respond to—the weight of the dead and the potential dissipation of the body in writing?

2. What is the relation between reading (or writing) for pleasure and the specter? Marx suggests that the dead—as the "figures" of history—feed revolutions; their bodies play leading roles in political movements and documents; their spectrality offers the metaphoric foundation of the new. If the specter provides the tropes we push away from in order to suggest other, more utopian orders, what can we conclude about the relation between the pleasure of "the new" and the spectral? Or, to make a more local intervention, how does excitement about new ideas depend on the specter, rest on the spectral properties—the tropics—of the dead?

3. Equally pressing, what is the status of griefwork and the thematics of loss within the fin de siècle academy? In what tones should we write about our obsessive recoveries of subsemantic histories? Are we inventing new "brands" of transgenerational haunting? Or is academic consumerism an inevitable outgrowth of the culture of late capitalism that, nevertheless, makes a crucial space for recovering the lost topos of transnational, trans-institutional mourning?

4. Finally, what does it mean to make the dead into "texts"? Is it possible to theorize other bodies, other cultures, while holding open a space for mourning, for the lost object? What relationship to theory will help us explore our repetitive love for the specter and our continual pleasure in being haunted by someone else's dead? Or, as my colleague Marlon Ross asked in a recent conversation, what are the dangers of doing anthropology with a dead subject?

E. Valentine Daniel tries to reformulate the relation between torture and theory in *Charred Lullabies: Chapters in an Anthropography of Violence,* a book that frames a new anthropological discourse to describe people killed or tortured during nationalist violence in Sri Lanka: "Many have died. To say more is to simplify, but to fathom the statement is also to make the fact bearable. Tellipali, Nilaveli, Manippay, Boosa, Dollar Farm, Kokkadicholai—mere place-names of another time—have been transformed into names of places spattered with blood and mortal residue. . . . Many have died. How to give an account of these shocking events without giving in to a desire to shock? And more important, what does it mean to give such an account? That is the burden of this book" (3). Daniel questions not only anthropology's narrative strategies but its deepest structures for confronting newly archaic remains. In "reading" atrocities, what good are methods "designed to enhance" our understanding of coherent social units like castes or clans? When do ordinary, structure-seeking explanations turn an ethnography of violence into "a pornography of violence"? Theory seems to offer one alternative. But in its flattening out of affect, its use of abstraction instead of prurience, theory refuses pornography but still risks the loss of intersubjectivity, obviating the stories of survivors "who wished to communicate with the anthropologist and through him to the outside world . . . the pain of violence in its brutal immediacy" (4).

In assessing the gap between theory and the anthropologist's human contracts, Daniel judges his own book a failure. But in *Charred Lullaby*'s odd rhythms, even when violence leaks in and theory advances as counter-vengeance, something haunting emerges. By refusing the easy marriage of theory to world, what Daniel performs is a *nervous* system, an anthropology anxious about its own logos, a writing that recognizes its status *as writing*, as "anthropo*graphy*."[3] Any theory pretending to account for the grim facticity of violence must stand both within and apart from the materiality it theorizes. Interpretation works only if it is nervous, if it refuses complacency and seeks the "jarring juxtaposition" of "places spattered with blood," with the heat of imperfect words.

This effort to reinvent the logos that drives both anthropology and cultural studies continues in *A Space on the Side of the Road*, Kathleen Stewart's disquisition on the coal mining regions of West Virginia. Stewart defines cultures and bodies as sites "hard to grasp": geologies lacking geography. She moves back and forth between the imperative voice—"imagine this, picture that"—and a concoction of voices: fragrant lists that conjure fragments of places. Jumping from someone's front porch to a violent car crash to a meditation on what it means to report "place" in this way, Stewart swerves into theory and back again. In reporting dialogue she tries to re-member the circumstance of the telling—including her own "aggravation" at proliferating stories that will not hold still. In refusing to galvanize grid-lessness into an order of things, Stewart asks, what if, instead of transcen-dent codes and systems, "there was only the anecdote"? What if we refused to rely on theories of culture and flooded our markets with contaminating voices? What if every academic appropriation grew "nervous in the wake of its own partial understandings and dense under the weight of its own political unconscious" (210). What then? What does the invocation of ner-vous writing (that is, of utterance embracing its status as stutterance) sug-gest about the specter? Doing anthropology with a dead subject already means that one is well outside the dialogic, talking with someone who can never talk back. But her writing suggests that stutterance may also be a technique that draws attention to text as performance, too much attention to the writer and too little to those who are written upon.

In *The Predicament of Culture* James Clifford also clamors for an anthro-pology of the incommensurable, a "discursive anthropology" that refuses to be a social "science" (as if social systems could be abstracted from em-pirical evidence and separated from the anthropologist's own aesthetic practice). When anthropology was new, the "authoritative" anthropol-ogist made herself into a specter or "participant observer" without notic-ing she provided another culture's phantasmatic ground. But even dur-ing "second-wave" anthropology when Clifford Geertz de-authorized the field and began his phantasm-busting, we find dangers abounding. In "interpretive anthropology," material that is excerpted as "text" may claim a stable relation to "context" with insufficient anxiety about the leap from whole to part, from "culture" to synecdoche. When texts (parts taken for wholes) become immobilized in the act of writing; when they hold very still, the ethnographer can assume the role of the traditional literary critic: someone "who sees the task at hand as locating the unruly meanings of a text in a single coherent intention" (Clifford 40). What gets lost is the colloquy of the colloquial, the situational basis of all fact-seek-ing interactions. Now there are two contexts missing—the ethnographers' and the informants'.

How to "resist the pull toward authoritative representation of the oth-er"? How "to maintain the strangeness of the other voice" as well as the quiddities of the exchange that produced that voice (Clifford 50)? If what emerges in both "authoritative" and "interpretive" anthropology is the problem of doing anthropology not only with abstracted subjects, but with a dead or missing anthropologist, the recent science of "discursive" anthropology also has its pitfalls. In trying to give the subject enough headroom the anthropologist compensates with ample quotation. But the danger here is in using quotation in a subordinate fashion as confirming testimony. How does one write an ethnography where the subject talks back? Even worse—how does one write such an ethnography with the dead? The body can become—not itself—but *an effect of reading*. It is transformed into an Ovidian site that can be manipulated for the sake of a certain form of academic mastery.

This absence beckons acutely in Feldman's *Formations of Violence,* which traces political violence between Republicans and Loyalists in Northern Ireland. Here, again and again, terrifying events are torn from context and "textualized." Often this involves extraordinary violations. Feldman anatomizes a scene of violence and then theorizes its sources in a professionalized nomenclature of cleanliness and contamination, with little apparent concern for this terror's victims—those murdered by inventive brands of territorial fury. How can we talk about those who are off-ed by political violence without replicating its dehumanizations? In Feldman's analysis there is no space for griefwork because he re-enacts what he analyzes: in IRA and Loyalist killings violence breaks the shackles of ideology and becomes its own site for intensifying still more circuits of violence.

In 1976 the "Blanketmen" (those IRA prisoners Feldman interviewed who refused to wear prison uniforms that could divest them of their political status by labeling them common "criminals") began a terrible vigil. When prison authorities refused to grant them political standing, numbers of men lived for years stripped of clothing—shivering in coarse blankets, extraordinarily vulnerable. For the Loyalist guards, every available opening became a portal for violation. Responding to repeated beatings and brutal searches of their anal cavities whenever they used the latrines, prisoners begin to cover the walls of their cells with their own feces—to stink the guards out.

Feldman's thick descriptions of these atrocities and the Dirty Protest that followed suggest a mode of creative interpretation stretched past the limit:

> The guards responded by transforming nakedness into an obvious surrogate tool of visual degradation in place of institutional clothing. The No Wash Protest by the prisoners reclothed their naked bodies with a new and repellent surface of resistance. The fecal cell, which the guards tended to

avoid and mainly entered to inflict quick terror, also interrupted compulsory visibility. . . . The stained walls and the stench endowed the cells with a sensory opacity, resistant depth, and blackness within which the prisoners could shelter. There was a strong analogue between the hiding of contraband by the prisoners in their rectal cavity and the withdrawal of the Blanketmen into the repelling depths of the scatological cell. Denied the surfaces of the inmate's body and the interior of the inmate's cell by fecal defilement, the prison regime extended its optic to the colon-ization of the physical interior of the prisoner with the rectal mirror search. (175)

Feldman describes the prison's rectal exams as "a ceremony of defilement and the highest expression of the prison regime's optical colon-ization of the captive body"—returning us to the question of the pun and whether the academic writer should abandon the temptation to hypertext an already violated body (174). The pun opens a site of readerly risibility and makes the bodies of others too available to the reader's objectifying gaze. That is, to pun about rectal extrusion and intrusion (to make the context of bodily invasion and privation so playful) is to risk excessive figuration. But *not* to mark this space of punning violation seems just as reprehensible. As Feldman argues, for Republican prisoners who transformed this continued defilement the colon became a powerful site of praxis and counter-defilement.

Here, I would argue, the practice of "texting" may go too far, but it also fails to go far enough. That is, Feldman's own colonic text defamiliarizes and disgorges a context so habitually violent that words can barely contain it. In stretching one's figurative capacities on behalf of bodies also stretched to the limit, in inventing puns that insist on making rhetorical capital out of someone else's body by means of an extravagant poiesis, Feldman becomes frighteningly mimetic. In immersing us so thoroughly, so viscerally in cloacal politics (running the gamut from highbrow theory to lowbrow wordplay), Feldman's version of "interpretive" anthropology veers deliberately off course and tries to become "discursive." This is thick description with an alienation-effect thrown in: rhetorical cavities held wide, figures violent and awkward—attempting to make readable (and therefore disruptable?) the space of the all too terrible and strange.

In criticizing the hard-troping, theory-hungry bent of Feldman's prose, I'm also arguing that its "evacuation" of griefwork or mourning is oddly compensated for by Feldman's own farfetched and farcical figurations—images that jolt us out of a pathos. Given this self-contradicting conclusion, why do I object so strenuously when Gildea constructs equally "creative" and objectifying figures to inscribe the mute surfaces of Mississippi's dead?

My objection is this: while Feldman tries to find a space to reinscribe the fecal contexts deliberately created by his informants, Gildea participates in a form of cultural criticism that doesn't recognize its own lack of information: namely, the complexities of doing anthropology with a dead subject who cannot talk back. In the face of this silence Gildea creates a system that forgets to be nervous about its own certainties:

> A convict who commits suicide out of the depths of despondency is an artist enacting a dream of expressive freedom upon his or her own body. . . . Self-violence in jail . . . needs to be witnessed to be validated as art. In large part because of the debate over their authorship and their journalistic depiction as unmakings, the Mississippi jail hangings have not been presented to a public audience as works of art. Once revealed as makings, however, the power of their iconic imagery rises before you. It speaks of stillness, of liminality and resistance. This is more than giving the finger to the establishment, or burning the flag, this is offering a dead body as an installation piece in a disciplinary space designed to be utterly devoid of artistic expression. (132–33)

Gildea describes the victims of violent deaths while in custody not only as "texts" but as self-texting integers (the ultimate fantasy of the body as text—of a body eager for the critic's resistant readings). Those who have died ambiguously in jail become death artists, deliberate artificers of their own transcendental critique.

But where are the voices of this writer's informants, where is his nervous system? To make such a grand argument out of anything but thin air, the cultural critic needs to cover a great deal of empirical ground—time spent in at least two different material contexts—in the streets, houses, and offices where incarcerated subjects roamed before their incarceration, and in the inferno of Mississippi's jails. Otherwise the dead offer a too-timely Rorschach for the writer's own fantasies—especially those deaths whose sources remain ambiguous. Any ventriloquism of these now-spectral lives must be largely theoretical or imaginary—and must acknowledge the potential arrogance and inaccuracies of its own hoped-for theories. Might we not see in these still bodies subjects who, meeting themselves on the way to jail, become frightened, confused, fragmented, insufficient—suggesting deaths that are just messy and meaningless rather than blithely agential and perverse? Might we not hear, in the margins of this essay, the murmurs of bodies that *do not* speak, because they did not ask to be unmade, but were tortured or murdered, or pushed into suicide? What kind of "installation space" would this make? The writer needs to stutter here, to explore the possibility that these incarcerated men and women might experience their "texting" as posthumous harm, might not consent to the critic's own figurations. Without this discursive doubt, the critical ecstasy and self-certainty that spins off these spectral bodies tells us too much. It creates the possibility that these hanged bodies tell us more about the cultural critic's own investments, and still more about the easy commodification of the dead in the face of a critic's own desire for an "installation piece."

THE ACADEMY AND THE COMMODIFICATION OF LOSS; OR, THE DEAD AS THE SOURCE OF THE NEW

So, what have I just installed? If "Consuming Trauma" exposes a quick trek from trauma to pleasure, if we can buy tenure by turning a trope or a page, then my own writing is also self-pleasing, self-consuming, enchanted at its own aporetics, adrift with the pleasures of merely circulating. What is the status of academic consumerism—of a world of words where we can channel-surf from trauma to pleasure and back to trauma again with so little cost?

Trying to reflect upon these diminutions, I recognize something perpetual; these feelings recur during those grim moments of (pseudo)consciousness I have while reading the *New York Times*. I'm horror-struck reading an article about Mexico, or Dakar, or Des Moines, or Dubuque, and then I glance at a body clothed by Lord and Taylor and feel reprieve (or anger, or desire, or bare nausea). On a really self-conscious day— shocked at the gargantuan presence of these ads next to tiny-print copy about people in pain—I think, what kind of world is this and why do I buy into it?—before buttering my bagel, folding the paper, and putting my thoughts away. How can these modes of protest and packaging coexist in the same paper, in the same consciousness, on the same page? Why is it so customary to mix our pleasures with our horrors?

Reading the *Times*, I know from Benedict Anderson, is a much more complicated act than simply gathering fads and facts about the world. To marry the apocalyptic delights of consumerism (brassy women in boas, quiet young women buckling their bras, young men staring back at me with their sweet, erect nipples) and the chaos of the recently dead or the long dead or the soon to be dead—is a ritual of nationalizing identity. I open my paper and the family across the street opens theirs—or used to, in any event. A sense of collectivity, of shared facts and shared modes of consumption (of consuming objects with our trauma) locates the self in a series of self-disciplining spaces.

What does it mean to give an academic audience "pleasure"? After thinking hard about "Estranged Fruit" and the anthropography of violence, I've begun to suspect that such pleasures have a great deal to do with the dead. As Marx comments in *The Eighteenth Brumaire:* "And just when they seem engaged in revolutionizing themselves and things, in creating something that has never yet existed, precisely in such periods of revolutionary crisis they anxiously conjure up the spirits of the past to their service and borrow from names, battle cries, and costumes in order to present the new scene of world history in this time-honoured disguise and this borrowed language" (103–4). Marx suggests that "new problems and paradigms" depend upon the dead's borrowed names. This means that revolutionary thinking is "never free of anxiety"; or, in Derrida's haunting of Marx, "conjuration is anxiety from the moment it calls upon death to invent the quick and to enliven the new, to summon the presence of what is not yet there" (Derrida 108–9). I would add that these narratives seek an infusion of pleasure by instigating a powerful and satisfying "out-sourcing" of pain—an observation based on the self-gratifying cling-ons of late commodity culture. The Nike swoosh manufactured under subhuman conditions in Vietnam, the Barbie dolls made in Malaysian sweatshops, represent an ultimate out-sourcing of the pain and alienation of labor that a "flexible" economy makes possible. Do academic communities that are pleasure-based work in a similar way? At the very least, the out-sourcing of pain into the traumatic narratives we read and write so freely may have the effect of creating a safely pleasurable source of self-shattering.

In thinking about *The Eighteenth Brumaire,* Derrida makes two more observations. First, those dead generations who weigh so thoroughly upon the "brains of revolutionaries" have a severe spectral density. "To weigh (*lasten*) is also to charge, tax, impose, indebt, accuse, assign, enjoin. And the more life there is, the graver the specter of the other becomes, the heavier its imposition. And the more the living have to answer for it. *To answer for the dead, to respond to the dead* . . . in the absence of any certainty or symmetry." But this debt of responsiveness to spectral thinking creates a strange paradox. The more "the new" demands change or crisis, "the more one has to convoke the old, 'borrow' from it" (109). The *spirit* of revolution depends upon, even as it tries to repudiate, history's *specters.* Facing this obstacle, Marx hopes for a sea change—a moment when the true revolutionary will find "the spirit of [a] new language . . . without recalling the old" (104). But is this anything other than a happy pipe dream?[4] According to Derrida, "Marx intends to distinguish between the spirit (*Geist*) of the revolution and its specter (*Gespenst*), as if the former did not already call up the latter, as if everything, and Marx all the same recognizes this himself, did not pass by way of differences *within a fantastics as general as it is irreducible.* Untimely, 'out of joint,' even and especially if it appears to come in due time, the spirit of the revolution is *fantastic and anachronistic through and through*" (112). We return to the image itself as commodity. In troping or turning death into figures, writing is once more exposed as an act of commodification and consumption: a space where death is converted into pleasure.

Suddenly, we are in the territory of psychoanalysis, of Freud's death wish and pleasure principle, where it is customary to be swept away by gallows humor so reprehensible and consoling and giddy that it can only repeat itself. That is, in the very act of telling or troping, the object world is refigured not as a source of pain but of pleasure: its tension veering toward zero. Can one write and remain in the unpleasure of death? A question terminable and interminable.

E. Valentine Daniel responds to these puzzles in his chapter on "Embodied Terror." In describing the pain of those tortured (by the Sri Lankan army and by Tamilese militants), Daniel notes the peculiar de-animation of the men and women who describe their own torture to others. "There were no signs of contained passion. Rather, attempts to extract information were met with expressions of utter listlessness. Months later I found out that it was not so much boredom that weighed down on the victim as it was the overwhelming sense of the sheer worthlessness of all attempts to communicate something that was so radically individuated and rendered unshareable" (143). But Daniel goes on to argue that those who have endured enormous pain may find some reprieve in terror—in the felt remembrance of pain. In "second" or therapeutic terror, "a seismic aftershock" goes through the body, terrifying those who are present when a torture victim is suddenly wracked by sobs or anger or violent shaking or numbing withdrawal. These convulsions have been described by a Siddha physician as "the pain coming out . . . the trembling and fear that comes through remembering terrible acts" (144). This terror is not an emotion that is simply gothic or void of knowing, but an overdetermined site for coming to deal with (not to heal; it offers no promise of healing) feelings so traumatic that they seem incommunicable—even to the self who endured them. In second or therapeutic terror, experiences that seemed utterly a-linguistic become something the psyche can discharge, recharge, find access to, if not control.

In the poetry and street theater that flourished during this period, Daniel discovers another opening where pain can be dislodged. Pain stuck "at the brink of language" can be freed into beauty—riding swiftly into our lives "on metaphor and icons of affect" (153). But just as swiftly, Daniel pulls back from the affective tug of his own aestheticizing argument. "Too easy," he insists, much too easy. In seeking comfort in the process of re-covering trauma for culture, we "need to ride our consolations between two echoes. . . . The poiesis of culture itself is a narcotic, and as such it summons us to respond to Emily Dickinson's charge that 'Narcotics can-not still the tooth / That nibbles at the soul'" (153). It seems that we can never be nervous enough.

Seeking such nervousness, let me turn to the letter "x." When I picked up my first copy of *Journal x,* its new and borrowed name gave me a small shock of pleasure. The "x" seemed so au courant and flexible, so wonder-fully twenty- and thirty-something, so outmodedly modish. But thinking about this "x" now through the scrim of pleasures derived from hanged bodies and the hard-to-read "scene of the gallant South," I see another "X" in the shadows: namely, the site of privation and violence that marks the loss of the African name. The capitalized "X" of a Black Muslim idiom is not cited here, and yet it resounds in the journal's margins—an unknown invariable that conjures up specters from the Middle Passage and beyond. What do we look for when we seek out the "x"? Do we seek the *pleasure* of the spectral unknown, or its *burden*? Perhaps, as a way of short-circuiting the proprietorship of the name, this "x" must resonate in both contexts, "between two echoes."

Let me end with my own echolalia. Last night at dinner we were play-ing a "Know Your U.S. Presidents" game with the kids. I asked Kiri, the seven-year-old, "Which president freed the slaves?" and Noah, just three, shouted—"Santa Claus!" We burst into laughter at his vehemence, his certainty, and his obvious pleasure in having such a good answer. He is learning his history from our culture's Old Masters—discovering, in ways that I'd never thought possible, the stinging pleasure, the consuming narcotic, the deadening hope, of recirculating the commodified name.

NOTES

An earlier version of this essay appeared in *Journal x* 1.2 (Spring 1997): 225–51. Reprinted by permission of the editors of *Journal x*. I thank Marlon Ross, Lauren Berlant, Barbara Johnson, Colin Johnson, Marjorie Levinson, Aamir Mufti, Anita Norich, Yopie Prins, Toby Siebers, P. A. Skantze, Valerie Traub, Bryan Wolf, Mako Yoshikawa, and many others for the invaluable ideas they contributed to this essay.

1. AP photograph in John F. Burns, "Biko's Case Now Offers Justice from a Travesty," *New York Times,* Sunday, Feb. 2, 1997: 4.

2. To investigate this idea in depth, see Christopher's Bollas's *The Shadow of the Object.*

3. The phrase "anthropography" is borrowed from Daniel's subtitle. Taussig details numerous nervous systems in his description of the social as an ongoing state of emergency in *The Nervous System.*

4. This is glossed in Gibson-Graham. "When Marx attempts to banish the specter, in that same moment he sets himself up for a haunting—by all that must be erased, denied, cast out, mocked as chimerical or belittled as inconsequential, in order to delimit a certain objectivity. Indeed, the attempt to banish the specter creates the possibility and the likelihood of a haunting. In the very moment of exorcism, the specter is named and invoked, the ghost is called to inhabit the space of its desired absence. The more one attempts to render it invisible, the more spectacular its invisibility becomes" (240).

WORKS CITED

Adorno, Theodor W. *Negative Dialectics.* Trans. E. B. Ashton. New York: Continuum, 1983.

Benjamin, Walter. "Theses on the Philosophy of History." *Illuminations.* Trans. Harry Zohn. New York: Schocken, 1969.

Bollas, Christopher. *The Shadow of the Object: Psychoanalysis of the Unthought Known.* New York: Columbia University Press, 1987.

Clifford, James. *The Predicament of Culture: Twentieth-Century Ethnography, Literature, and Art.* Cambridge, Mass.: Harvard University Press, 1988.

Daniel, E. Valentine. *Charred Lullabies: Chapters in an Anthropography of Violence.* Princeton: Princeton University Press, 1996.

De Certeau, Michel. *The Practice of Everyday Life.* Trans. Steven Rendell. Berkeley: University of California Press, 1984.

Derrida, Jacques. *Specters of Marx: The State of the Debt, the Work of Mourning, and the New International.* Trans. Peggy Kamuf. New York: Routledge, 1994.

Feldman, Allen. *Formations of Violence: The Narrative of the Body and Political Terror in Northern Ireland.* Chicago: University of Chicago Press, 1991.

Gibson-Graham, J. K. *The End of Capitalism (As We Knew It).* Oxford: Blackwell, 1996.

Gildea, Barry. "Estranged Fruit: Making and Unmaking in Mississippi's Jails." *Journal x* 1 (1996): 113–44.

Hertz, Neil. "More Lurid Figures." *Diacritics* 30 (1990): 2–27.

Homer. *The Odyssey of Homer*. Trans. Richmond Lattimore. New York: Harper, 1965.

Kamps, Ivo, and Jay Watson. "Editors' Preface." *Journal x* 1 (1996): 1–4.

Marx, Karl. *The Eighteenth Brumaire of Louis Bonaparte*. Vol. 11 of Karl Marx and Frederick Engels, *Collected Works*. New York: International Publishers, 1979.

Spillers, Hortense. "Interstices: A Small Drama of Words." *Pleasure and Danger: Exploring Female Sexuality*. Ed. Carole S. Vance. Boston: Routledge, 1984. 73–100.

Stallybrass, Peter. "Worn Worlds: Clothes, Mourning, and the Life of Things." *Yale Review* 81 (1993): 35–75.

Stevens, Wallace. "The Pleasures of Merely Circulating." *The Palm at the End of the Mind*. Ed. Holly Stevens. New York: Vintage, 1972. 96–97.

Stewart, Kathleen. *A Space on the Side of the Road: Cultural Poetics in an "Other" America*. Princeton: Princeton University Press, 1996.

Taussig, Michael. *The Nervous System*. New York: Routledge, 1992.

Z Magazine: A Political Monthly (Feb. 1994): 17.

PART TWO

Holocaust Legacies

TWO

Between the Extreme and the Everyday: Ruth Klüger's Traumatic Realism

Michael Rothberg

Everyday problems do not interest us.

—Heinrich Himmler

The program that followed from Himmler's dismissal of daily life rapidly left the realm of the everyday to become a defining moment in what Eric Hobsbawm has called the "age of extremes."[1] But the traffic between the extreme and the everyday is never simple. As Ruth Klüger's memoir *weiter leben: Eine Jugend* (Living on: A youth) makes clear, the inevitable overlap of ordinary and extraordinary experiences constitutes one of the most troubling legacies of genocide—and one of the most difficult problems for autobiographical writers. Through its combination of autobiographical narration and essayistic commentary, Klüger's memoir maps the world of the concentration camps as a borderland in which extremity and everydayness coexist.[2]

In *weiter leben,* the extreme and the everyday are neither opposed, collapsed, nor transcended through a dialectical synthesis—instead, they are at once held together and kept forever apart in a mode of representation and historical cognition I call traumatic realism. My notion of traumatic realism parallels that in Hal Foster's important book on neo-avant-garde art, *The Return of the Real.* However, developing this concept in the context of a response to historical extremity—and in terms of literary instead of visual texts—critically alters the category. Drawing on Fredric Jameson's notion of realist discourse as a form of cognitive mapping, I use traumatic realism as both an epistemological and a social category in order to work through the dilemmas of Holocaust representation.[3] As supplementary examples from the writings of Charlotte Delbo will demonstrate, the practice of traumatic realism is by no means unique to *weiter leben,* but rather constitutes a crucial, if too often overlooked, feature of testimonial writing. In representing a site of violence, traumatic realism simultaneously produces knowledge of the extreme and prompts public recognition of a post-traumatic social context.

• • •

Weiter leben tells the story of Ruth Klüger's coming of age as a Jewish child under National Socialism in Vienna and of her early teen-age years spent in concentration camps. After the war, Klüger and her mother spent a few years in Germany before emigrating to the United States, where she later became a professor of German. The combination of reflection and autobiography through which Klüger narrates her story, as well as her characteristic sharp wit and biting analysis of the postwar world, makes her text an especially rich object of critical interrogation. While the memoir would repay many different approaches, I have chosen to focus on the types of knowledge that autobiographical writings such as *weiter leben* can produce about the Nazi genocide and particularly about the world of the camps, a world that David Rousset famously named the "concentrationary universe." Such an approach teaches us something about the nature and epistemology of "extremities" and about a mode of autobiographical discourse that attempts to grapple with the extreme.

Klüger's mapping of the concentrationary universe can be glimpsed through attention to the primary and often-repeated image through which she figures boundaries: barbed wire. A frequently reproduced and cited "piece" of the camp world, barbed wire serves in much Holocaust literature not only as a metaphor that immediately calls up certain well-worn associations of evil, but as a metonymy that evokes a particular topography. As Sidra Ezrahi has shown, such internally chosen, metonymic figures generally function to emphasize the "closedness" of the camp world, since through them language itself is revealed as trapped within the limited options of the concentrationary (49–66; esp. 55). Through a critique and refunctioning of this stereotypical image, Klüger transforms barbed wire into a tool for prying open the multiplicity of relations within the camps and between victims and their non-victimized contemporaries (both during and after the war).

In an epilogue to her memoir, Klüger describes the "primal scene" that generates the literary narration of her life story. Back in Germany as a visiting professor of German literature, Klüger is run down by a bicyclist on Göttingen's Jüdenstraße [Jew Street]. It is during her recovery from this accident that she begins to write her memoirs. In her reconstruction of her thoughts as the bicyclist bore down on her, the bicycle and headlight are transformed into barbed wire and a spotlight: "I believe he is pursuing [*verfolgt*] me, wants to run me down, bright desperation, light in the dark, his headlight, metal, like a spotlight over barbed wire, I want to defend myself, push him back, both arms outstretched, impact, Germany, a moment like a hand-to-hand fight, *that* struggle I lose, metal, Germany again, what am I doing here, what did I come back for, was I ever gone?" (272). In her description of this occurrence, Klüger creates a constellation consisting of the constricting threat of barbed wire, the accidental impact of extreme events, and the restlessness of the memory of the camps that reverberates back through the entire memoir. By merging divergent locations in time and space, she suggests the essentially traumatic origin of her story. This "origin" is at once located at the moment of the memoir's enunciation and in the open wounds of the memories that it probes. Because it suggests a simultaneously porous but painful marking of boundaries, barbed wire in *weiter leben* comes to play a significant role in figuring the complex relationship between past and present, and here and there. While all memoirists must negotiate this charged borderland of experience and memory, survivors of trauma bear the added burden of having to grapple continuously with the interplay of the extreme and the everyday.

Barbed wire imagery begins in the section of *weiter leben* entitled "The Camps" and continues throughout the rest of the book. Significantly, however, the image first appears not in a description of the author's experience, but rather in the lengthy essayistic discourse that opens "The Camps." This reversal of the expected order of memoiristic presentation—ordinarily, reflection follows experience—serves to highlight the impossibility of direct access to events and the necessity of working through the preexisting discourses that mediate and circumscribe experience. Introducing her time in Theresienstadt, Auschwitz-Birkenau, and Christianstadt, Klüger reflects on the multiple types of camps and ghettos in the concentrationary universe and on the reluctance of the general public to recognize them:

> The disinclination of most people . . . to note the names of smaller camps perhaps is attributable to the fact that one would like to keep the camps as unified as possible and under the large labels of the concentration camps that have become famous. That is less tiring for the mind and emotions than coming to terms with differentiations. I insist on these distinctions . . . in order to break through the curtain of barbed wire that the postwar world has hung before the camps. There is a separation between then and now, us and them, which doesn't serve truth, but rather laziness. (82)

In her insistence on differentiation and her critique of separation, Klüger provides tools for thinking beyond the dominant tendencies within Holocaust studies, which often homogenize the camps either through a hyperbolic discourse of extremity or through their banalization. The barbed wire curtain not only screens out distinctions between camps, it also installs a lazy separation between the camps and the postwar world. Differentiation does not mean distancing the events from the present; this passage implies that—for outsiders and perhaps for former inmates as well—overcoming that distancing is in fact a prerequisite for understanding and coming to terms with the specificities of the concentrationary universe. Breaking through the barbed wire means learning to differentiate between differentiation and separation. Unlike separation, which marks out clear boundaries, differentiation can be seen as a non-totalizing process of distinction whereby differences are held together, while simultaneously a "displacement of the clear borderlines of thought" also takes place (86). The proximity in Klüger's text of borderlines of thought to the material borders of the camps makes clear that undermining the "disciplinary" function of barbed wire means challenging not only *what* we think about the camps, but the *way* we think about them. Displacement of borderlines is not equivalent to their erasure; indeed, it throws into question all attempts at equation.[4]

The challenge to the thinking of the camps that Klüger's text poses in the passage on the barbed wire of the postwar world has particular resonance for the problem of autobiographical discourses by survivors of extremity. If Klüger is caught between the everyday and the extreme, she also makes clear that the memoirist and her interlocutors are all too easily trapped in approaches to the extreme that fetishize or erase differences. Pondering the communicability of extreme experiences, Klüger criticizes Gisela, her foil throughout the book, out of whose comparisons equations continually emerge, and yet she notes that "one cannot get by without comparisons" (111). Differentiation, comparison, and displacement constitute the conceptual tools through which Klüger both experiences and represents the events of the Holocaust. The "truth" of the concentrationary universe is that it is not one—in Klüger's words, "Behind the barbed-wire curtain everyone is not the same; concentration camp does not equal concentration camp" (83). Barbed wire is, nonetheless, not only the name for a negative rhetorical tool that must be dispensed with since it produces only equation or separation. It remains simultaneously a metonymy tied to the material conditions of the camps, a border behind which "literal" death indeed took place. And yet literal death cannot be represented, not only because language always has a figural side, but because, as Klüger notes, "she who writes, lives" (140). The "living" medium itself gives the lie to its message of death. How does the memoirist represent realistically this space of death behind the barbed wire curtain? How can a language that must remain ordinary portray the heterogeneity of the extreme without neutralizing it? By highlighting the fact of survival as a factor in the figuring of death, Klüger reminds us that the theory of the "death of the author" and the critique of realism that accompanied it in theoretical discourse of the 1960s and 1970s targeted a far different context from that of the testimonial autobiography—a genre in which the survival of the author is as troubling as the failure of language to correspond to reality.

Klüger's text implies that extremity is not only that which falls out of language, it is also what remains caught in its net. Drawing on the physical topography of Birkenau, in which various subcamps were situated adjacent to each other and separated only by barbed wire, Klüger represents a situation in which proximity and distance coexist. A brief paragraph describes the encounter of the narrator and her mother with two Hungarian prisoners, victims of one of the last and most massive phases of the Nazi genocide:

> One day, the camp next to ours was full of Hungarian women. They had come directly from home, and they knew nothing yet. Through the barbed wire we talked with them, quickly, hectically, without being able to say much. I realized how far ahead of them I was with my experience from Theresienstadt. There was a woman who spoke good German, and her daughter, approximately my age. . . . My mother remembered that we had an extra pair of wool socks, went to fetch them, and set about throwing

them over the wire. I interfered, I could throw better, give them to me. My mother refused, threw, threw badly, and the socks remained hanging overhead in the barbed wire. Words of regret on both sides. Futile gestures. The next day the Hungarian women were gone, the camp stood ghostly empty, in the barbed wire our socks still hung. (123)

In this passage, Klüger mixes identification and dis-identification, familiarity and estrangement. The Hungarian mother-and-daughter pair mirrors the narrator and her mother. They speak the same language, the daughter is the narrator's age, and they seem to be accessible across the barbed wire. At the same time, the throwing of the socks is an everyday gesture of care for the body's extremities. And yet, the homeliness and familiarity of the women, and the everyday gesture of the mother, are rendered uncanny by the context—an uncanniness that helps the narrator to see her own self-estrangement through the experience of the camps. The same barbed wire whose porousness allows communication between camps also establishes a limit beyond which gestures are futile, words tinged with regret. When the Hungarian women disappear, their end can be conceived, but not represented through a mimetic gesture. Nevertheless, their absence is marked by the socks that hang in the barbed wire. Not quite across the line into the ghostly emptiness, but no longer in the possession of the living on the near side, the socks mediate between the everyday and the extreme. The dead possess the living insofar as they dispossess them—of words, gestures, and other everyday objects.

Klüger's memoir teaches us to reconceive the relationship between language and death—a relationship that has been a regular concern in studies of autobiography since at least Paul de Man.[5] As victims of extremity, the dead in *weiter leben* cannot be the objects of an everyday autobiographical realism, because they embody "something more real than the reality we ordinarily inhabit" (Hartman 542). They are, instead, traumatically real. Indeed, the extreme, as I have described it thus far, bears a strong resemblance to the Lacanian notion of the real.[6] Hal Foster has drawn on the Lacanian real to describe an aesthetic of "traumatic realism" (Foster 130). In Foster's fine reading, Andy Warhol's repetitive images of accidents both "*screen* the real understood as traumatic" and *point* to the real that "*ruptures* the screen of repetition" (132). The repetition produces a paradoxical situation: "we seem almost to touch the real, which the repetition of images at once distances and rushes toward us" (136). In Klüger's text, what I call traumatic realism has a similar double relationship to the real. The barbed wire seems both to offer access to the real and to frustrate attempts to touch it; the socks provide a condensation of this doubleness. Yet, if the extreme bears a strong resemblance to the real in *weiter leben,* it does not equal it, and neither can it be equated with trauma—the relationship is more complex and demands further distinctions.

The evocation of the traumatic relationship between the extreme and the everyday through the tracking of a homely object in an unhomely landscape is not unique to *weiter leben* but rather constitutes a significant, traumatic realist subgenre of recent autobiographical writings and art. In her trilogy *Auschwitz and After,* for example, the French political prisoner and memoirist Charlotte Delbo employs disjunctive strategies not unlike Klüger's in order to suggest the traumatic complexity of life in the face of the extreme. One chapter in *Useless Knowledge,* the middle volume of Delbo's trilogy, begins, innocuously enough, with the description of a Christmas spent in the Raisko laboratory, where Delbo served part of her time at Auschwitz. While certainly melancholy, this episode seems to represent one of those "moments of reprieve," as Primo Levi named them, during which these privileged prisoners were almost able to obtain an experience of normality at the heart of extremity. The festivities conclude with the exchange of small gifts, one of which, given to a young girl, is a teddy bear. This most innocent of gifts turns out to have a terrible provenance, which, recounted by the narrator, shatters the normality of the entire scene.

> One morning, as we passed near the railway station on our way to the fields, our column was stopped by the arrival of a Jewish convoy. . . . This is how a doll, a teddy bear, arrives in Auschwitz. In the arms of a little girl who will leave her toy with her clothing, carefully folded, at the entrance to "the showers." A prisoner from the "heaven commando," as they called those who worked in the crematoria, had found it among the objects piled up in the showers' antechamber and exchanged it for a couple of onions. (166)

In this small but emblematic anecdote, a chain of contamination connecting the murder of a Jewish girl with the celebration of a Christian holiday stretches across various regions of the camp world—from the crematoria, through the chambers and antechambers of death, into the commerce of concentrationary society. The very same process that produces an extraordinary genocide is revealed as enhancing an ordinary celebration at the privileged end of the camp hierarchy. In its circulation from one little girl to another, the narrator recognizes the bear as the carrier (bearer?) of an

uncanny double heritage. In the face of the extreme, the price of normality is high indeed. And yet, it is not clear that the Christmas party has been
a failure. Except that the narrator has by chance seen the bear's original
owner, an accident that ensures that the chain of evidence leading from
murder to celebration will survive. From that accidental survival comes
the testimony of traumatic realism—the delivery of a terrible message that
contaminates the receiver with useless knowledge.[7]

Unlike the barbed wire curtain of the postwar world—which attempts
to avoid the traumatically real by separating now and then, us and them,
the extraordinary and the banal—Klüger's barbed wire and Delbo's useless knowledge occupy an intermediary space and reveal a tangled legacy
of differentiation. The story of the Hungarian women, like the story of the
teddy bear, illustrates how, even in the middle of the concentrationary
universe, the relationship between extremity and normality is constantly being displaced according to position and perspective: while situated
within the shadow of the crematorium, the narrator and her mother find
themselves, incredibly, on this side of extremity and returned to a care-
taking, everyday role. Although it is produced from within the ordinary,
the extreme remains an outside limit, always situated on the other side of
the fence. Having returned from the land of the dead, the witness attempts
to climb back over that fence through an act of testimony. But when she
tries to grab hold of the extreme with language, it slips away, leaving the
grounds "ghostly empty." When she tries to avoid the extreme, however, it returns, or rather, reveals that it was there all along, like socks caught
in barbed wire.

Besides exposing the memoirist's dilemma in the face of the contra-
dictory quality of the extreme—the fact that it always exceeds language
but still inhabits it—Klüger also reveals extremity's implication in the
everyday. This implication represents in turn the traumatic potential of
extremity, and Klüger's depiction of extremity modifies predominant
notions of trauma. In *weiter leben,* trauma resides not in the extreme event
itself, but in the barbed wire that holds together and separates life and
death, the inside and the outside, the familiar and the radically foreign.
This understanding of trauma is slightly, but significantly, at an angle to
dominant contemporary understandings. Foster suggests that "a confusion of subject and world, inside and outside . . . is an aspect of trauma;
indeed it may be this confusion that *is* trauma" (134).[8] At least in Klüger's
representation, however, the traumatic nature of the experience results
not so much from a confusion of inside and outside, but rather from the

narrator's location in the face of an unsurpassable coexistence of inside and outside, subject and world. This shared/divided place—where, for instance, Klüger encounters the Hungarians—is a place of trauma because its coincidence of opposites overwhelms the everyday structures of understanding, which nevertheless remain present.[9] As Cathy Caruth writes, trauma is not an event, but a *"structure of . . . experience"* ("Trauma and Experience" 4; emphasis in original) in which events remain unintegrated into narrative memory. This lack of integration recalls the socks that mark the crossroads of inside and outside, but also the maintenance of the boundary. Klüger's text suggests that it may be the insistence of a seemingly banal object within a context of extremity, rather than some absolute quality of the Extreme Event, that poses the greatest challenge to understanding: "[f]or the survivor of trauma . . . the truth of the event may reside not only in its brutal facts, but also in the way that their occurrence defies simple comprehension" (Caruth, "Recapturing" 153). What is crucial here, but easily unremarked, is that the "defi[ance of] *simple* comprehension" does not simply annihilate comprehension, but rather *displaces* it. This displacement, as both Klüger and Caruth make clear, derives from the fact that trauma involves both "the encounter with death" and "the ongoing experience of having survived it." Thus traumatic texts, such as Klüger's, represent "the inextricability of the story of one's life from the story of a death" (Caruth, *Unclaimed Experience* 7, 8). She who writes lives—but she lives an other life.

Trauma theory, as it has been developed recently by Caruth, Hartman, Zizek, and Foster, among others, helps to overcome the fetishistic separation identified by Klüger as the denial of trauma's impact. To claim that the extreme is implicated in the everyday as a nonintegrated presence, and that this implication constitutes the traumatic, is not necessarily to claim, however, that the reverse is also true. That is, the everyday is not always implicated in the extreme and is not only a place of trauma. Without this distinction, Klüger teaches us, a trap different from separation emerges: equation threatens to replace comparison and differentiation. A potential risk of trauma theory based on Lacan's rereading of Freud is the collapse of distinction between the real and the traumatic—the notion, in Foster's reading for instance, of "the real understood as traumatic" (132). Because Klüger presents a more complicated picture, I depart from Foster and seek to install a rift between the two categories in order to specify the differentiated relationship between the real, the everyday, the extreme, and the traumatic.[10]

As Klüger suggests when she describes how she came to write her memoir after being run down by a bicyclist on a German street, trauma and its witnessing emerge in the context of accidents. The real is always a "missed encounter," as Lacan famously notes, but he also makes clear that within the category of the missed encounter only trauma is radically "unassimilable" and "accidental" (55).[11] To equate the real with the traumatic would be to generalize the unassimilable and thus deprive it of its accidental nature.[12] Under nontraumatic, everyday circumstances, the missed encounter that characterizes confrontation with the real does not have the status of the "shocking and unexpected occurrence of an accident" (Caruth, *Unclaimed Experience* 6). Rather, the *méconnaissance* of the real under everyday circumstances is precisely that which is expected, and thus its potentially traumatic nature is mediated by social structures of community, communication, and empathy.[13] Under extreme circumstances, in contrast, the unexpected and overwhelming breakdown of communicative structures results in what Shoshana Felman calls an "accidenting" of knowledge (Felman and Laub 17–25). Through the practice of traumatic realism, Klüger brings together knowledge and the accident in a constellation bound by barbed wire. Such a constellation of suffering, chance, and cognition represents an unlikely combination, indeed, for positivist and traditional realist accounts of first-person knowledge. But precisely for that reason, Klüger's traumatic realism helps to reveal what is most particular to autobiography as a form of historical understanding.[14]

Klüger's text makes clear that trauma's conditions of possibility lie in surviving the accident of the extreme. In the narrator's missed encounter with the disappearance of the Hungarian women, it is not the women who are traumatized by the extreme; they are its victims. The narrator is traumatized in so far as she lives on beyond extremity into a new world of everydayness—hence the book's title, *weiter leben*. Without the distinction between the traumatic and the extreme, the difference so crucial to Klüger between the dead and the living, both surviving victims and nonvictims, disappears. The extreme's implication in the everyday is spatial, but trauma's relationship to that place is temporal. Trauma always entails a coming after: "the impact of the traumatic event lies precisely in its belatedness, in its refusal to be simply located" (Caruth, *Trauma* 9). The socks snared in the barbed wire don't only testify to the spatial inextricability of the extreme and the everyday. They *hang* there, they persist beyond the murder of the women, and this persistence invokes the "ghostly" belatedness of trauma.

Once again, the texts of Charlotte Delbo produce a related insight into trauma's temporality. In "Kalavrita of the Thousand Antigones," published first in 1979 and then integrated into *La mémoire et les jours,* Delbo provides a stunning image of the doubleness of trauma's belated temporality: the past is at once completely present, because trauma stops time, and completely distant, because such time is not susceptible to transformation. In this narrative, a Greek woman recounts to a "voyager," Delbo, how, in December 1943, the Germans entered Kalavrita, a Peloponesian village, and massacred all of the men, while the women were held in the village school. Much of "Kalavrita" recounts the efforts of the women to bury the thirteen hundred men, hence the reference to Antigone.

For the women of Kalavrita, the result of such a genocidal war on civilians is a disruption of the conventions of the mourning process, and this disruption impinges upon the very experience of time. Faced with the masses of the dead, the women found themselves "immobile. Mute. What should they do? What should they really do? For ordinary deaths, one knows. But for those . . . That enormous heap of the dead. The enormous heap" (114; Delbo's ellipses). The narrative makes clear that the difference between genocide and ordinary death is not one of scale, but of social organization. "For the funerary toilet, everyone knows what to do. / For the burial . . . The gravedigger was there, dead with the others. [. . .] And the coffins? The carpenter was there, dead with the others" (119; first ellipses Delbo's). The problem of burying thirteen hundred men exceeds the individual faculties, which might accomplish the "toilet," but which are rendered helpless by genocide's utter destruction of the community. "Ordinary" means for burying extraordinary dead prove insufficient when the grave-digger, the carpenter, and even the priest have been murdered together.

In improvising a communal grave for the men, the women of the village also show extraordinary commitment to the task of burying and honoring the dead—"we performed for our dead all of the duties that one owes to the dead" (123). But the tale's uncanny end reveals the extent to which the standards and practices of the everyday have been destroyed, at least for the survivors of the massacre: "Goodbye, voyager. / When you cross the village to find the road and return home, look at the hour on the clock in the square. / The hour that you will read on the face of the clock is the hour of that day. The spring of the clock broke with the first volley. We didn't repair it. It's the hour of that day" (124). As material evidence of a crime, the stopping of the Kalavrita clock becomes a monumental index of genocide and a metaphor for its traumatic persistence. The narrator's *envoi* and Delbo's recording of it also attempt to transmit this trauma to the reader/voyager, who is able to read the signs of violence but is also safely on the tourist's path home—a path not so different from that taken by the perpetrators as they proceeded home unscathed. The narrator's trauma lies in part in the recognition of this tension between the rupture of home and time in the village and the continuity which will finally bury the traces of the dead. That different times and places coexist can itself be traumatic, but it also represents the only possibility for memorialization. In order for the story to be passed on, "so that one remembers," the narrator needs the voyager, even if the voyager's experience can only be the vicarious one of the gilded memorial stairs that mark the site of the slaughter. The dilemma of the modern Antigone lies in this traumatic dialectic between the eroding passage of time, which threatens the preservation of memory, and the fixing of time, in which memory overwhelms the activities of the present.

In their recognition of trauma's disruption of everyday space and time, Klüger and Delbo force a rethinking of testimony beyond the assumptions of traditional realist accounts of mimesis and reference. Even under everyday circumstances, the missed encounter of the real—its resistance to full and transparent symbolization—certainly troubles dominant theories of realism. It is indeed not easy to penetrate beyond the surface reality of the world to the real of the historical totality, as Lukács proposes in the marxist tradition (Lukács). Nor is the "serious treatment of everyday reality"—a phrase with which Auerbach famously characterizes the realist project (491)—as straightforward as it may sometimes appear. The problems with these assumptions from theories of realism become especially glaring under what I have characterized as traumatic circumstances. On the one hand, something always slips away—in this case, the Hungarian women and the men of Kalavrita—leaving a gap that undermines the movement from the microcosm of the text to the macrocosm of the social world. On the other hand, something always inexplicably persists as a remainder/reminder—like the socks, the teddy bear, and the stopped clock—that links surface to depth without allowing passage from one into the other. In a sense, then, to carry on the classical project of realism in relation to an extreme event such as the Holocaust is to risk falling into what Eric Santner has called "narrative fetishism": "the construction and deployment of a narrative consciously or unconsciously designed to expunge the traces of the trauma or loss that called that narrative into being in the first place" (144). Like the fetishist, the realist attempts to use a piece of reality to convert a hole in the real into a real whole.

But, despite the risks of fetishism, Klüger and Delbo do not therefore give up the need for some form of documentation. Rather, they situate the autobiographical project at the intersection of the extreme and the everyday and forge a new traumatic realism out of the haunting memories of the past. Such memoirs seek to bring forth traces of trauma, to preserve and even expose the abyss between everyday reality and real extremity. But traumatic realism differs from other forms of writing and art that also recognize the non-symbolizable remainder of the real and move in the direction of nonrepresentational or nonreferential aesthetic practices. If traumatic realism shares a distrust of representation with modernist formal experimentation and postmodern pastiche, it nevertheless cannot free itself from the claims of mimesis and it remains committed to a project of historical cognition through the mediation of culture. The abyss at the heart of trauma not only entails the exile of the real but also its insistence. Traumatic realism is marked by the survival of extremity into the everyday world and is dedicated to mapping the complex temporal and spatial patterns by which the absence of the real, a real absence, makes itself felt in the familiar plenitude of reality. In the wake of modern and postmodern skepticism, traumatic realism revives the project of realism—but only because it knows it cannot revive the dead.

Yet traumatic realism is not turned only toward the past and its tendency to reappear in haunting repetition. By virtue of its performative address to a post-traumatic context, this kind of writing possesses a future orientation.[15] The traumatic realist project is not an attempt to reflect the traumatic event mimetically, but to *produce* it as an object of knowledge, and to *transform* its readers so that they are forced to acknowledge their relationship to post-traumatic culture. Hence, barbed wire functions in *weiter leben* both as a metaphor for the postwar generation's refusal to acknowledge extremity and as a textual screen across which that generation is given a controlled access to the past. Klüger's self-reflexive use of the concentration camp stereotype does not allow a naturalized, mimetic consumption of the extreme, but it also refuses to accept the postmodern version of the bystander's lament whereby "we didn't know" is transformed into "we can't know." Because it seeks both to construct access to a previously unknowable object and to instruct an audience in how to approach that object, the stakes of traumatic realism are at once epistemological and pedagogical, or, in other words, political.

NOTES

An earlier version of this essay appeared in *a/b: Auto/Biography Studies* 14.1 (Summer 1999): 93–107. Reprinted by permission of the editors of *a/b: Auto/Biography Studies*. I am grateful to Nancy K. Miller for her comments on this essay and her continued support. The work of Yasemin Yildiz on Klüger was an inspiration for my own, and her readings of this essay were essential to its completion. Neil Levi was also a valued respondent, as were audiences at Cornell University and the MLA convention in San Francisco, where versions of the essay were presented.

1. Hobsbawm's notion of the "age of extremes" encompasses the wars, genocides, and other acts of extreme violence, as well as the enormous technological progress, that have characterized the twentieth century. The quotation from Himmler is in Arendt (378).

2. All translations from Klüger's German are my own. The English-language edition of Klüger's memoir, titled *Still Alive: A Holocaust Girlhood Remembered* (Feminist Press, 2001), appeared as *Extremities* was in press. On *weiter leben*'s duality of genre, see Lezzi. Lezzi refers to Saul Friedlander's call for the self-conscious inclusion of commentary in the writing of Holocaust history. See "Trauma and Transference" in Friedlander, *Memory, History,* 117–37.

3. See Jameson, esp. 158, 165, 166. For a brief, but suggestive, commentary on the relationship between epistemological and social approaches to realism, see Robbins.

4. Although developed in a very different context, Leslie Adelson's insightful discussion of Klüger's "positionality" is similar to my reading of "displacement" and "differentiation."

5. See de Man's "Autobiography as De-facement." For an insightful and moving study of the terrain of autobiography and death, see Nancy K. Miller's *Bequest and Betrayal.*

6. The Lacanian notion of the real has been helpfully characterized by Slavoj Zizek in sentences that resonate nicely with the passage from Klüger: "it is impossible to *occupy* its position. But, Lacan adds, it is even more difficult simply to *avoid* it. One cannot *attain* it, but one also cannot *escape* it" (Zizek 156; emphasis in original).

7. For an extensive treatment of Delbo as a practitioner of traumatic realism, see my book *Traumatic Realism.*

8. Mark Seltzer also defines trauma as the breakdown in such distinctions. See "Wound Culture" and *Serial Killers.*

9. The notion of a "shared/divided place" is borrowed from Yasemin Yildiz's reading of Klüger and Jean Améry. Her concept of "geteilte Zeiten" puns on the German verb "teilen," which can mean both to share and to divide.

10. A related point is made by Judith Butler in her critique of Zizek and his deployment of the concept of the real. Butler's convincing critique turns, in part, on the question of Zizek's analysis (or non-analysis) of concentration camps as instantiations of the real (201–3).

11. I discuss and critique the Lacanian dimensions of trauma theory in greater detail in *Traumatic Realism.*

12. I have found Dominick LaCapra's important distinction between "structural" and "historical" trauma quite helpful here (see esp. 47). On the importance of accidents for trauma theory, see Caruth, *Unclaimed Experience* 6–7.

13. On the importance of lack of community, communication, and empathy in the constitution of trauma, see Laub and Auerhahn.

14. For more on Klüger and trauma, see Lezzi.

15. On Klüger's modes of address to the postwar world, see Yildiz, "Sharing Divided Times."

WORKS CITED

Adelson, Leslie. "Ränderberichtigung: Ruth Klüger and Botho Strauß." *Zwischen Traum und Trauma—Die Nation: Transatlantische Perspektiven zur Geschichte eines Problems.* Ed. Claudia Mayer-Iswandy. Tübingen: Stauffenburg-Verlag, 1994. 85–97.

Arendt, Hannah. "Social Sciences Techniques and the Study of Concentration Camps." *Echoes from the Holocaust: Philosophical Reflections on a Dark Time.* Ed. Alan Rosenberg and Gerald Myers. Philadelphia: Temple University Press, 1988. 365–78.

Auerbach, Erich. *Mimesis: The Representation of Reality in Western Literature.* Trans. Willard Trask. Princeton: Princeton University Press, 1953.

Butler, Judith. *Bodies That Matter: On the Discursive Limits of "Sex."* New York: Routledge, 1993.

Caruth, Cathy. "Recapturing the Past: Introduction." Caruth, *Trauma* 151–57.

———. "Trauma and Experience: Introduction." Caruth, *Trauma* 3–12.

———. *Unclaimed Experience: Trauma, Narrative and History.* Baltimore: Johns Hopkins University Press, 1996.

———, ed. *Trauma: Explorations in Memory.* Baltimore: Johns Hopkins University Press, 1995.

Delbo, Charlotte. *Auschwitz and After.* Trans. Rosette Lamont. New Haven: Yale University Press, 1995.

———. *La mémoire et les jours.* Paris: Berg International, 1995.

De Man, Paul. "Autobiography as De-facement." *Modern Language Notes* 94 (1979): 919–30.

Ezrahi, Sidra. *By Words Alone: The Holocaust in Literature.* Chicago: University of Chicago Press, 1980.

Felman, Shoshana, and Dori Laub. *Testimony: Crises of Witnessing in Literature, Psychoanalysis, and History.* New York: Routledge, 1992.

Foster, Hal. *The Return of the Real: The Avant-Garde at the End of the Century.* Cambridge, Mass.: MIT Press, 1996.

Friedlander, Saul. *Memory, History, and the Extermination of the Jews of Europe.* Bloomington: Indiana University Press, 1993.

Hartman, Geoffrey. "On Traumatic Knowledge and Literary Studies." *New Literary History* 26 (1995): 537–63.

Hobsbawm, Eric. *The Age of Extremes: A History of the World, 1914–1991.* New York: Pantheon, 1994.

Jameson, Fredric. *Signatures of the Visible.* New York: Routledge, 1992.

Klüger, Ruth. *weiter leben: Eine Jugend.* 1992, Munich: dtv, 1994.

Lacan, Jacques. *The Four Fundamental Concepts of Psycho-Analysis.* Trans. Alan Sheridan. New York: Norton, 1981.

LaCapra, Dominick. *History and Memory After Auschwitz.* Ithaca: Cornell University Press, 1998.

Laub, Dori, and Nanette C. Auerhahn. "Failed Empathy—A Central Theme in the Survivor's Holocaust Experience." *Psychoanalytic Psychology* 6.4 (1989): 377–400.

Lezzi, Eva. "'weiter leben': Ein deutsches Buch einer Jüdin?" *Rundbrief: Frauen in der Literaturwissenschaft* 49 (Dec. 1996): 14–20.

Lukács, Georg. "Realism in the Balance." *Aesthetics and Politics.* Ed. Ernst Bloch et al. London: New Left Books, 1977. 28–59.

Miller, Nancy K. *Bequest and Betrayal: Memoirs of a Parent's Death.* New York: Oxford University Press, 1996.

Robbins, Bruce. "Modernism and Literary Realism: Response." *Realism and Representation: Essays on the Problem of Realism in Relation to Science, Literature, and Culture.* Ed. George Levine. Madison: University of Wisconsin Press, 1993. 225–31.

Rothberg, Michael. *Traumatic Realism: The Demands of Holocaust Representation.* Minneapolis: University of Minnesota Press, 2000.

Rousset, David. *L'univers concentrationnaire.* Paris: Pavois, 1946.

Santner, Eric. "History beyond the Pleasure Principle: Some Thoughts on the Representation of Trauma." *Probing the Limits of Representation: Nazism and the "Final Solution."* Ed. Saul Friedlander. Cambridge, Mass.: Harvard University Press, 1992. 143–54.

Seltzer, Mark. *Serial Killers: Death and Life in America's Wound Culture.* New York: Routledge, 1998.

———. "Wound Culture: Trauma in the Pathological Public Sphere." *October* 80 (Spring 1997): 3–26.

Yildiz, Yasemin. "Sharing Divided Times: Responses to the Uses of the Holocaust in the Works of Ruth Klüger and Jean Améry." *Hearing the Voices: Teaching the Holocaust to Future Generations.* Ed. Michael Hayse et al. Merion Station, Pa.: Merion Westfield, 1999. 173–80.

Zizek, Slavoj. *The Sublime Object of Ideology.* New York: Verso, 1989.

THREE

Marked by Memory: Feminist Reflections on Trauma and Transmission

Marianne Hirsch

Toni Morrison's Sethe meets her own mother only once. As she tells her two daughters, one day, when she was still a little girl, raised primarily by Nan who spoke to her in a language she has since forgotten, her mother took her behind the smokehouse, opened her dress, and showed her the mark under her breast: "Right on her rib was a circle and cross burnt right in the skin. She said, 'This is your ma'am. This,' and she pointed. 'I am the only one got this mark now. The rest dead. If something happens to me and you can't tell me by my face, you can know me by this mark" (61). Sethe's answer expresses her sense of her own vulnerability, and her desire for mutuality and maternal recognition: "'Yes Ma'am,' I said. 'But how will you know me? How will you know me? Mark me too,' I said. 'Mark the mark on me too.' Sethe chuckled. 'Did she?' asked Denver. 'She slapped my face.' 'What for?' 'I didn't understand it then. Not till I had a mark of my own.'"

In telling this story to her daughters, Sethe claims the mark of her slavery as a thing that can be spoken about to those in the next generation who, like Denver, were not there to be marked themselves. For survivors of trauma, the gap between generations is the breach between a traumatic memory located in the body and the mediated knowledge of those who were

71 •

born after. *Trauma,* in its literal meaning, is a *wound* inflicted on the body. Roberta Culbertson stresses that "no experience is more one's own than harm to one's own skin, but none is more locked within that skin, played out within it in actions other than words, in patterns of consciousness below the everyday and the constructions of language" (170). The wound inflicted on the skin can thus be read as a sign of trauma's incommunicability, a figure for the traumatic real that defines the gap between survivors and their descendants. Paradoxically, the writing on the body that most objectifies its victims by identifying them as slaves or concentration camp prisoners is enclosed within the boundaries of skin, ultimately and utterly private and incommunicable, in Sethe's terms, "a mark of *my own.*"

While theorists like Shoshana Felman and Geoffrey Hartman in writing about the Holocaust have consistently seen literary language as a privileged medium for the transmission of trauma, recent literary, artistic, and theoretical representations have forged a *visual* discourse of trauma that often gets expressed through the figure of the bodily mark, wound, or tattoo. Visual images, the art historian Jill Bennett has argued, do more than to *represent* scenes and experiences of the past: they can communicate an emotional or bodily experience to us by evoking our own emotional and bodily memories. They *produce* affect in the viewer, speaking *from* the body's sensations, rather than speaking of, or representing the past. Bennett comments specifically on the language of sense memory: "It is no coincidence that the image of ruptured skin recurs throughout the work of artists dealing with sense memory. . . . If the skin of memory is permeable, then it cannot serve to encase the past self as other. It is precisely through the breached boundaries of skin in such imagery that memory continues to be felt as a wound rather than seen as contained other. . . . it is here in sense memory that past seeps back into the present, becoming sensation rather than representation" (92).

I want to consider this visual discourse of trauma and, particularly, the dynamics of identification by which the mark, and thus the sense memory that it represents, can, however partially and imperfectly, be transmitted across subjects and generations. When Gayatri Spivak reads the above scene in *Beloved* in relation to the novel's repeated assertion that "this is not a story to pass on," she reflects on the mother's slap: "even between mother and daughter a certain historical withholding intervenes. . . . And yet," she continues, "it *is* passed on with the mark of untranslatability on it, in the bound book *Beloved* that we hold in our hands" (169). The mark of untranslatability becomes the untranslatability of the mark. The implication, on the one hand, that interest and empathy are heightened within the matrilineal family in particular, and the articulation, on the other, of the "historical withholding" that intervenes even between mothers and daughters, make of Morrison's novel a theoretical text for the contradictions that define the intergenerational transmission of trauma. This is why I begin this discussion of the bodily memory and transmission of the Holocaust with *Beloved*—not to compare the Holocaust and slavery but to find in Morrison's mother/daughter story a model through which one might read the transmission of bodily memory in instances of cultural trauma.

When Sethe's mother points out that "this your ma'am" she identifies the mother with the burned circle and cross on her skin. The mark *is* the mother—"this your ma'am"—and it is also the vehicle for mother/daughter recognition—"you will know me by this mark." When physical identity is altered by the mark of slavery, and the daughter is separated from the mother by a radically different history, she both fears having to repeat her mother's story and longs for the recognition that ensures her identity as her mother's daughter. "How will you know me?"[1] The ambivalent desire to be marked, and thus to repeat the mother's trauma, is understandable between mothers and daughters whose bodily resemblance is so violated by the mark as no longer to be the vehicle of mutual recognition at the heart of the mother/daughter bond.

What concerns me here is how writers and visual artists of the second generation have been able to represent this intergenerational dynamic— the desire and the hesitation, the necessity and the impossibility of receiving the parents' bodily experience of trauma manifested in the visual mark or tattoo. Witnessed by those who were not there to live it but who received its effects, belatedly, through the narratives, actions, and symptoms of the previous generation, trauma both solidifies and blurs generational difference.[2] What forms of identification can enable this transmission of body memory, and what artistic idioms can represent them? And what is the role of "historical withholding" in the transmission of trauma? Because of the distinctive cultural expectations bestowed on daughters and the gendered dynamics of subject-formation by which they are shaped, I am particularly interested in exploring the specificity of the role of *daughters* in this line of transmission.

• • •

In the literature on trauma inspired by readings of Freud's work on mourning and melancholia there is a familiar distinction between two modes of remembering. Variously labeled "mémoire profonde" and "mémoire ordinaire" (Delbo), "acting out" and "working through" (LaCapra), "perception" and "memory" (Mitchell), "traumatic memory" and "narrative memory" (van der Kolk and van der Hart), these modes are neither oppositional nor mutually exclusive. Rather, relying on a performative notion of language and other forms of expression, they account for varying degrees of coming to terms with or gaining distance from the past. But the second generation—those who are deeply affected by events they themselves did not experience but whose memory they inherited—are also subject to different, if always overlapping, modes of "remembering." In the stories of transmission on which I will focus, I see a *range* between what Morrison has called "rememory" and what I have termed "postmemory"[3]—between, on the one hand, a memory that, communicated through bodily symptoms, becomes a form of repetition and reenactment, and, on the other hand, one that works through indirection and multiple mediation.[4]

In her extensive psychoanalytic discussions of children of Holocaust survivors, Judith Kestenberg has found the notion of "identification" insufficient in describing their relationships with their parents: "The mechanism goes beyond identification. I have called it 'transposition' into the world of the past, similar—but not identical—to the spiritualist's journey into the world of the dead" (148–49). Morrison's *rememory* is such a form of "transposition," a descent through what Kestenberg calls a "time tunnel of history" into the world of the dead. "Rememory" is a noun and verb, a thing and an action. Communicable, shared, and permanent, because it is spatial and material, tactile, it underscores the deadly risks of intergenerational transmission: "'Some things you forget. Other things you never do. . . . Places, places are still there. If a house burns down, it's gone, but the place—the picture of it—stays, and not just in my rememory but out there, in the world. . . .' 'Can other people see it?' asked Denver. 'Oh yes. Oh, yes, yes, yes. Some day you be walking down the road and you hear something or see something going on. So clear. And you think it's you thinking it up. A thought picture. But no. It's when you bump into a rememory that belongs to somebody else" (Morrison 36). In this passage Sethe underscores the materiality and the intersubjectivity of memory and the dire consequences of one person's empathic over-identification and adoption of another's memories. In *Beloved,* the ultimate ghost story, haunting takes on material shapes. Rememory is the same for the one who was there and the one who was never there, for the I and the you in Sethe's conversation: "'Where I was before I came here, that place is real. It's never going away. Even if the whole farm—every tree and grass blade of it dies. The picture is still there and what's more, if you go there—you who never was there—if you go there and stand in the place where it was, it will happen again; it will be there for you, waiting for you.'" The "re" in rememory signals not just the threat but the certainty of repetition: "It will happen again."

Children of Holocaust survivors often describe their relationships to their parents' memories in these very terms. In her memoir *The War After,* for example, the British journalist Anne Karpf, the daughter of an Auschwitz survivor, enumerates the bodily symptoms through which she experiences her mother's sense memories of the camps. The mark on the skin is the focus of her discussion. For a long period in her young adulthood she develops terrible eczema and scratches herself irresistibly first on her hands and arms and later her entire body:

> I wanted to divest myself of my skin, slip out of it like a starched dress left standing while my self crept away to hide. . . . My skin no longer seemed able to keep what was inside in. . . . After years of my scratching, a close friend asked whether the place on my inside forearm that I was repeatedly injuring wasn't the same place, indeed the very same arm, where my mother's concentration camp number was inked. I was astonished—it had never occurred to me. But I couldn't believe that the unconscious could go in for such crude symbolism, the kind you find in made-for-TV movies— it seemed like a base attempt to endow my own flimsy desolation with historical gravitas and dignify it with reference to my mother's. (I remain unconvinced). (102, 103, 106)

Her own welcome skepticism notwithstanding, Karpf's symptoms, like Sethe's intense desire to be marked with her mother's mark, illustrate what can happen in the absence, or even in spite of, "a certain historical withholding" between mother and daughter. Anne Karpf's relationship to her mother becomes incorporative and appropriative—more a form of "transposition" than identification. Memory is transmitted to be repeated and reenacted, not to be worked through: "I'd always envied my parents their suffering. This was so obviously shocking that I couldn't have admitted it, had I even been conscious of it. . . . their terrible experiences seemed to diminish—even to taunt—anything bad which ever happened to us" (Karpf 126). In the absence of a bodily identity with her mother, Karpf, like Sethe, risks losing her sense of herself: she has to feel the same sense of cold and warmth, the same marking of her skin, the same danger and misery. "It was as if I'd finally managed to prise off some particle of my mother's suffering and make it my own. I'd grafted on to myself a bit of her pain" (Karpf 126).

The child of survivors who "transposes" herself into the past of the Holocaust lives the "burden of a double reality" that makes "functioning" extraordinarily "complex" (Kestenberg 156, 150). Karpf receives her mother's memories in her own body as symptoms that plague even as they fail to lead to understanding. In the sense that they repeat the trauma of the past in what she calls an "awful, involuntary mimetic obsession" (Karpf 253), her mother's memories are *rememories* engaging both mother and daughter with equal vehemence. But Karpf's memoir allows us also to distinguish "transposition" from a different form of "identification," and thus "rememory" from "postmemory." When the mother's experiences are communicated through stories and images that can be narrativized, integrated—however uneasily—into a historically different present, they open up the possibility of a form of second-generation remembrance that is based on a more consciously and necessarily mediated form of identification. Postmemory is a powerful form of *memory* precisely because its connection to its object or source is mediated not through *repetition* or *reenactment* but through previous *representations* that themselves become the objects of projection and recreation. Postmemory is defined through an identification with the victim or witness of trauma, modulated by an admission of an unbridgeable distance separating the participant from the one born after. Geoffrey Hartman has written about "witnesses by adoption" (8–9) and I like the connection to and enlargement of family that this term implies, the acknowledged break in biological transmission. Postmemory thus would be *retrospective witnessing by adoption.* It is a question of adopting the traumatic experiences—and thus also the *memories*—of others as experiences one might oneself have had, and thus of inscribing them into one's own life story. This form of identification means the ability to say, "It could have been me; it was me, also," and, *at the same time, categorically,* "but it was not me." It corresponds to what Eve Sedgwick terms "allo-identification" or "identification with" as opposed to "auto-identification" or "identification as" (59–63).

But how can such identification resist appropriation and incorporation, resist annihilating the distance between self and other, the otherness of the other?[5] How can it resist the envy and competition we see in Morrison and Karpf's texts? How, particularly, can the bodily memory of the mark be transmitted and received without the violent self-wounding of transposition?

For postmemorial artists, the challenge is to define an *aesthetic* based on a form of identification and projection that can include the transmission of the bodily memory of trauma without leading to the self-wounding and retraumatization that is rememory. The desire for this type of nonappropriative identification and empathy and, of course, its often painful and disastrous flaws and failures have formed the core of feminist theory and practice in the last thirty years. As Sedgwick says, "For a politics like feminism . . . effective moral authority has seemed to depend on its capacity for conscientious and nonperfunctory enfoldment of women alienated from one another in virtually every other relation of life" (61). Strangely, however, much of the work on trauma and memory has been resistant to gender differentiation and has not been overtly informed by feminist thinking. In this light, we might examine Spivak's implications that mothers and daughters are privileged intergenerational interlocutors when it comes to traumatic memory. Can the daughter, in particular, both maintain the distance of allo-identification and become the recipient of a bodily memory that enables the transgenerational transmission of trauma?

The work of postmemory defines the *familial* inheritance and transmission of cultural trauma. Still, I believe that this form of remembrance need not be restricted to the family, or even to a group that shares an ethnic or national identity marking: through particular forms of identification, adoption, and projection, it can be more broadly available. Thus, postmemory need not be *strictly* an identity position. But if identifications learned and practiced within the family can be expanded to cross the boundaries of gender, family, race, and generation, then the identification between mothers and daughters forms a clear example of how a shared intersubjective transgenerational space of remembrance, based in bodily connection, can be imagined. Because of a bodily closeness that is reinforced by cultural expectations, the case of mothers and daughters might indeed acutely exemplify the danger of an over-identification through which the more distant idioms of postmemory slide back into the appropriations of rememory. Through the caregiving role traditionally ascribed to daughters, the pressures of intersubjective relationships marked by trauma emerge in especially sharp focus. In looking at postmemory through the lens of the daughter, I am trying to bring the feminist negotiation between commonalities and differences, and the feminist theorization of subjectivity and intersubjectivity, and of political solidarity, to bear on the theorization of memory and trauma. Daughters

become paradigmatic insofar as they enable us to define the range of identificatory practices that motivate the art of the second generation.

• • •

> I have known since I was a child that my parents were concentration camp
> survivors, since both of them had a number tattooed on their left arm. I
> used to spend a lot of time studying their tattoos, wondering what it must
> have been like. My mother never talked about her experiences. My father
> only talked about it when he was scolding us, especially about eating ev-
> erything on our plates. Once when I was at his side on an after-dinner walk,
> he told a friend the stories of the medical experiments performed on him
> and the ten-day transport when people began devouring each other. I
> think he must have forgotten I was there. I didn't inquire any further for
> fear of hurting him.[6]

Tatana Kellner's two artists' books *71125: Fifty Years of Silence* and *B-
11226: Fifty Years of Silence,* which both begin with the above passage, are
the work of a daughter of survivors, born and raised in postwar Prague.
After emigrating to the United States and becoming an artist, Kellner in-
vited her parents to help her with a work that would be based on their

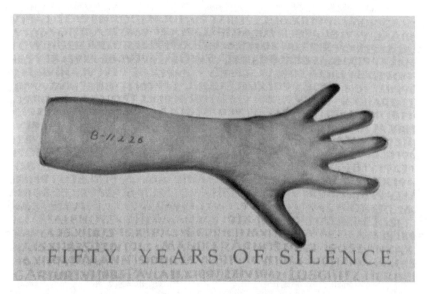

Tatana Kellner, cover, *B-11226: Fifty Years of Silence,* 1995 (courtesy of the artist)

reminiscences of the war. She wanted to tape their stories, but they preferred to write them for her in Czech and she undertook to translate their texts into English. "Except for questions I had in terms of accuracy, this is still not something we can talk about," she told me.

The two books of *Fifty Years of Silence* are the product of a collaboration between the parents and the daughter. Each parent's text—the mother's stories in *71125*, the father's in *B-11226*—handwritten in Czech in blue ink on translucent pages, faces its typewritten translation (on opaque white pages) by the daughter. Superimposed on both versions are large silk-screened photographs. Some were taken by Tatana Kellner on a trip to Prague and Auschwitz and are mostly of roads, train stations, and what look like remains and memorial sites in the camp; others are family photographs from the more than fifty years between the parents' youth in Prague before the war and their old age in an American suburb. On some pages, the superimposed photographs are combined with lists of names and with birth and death dates, taken from the memorial wall of Prague's Pinkasova synagogue. Strikingly, embedded in the middle of each book there is a handmade paper cast of the parent's tattooed arm; the daugh-

Tatana Kellner, layered pages, *B-11226: Fifty Years of Silence,* 1995 (courtesy of the artist)

ter took casts to make the handmade paper arms, and photographed the tattoos so as to copy them exactly, in her own hand, onto the pink surfaces. Each book page contains a hole in the shape of the protruding cast. The parents wrote their stories around the void left by the cast.

By embedding her parents' stories, written in their own language and their own handwriting, into her artwork, Kellner is able, in Paul Celan's terms, to "witness for the witness." In editing and translating her parents' texts, in going to Poland to visit the camp where her parents had been interned, and in constructing her books, Kellner has found a mode of receiving and transmitting their testimony even as she attempts to respect their fifty years of silence. Like the stories of Sethe and Paul D. in *Beloved,* Eva and Eugene Kellner's are not stories "to pass on." But in the art work of their daughter, they are passed on, and with them is the process of transmission, the work of postmemory. *Fifty Years of Silence* suggests the silence with which Tatana Kellner grew up, as well as her own determined need to know. It represents the daughter's responsive and protective "allo-identification," her effort to elicit the stories and her continued childhood fear of "hurting" them further. And Kellner's visual text enables her to respect her parents' "historical withholding," their need for silence and the untranslatability of their story—"this is still not something we can talk about." But, of course, in publishing their narratives, she does inevitably violate the silence they had determined to keep. Kellner's work, like all postmemorial texts, situates itself in this paradoxical space.

Rather than listen and talk with her parents, Kellner looks at their tattoos. Like Sethe's paradigmatic look at the mark beneath her mother's breast—a look both of recognition ("you will know me by this mark") and of nonrecognition ("but how will you know me?")—Tatana's look fundamentally structures her text. She suggests that a visual textuality might expand the current emphasis on oral testimony and active listening as privileged modes of transmission. And the graphic modes she has chosen—casting, tracing, and photography—attempt precisely to convey to her own readers/viewers her parents' bodily wounding. For Kellner, as for other postmemorial artists, visuality is both a *figure* and a *vehicle* for the transmission of sense memory. The enlarged photographs dominate the pages of the two books in such a way that the written text itself becomes photographic—more a visual than a textual image—especially since the reception of the books in a museum setting, for example, precludes detailed *reading* of the texts and relegates viewers to an uncomfortable shuttling between the impulse to look and the compulsion to read.

Like the tattoos, the photograph's indexical relation to its object and the haunting, ghost-like presence of the referent it evokes makes the photographic image a privileged link between memory and postmemory—a vehicle of the *productive look* that can supplement the active listening of postmemory.[7] Photography offers a material indexical medium through which one might literally re-call—and thus make present—a past that remains unreachable. Photographs, like numbers written on an arm, are stubborn survivors of death, ghostly revenants from an irretrievable past. But photographic images are ultimately two-dimensional, moments frozen in time and mere surfaces—*photo-graphy* is literally written (in light) on the skin of the paper. They signal absence as well as presence—the irreparability of loss, the pastness of the past. Photographic images are and also, decidedly, are *not* material traces of an unreachable past. They invite us in, grab us, giving the illusion of depth and thus deep memory, and they also repel us. They convey the spatial dimension of postmemory where, trapped on the surface, we nevertheless fall for the promise of a glimpse into the depths of remembrance. Holocaust photographs, the leftovers and debris of a destroyed culture, made precious by the monumental losses they inscribe, certainly have the capacity to retain a radical otherness that evades a too easy identification. Postmemorial artists use photography precisely to stage a productive look of "allo-identification" that can see beyond the familiar, displacing an incorporative, ingestive look of self-sameness and familiarization in favor of an openness to the other, a granting of alterity and opaqueness. The images they produce have the power both of screening the real and of piercing holes that allow the real to show through.

Kellner's text is literally built around a hole and thus this paradoxical dilemma of transmission structures Kellner's work nowhere more obviously than in the tattooed arm at the center of each book. The arm is almost unbearable to look at in its truncated presence but it also leaves an empty space in the center of each turned page. Kellner has said that for her, visually, "it began with the arms" and she built the books around them. The arms communicate visually and sensually the wounded skin and thus the bodily memory of trauma by recalling the viewer's own bodily memories. At the same time, on the other side of the page, it is the reminder of absence, secrecy, silence, untranslatability.

After turning all the pages of *Fifty Years of Silence* one reaches the base on which each book rests: a sheet of pink handmade paper holding the cast of the amputated tattooed arm, a sculpture signed and numbered by

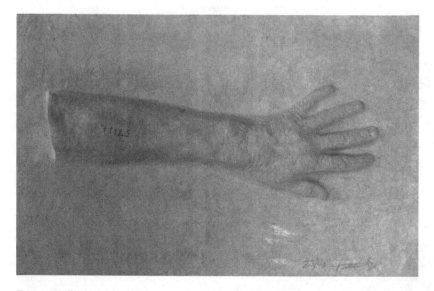

Tatana Kellner, layered pages, *71125: Fifty Years of Silence,* 1995 (courtesy of the artist)

the artist. The numbers tattooed on the two arms are thus mirrored in the numbers indicating the edition of the artwork, signed in the artist's hand. Here ultimately is the unbridgeable distance between the experiences of the two generations: while the artist numbers her own work, separate from her body, the parents' arms were themselves numbered—not as works but as bodies deprived of human agency—by their Nazi victimizers. On the daughter's part, creative choice, the sign of artistic power; on the parents' part, a reminder of forcible dehumanization and powerlessness (Hirsch and Suleiman, 101–2).

One might ask, however, whether Kellner, in numbering her work, has taken care to mark the gap separating her own process of knowledge and *marking* from her parents' experience of *being marked.* Has Kellner, in casting the arm, made too literal a signifier, has she revealed too much, has she slipped into the mimetic repetition that is rememory? She might indeed have, had the arm not been inscribed in the layered, mixed-media work that is *Fifty Years of Silence.* The photographs, the paper casts, and tattoos, combined with the writing, work together to engage us in multiple and complex ways, inviting us to look, to turn pages, to read, to confront the empty space left by the arm. As we shuttle, uneasily, between modes of reception, the text resists understanding and consumption.

Indeed, in its very form, *Fifty Years of Silence* comments self-consciously both on the difficulties of remembrance and transmission and on the problematics of the artistic representation of the Holocaust from a present vantage point. In its sculptural mode and book form, in its conjunction of narrative and image, Kellner's work creates a sense of depth and the promise of revelation. At the same time, the excess of text, the flatness and illegibility of the superimposed images, the materiality of the arm we reach at the end of our reading, and the gaps left in the stories, cannot remove frustration, incomprehension, and unreality. Kellner's work is an attempt at translation, from Czech to English, from the past to the present, from the camp world to ours. And in that process of failed translation, the second-generation daughter can *hold* the memory with which she has been entrusted, because she can respect and perpetuate her parents' act of historical *withholding*. And, at the same time, she can acknowledge the inevitability of her own act of violation that emerges from the lack of *recognition* that marks the relationship of survivors to their children. But in Kellner's text, it is the *father* who talks, and the *mother* who withholds: "I think he must have forgotten I was there."

• • •

Jeffrey Wolin's 1997 exhibition and book *Written in Memory: Portraits of the Holocaust* offers another cross-generational moment of visual and verbal transmission of trauma. In these portraits, Wolin, an American artist born in 1951 as a descendant of Polish and Lithuanian Jews, photographs survivors and records excerpts from their edited testimony by writing them in his own handwriting right on the print. In one of his images, we can study his representation of the dynamics of mother-daughter transmission. The example of this particular image enables us to envision mother-daughter transmission and postmemory as a figure, available to male and female artists both, and thus not as an identity position.

In the image of Irma Morgensztern, born in 1933 in Warsaw, Irma stands hugging a young woman who must be her adult daughter and they both hold a portrait of a woman who must be Irma's mother. On the facing page in Wolin's book is a 1945 photo of the twelve-year-old Irma taken in Warsaw at the end of the war. The text describes the night Irma escaped from the ghetto. While it tells about her mother and father, no mention is made of the daughter, who is depicted as an earnest listener, witness, and inheritor. The narrative describes the complicated name and identity change Irma had to undergo in hiding. "It was terribly tragic the night before I left the Warsaw ghetto when they knew I'm going to be gone the next night. So we were sitting and talking and they were trying to put into my head who I am, that I'm from Warsaw and my name is Barbara Nosarewska, I never should forget. . . . And on the other hand they were trying to put into the other side of my brain that after the war I am Jewish and my name is Irma Morgensztern."

Mother, daughter, and grandmother are intertwined in the image, but there is something terribly anachronistic about it: the woman in the portrait, the grandmother, is younger than the adult Irma, perhaps not much older than Irma's daughter, and she will never age or have aged enough to act as a grandmother to the young woman in the picture. There are several mother-daughter pairs in the image: Irma and her daughter, in the present; Irma and her mother in the past looking at each other across the break of the white page, both smiling; and Irma and her mother in the

Jeffrey Wolin, Irma Morgensztern and Her Daughter, 1997, from *Written in Memory* (courtesy of the artist)

Irma Morgensztern, 1945, from *Written in Memory* (courtesy of the artist)

present: but here the mother is just a portrait, younger than her daughter, frozen in an eternally past present.

Nor is the mother's story told—did she die in the war, did Irma ever find out what happened to her mother and father? The gesture with which Irma and her daughter hold her mother's portrait is protective and tender, as is the gesture with which they hold one another, but their eyes do not meet, each is in her own space, each in her own time zone. Even as the women hug, we sense that this is a fractured family, that the chain of transmission has been broken. With her mother covering most of her chest and the words of her story crowding around her body, Irma is shuttling between that night before she left the ghetto and the present moment, over fifty years later. Her daughter, like us as viewers, is in the present, trying to understand that past moment, to gain access to it. But just as Irma rehearses her separation from her mother and father, and from her past identity—"So while I was sitting with the cows in the pasture I was thinking 'that's me or not me?'"—so her daughter looks to her for a form of recognition that might assure her identity. But Irma's gaze is elsewhere: she does not return her daughter's look.

Wolin explains the role of the intercalated archival images when he discusses the founding photo of the exhibit, the image of Miso Vogel. "I wanted to show his tattoo, which is in and of itself a powerful visual statement. . . . I also had him hold a photograph of his father who died in Auschwitz. This image acted as a window and Miso was, for a moment, transported back to a terrible time in his past." So is Irma transported back to a terrible time in her past, and by holding onto her daughter, she takes her back with her, even as she needs her daughter to take her back out to the present again. The photo is a window to the past, reinforced by the partly open door at the edge of the picture marking perhaps the invitation to go back and also the threshold that is so difficult to cross.

The stylized, obviously posed figures, the framing by the door and the plant, and, especially, the writing on the print create a two-dimensionality that removes depth and thus temporality, showing memory to be firmly situated in the present. The past is in the present, spatially in the room, crowding out the figures, encasing them in a story that determines their very movements. Irma's daughter stares at the writing that surrounds her. The writing on the print is "written in memory"—both written in *memory*, out of one's memory, and *written-in* memory, a memory inscribed on the skin of the image itself, as a tattoo might be, as tattoos are in a great number of Wolin's images. Written-in memory, like photography (writing in light), mediates the transmission between memory and postmemory. But the handwriting here, and the photographic gaze itself, expand the familial circle. The artist—in this case a male artist—inserts himself as another witness, another viewer and listener who is able to receive the stories and to transmit them, sharing in the familial, mother-daughterly network of looking which he mediates and enables. Through his indirection, his extra-familial presence, he can become the agent of the allo-identification, the medium of the historical withholding that precisely prevents mother-daughter transmission from becoming incorporative rememory. But it is not thereby any less appropriative or violating.

In *Written in Memory* Jeffrey Wolin begins to articulate the aesthetic strategies of identification, projection, and mourning that specifically characterize postmemory. In the image of Irma Morgensztern, he stages and shares in a moment of knowledge for the daughter, who is literally, bodily surrounded, marked, by traumatic memories that preceded her birth but that nevertheless define her life's narrative. Along with the unnamed daughter, Jeffrey Wolin becomes an extra-familial "witness by adoption," who, in his own hand, reenacts the split identity of Irma Morgensztern (written on the right side of the image)/Barbara Nosarewska (written on the left). The two sides of the photograph mirror the two sides of young Irma's brain. Wolin both creates and severely delimits the space of the encounter between memory and postmemory.

These transgendered and transgenerational affiliations mark the subjects of these memories as members of a generation and as witnesses of a particular historical moment: born after World War II, as a Jew, Wolin represents this daughter and, through identification, himself as literally branded by the harrowing memory of Nazi genocide. His texts, shaped by identification with the victims, invite viewers to participate in a cultural act of remembrance, or in Shoshana Felman's terms, "to perceiv(e) history *in one's own body,* with the power of sight (of insight) usually afforded only by one's own immediate physical involvement"(108). The daughter's body, like the mother's, is surrounded by the inscription of her mother's story, and as their bodies intertwine, the two women risk losing their physical boundaries and merging with one another. Yet their eyes do not meet, their hands do not touch.

Photographic writing and the affect it can engender allow bodily experiential memory to be represented and transmitted beyond the family to those who would witness "by adoption." Describing his relationship with survivors, James Young has said that their stories are "grafted indelibly into my own life story" (19). Wolin's images reproduce this "indelible grafting." His photographic writing demands reading as well as looking, thus drawing viewers in even as it pushes us back out. Wolin, this "witness for the witness," re-produces the marking of trauma by enabling the narrative and bodily encounter between mother and daughter and by staging it for others to witness. The challenge for the postmemorial artist is precisely to allow the spectator to enter the image, to imagine the disaster *"in one's own body,"* yet to evade the transposition that erases distance, creating too available, too direct an access to this particular past.

• • •

Our access to the postmemory of the Holocaust has, until recently, been largely shaped by works by and about men, fathers and sons. Male narrators have dominated not only in the first generation (Levi, Wiesel) but also in the second: Art Spiegelman's *Maus,* David Grossman's *See under Love,* the work of Patrick Modiano, Christian Boltanski, Alain Finkielkraut. Even Anne Michaels, a woman writer, envisions the transmission of the Holocaust along masculine lines in her *Fugitive Pieces*. The question of gender, moreover, is a particularly fraught one in regard to the memory of an event that was meant to annihilate an entire people regardless of gender, class, age, or other identity markers. Vladek Spiegelman boldly erases any gender differentiation when he states about his wife, Anja, who could no longer testify for herself: "She went through the same what me, *terrible!*" (I, 158). Does it then make sense, even in the second generation, to single out the daughter as an agent of transmission? Of course, just as Anja did not go through "the same what me," so the position of the daughter as historical agent is not the same as that of the son.

Yet in thinking about postmemory as a feminist, I have found it fruitful not only to search for female witnesses of the first and second generation, but also to think about a feminist mode of knowing this past. In this effort, it seems to me that the works by Morrison, Karpf, Kellner, and Wolin, and their focus on the position of the daughter, might allow us to theorize not a female or daughterly but a *feminist* postmemory. It is a question, then, of a particular mode of knowledge about the other, a particular intersubjective relation or "allo-identification." It is a question of how memory is constructed, of what stories are told, to whom, and by whom.

Thus I would say that some of the characteristics of Kellner's and Wolin's postmemorial textuality can be fruitfully read through the lens of feminist theories of commonality and difference. These artists both search for forms of identification that are nonappropriative. The mixture of media and the multiple responses they elicit, the oscillation between reading and looking, in particular, create a resistant textuality for the viewer. The mediated access that they open allows for a historical *withholding* that does not absorb the other, but grants the pastness and the irretrievability of the past, the irreducibility of the other, the untranslatablity of the story of trauma. The modes of knowledge they engage in are embodied, material, located and thus also responsive and responsible to the other. But they also thematize the act of *holding*—caring, protective, and nurturing—made palpable in the use of hands as primary figures in their works. The lines of transmission they enact, moreover, are capacious enough to transcend gender and familial role and thus they expand the circle of postmemory in multiple, inviting, and open-ended ways. In casting *daughters* as agents of transmission, and, through them opening the space of remembrance beyond the line of family, such a practice of postmemory, particularly, can become an ethical and political act of solidarity and, perhaps, agency, on behalf of the trauma of the other. Significantly, however, both artists enable us also to understand the risks of even such a well-intentioned identificatory practice, and the inevitable appropriations that inflect an empathic aesthetics. The particularities of mother-daughter relations provide the clearest insight into these messy contradictions.

It would be easy to protest that Kellner's and Wolin's art is an act of co-optation of a story that is not theirs, as can of course be said of my own earlier invocation of Toni Morrison and the story of slavery. In response to this objection, I would like to conclude with a remarkable passage about the transmission of bodily memory and the risks of appropriation, from Patricia Williams's *The Rooster's Egg*. This passage best exemplifies the feminist postmemory I have tried to identify. This is a story about how the mark of memory gets erased to make space so that—generations later—it may again be found and re-adopted across lines of difference. It is a story of a bold and risky and deeply *feminist* act of making connections across the differences of gender, race, and generation. And it is a great-great-granddaughter's story marked by the anxious desire for mutual recognition that is constitutive of memory and identity:

> Many years ago, a friend invited me to her home for dinner. As it turned out, her husband was a survivor of Auschwitz. He has been an artist before he was captured by the Nazis, and, while he had made his living in an entirely different way since coming to the United States, his wife told me that he still painted as a hobby. She took me to their garage and showed me the immense collection of his work. There he had stored paintings that probably numbered in the hundreds—circus-bright landscapes with vivid colors and lush exquisitely detailed vegetation. Yet in every last one of them there was a space of a completely bare canvas, an empty patch in the shape of a human being. "He never finishes anything," my friend whispered, but I could hardly hear her, for I had never seen such a complete representation of the suppression of personality, the erasure of humanity that the Holocaust exacted.
>
> A few weeks after this, my sister sent me a microfiche copy of the property listing from the National Archives, documenting the existence of our enslaved great-great-grandmother. The night after I received my sister's letter, I dreamed that I was looking at my friend's husband's paintings, all those vivid landscapes with the bare body-shapes and suddenly my great-great-grandmother appeared in the middle of each and every one of them. Suddenly she filled in all the empty spaces, and I looked into her face with the supernatural stillness of deep recollection. From that moment, I knew

exactly who she was—every pore, every hair, every angle of her face. I would know her everywhere. (208–9).

NOTES

I thank Ivy Schweitzer, Susan Suleiman, and Nancy K. Miller for their helpful comments on this essay. I am also grateful to audiences at York University, Indiana University, Ohio State, Georgetown, Yale, and the Dartmouth Feminist Inquiry Seminar who heard earlier versions of this argument.

1. Juliet Mitchell sees recognition as a fundamental element of subject-formation which, when breached, can cause trauma; see esp. chap. 9. On maternal recognition, see Kahane.

2. Juliet Mitchell goes so far as to suggest that "an actual trauma in one generation may not be induced until the next" (280).

3. For an evolving definition of postmemory, see my *Family Frames;* "Projected Memory"; and "Surviving Images." See also Liss's related use of the term in relation to post-Holocaust photography. On rememory in *Beloved* see my "Maternity and Rememory."

4. On reenactment in the work of post-Holocaust artists, see Van Alphen.

5. See Susan Gubar's essay in this volume and also my essay "Projected Memory" for other attempts to theorize such a nonappropriative form of identification in relation to Kaja Silverman's notion of "heteropathic memory."

6. The following discussion of Tatana Kellner's work is in part based on an essay with a different focus that I co-wrote with Susan Suleiman (2001). I am grateful to Suleiman for her permission to continue thinking and writing about Kellner's work, building on our work together.

7. The "productive look" is Kaja Silverman's term; see esp. her chap. 5.

WORKS CITED

Bennett, Jill. "The Aesthetics of Sense-Memory: Theorising Trauma through the Visual Arts." *Trauma und Erinnerung/Trauma and Memory: Crosscultural Perspectives.* Ed. Franz Kaltenbeck and Peter Weibel. Vienna: Passagen Verlag, 2000. 81–96.

Caplan, Jane. *Written on the Body: The Tattoo in European and American History.* Princeton: Princeton University Press, 2000.

Culbertson, Roberta. "Embodied Memory, Transcendence, and Telling: Recounting Trauma, Re-establishing the Self." *New Literary History* 26.1 (1995): 169–95.

Felman, Shoshana, and Dori Laub. *Testimony: Crises of Witnessing in Psychoanalysis, Literature and History.* New York: Routledge, 1992.

Hartman, Geoffrey H. *The Longest Shadow: In the Aftermath of the Holocaust.* Bloomington: Indiana University Press, 1996.

Hirsch, Marianne. *Family Frames: Photography, Narrative, and Postmemory.* Cambridge, Mass.: Harvard University Press, 1997.

———. "Maternity and Rememory." *Representations of Motherhood.* Ed. Donna

Bassin, Margaret Honey, Meryle Kaplan. New Haven: Yale University Press, 1994. 92–110.

———. "Projected Memory: Holocaust Photographs in Personal and Public Fantasy." *Acts of Memory*. Ed. Mieke Bal, Jonathan Crewe, and Leo Spitzer. Hanover, N.H.: University Press of New England, 1998. 3–23.

———. "Surviving Images: Holocaust Photographs and the Work of Postmemory." *Visual Culture and the Holocaust*. Ed. Barbie Zelizer. New Brunswick, N.J.: Rutgers University Press, 2001. Also *Yale Journal of Criticism* 14.1 (2001): 5–38.

Hirsch, Marianne, and Susan Suleiman. "Material Memory: Holocaust Testimony in Post-Holocaust Art." *Shaping Losses: Cultural Memory and the Holocaust*. Ed. Julia Epstein and Lori Hope Lefkovitz. Urbana: University of Illinois Press, 2001. 87–104.

Kahane, Claire. "Dark Mirrors: A Feminist Reflection on Holocaust Narrative." *Feminist Consequences: Theory for the New Century*. Ed. Elisabeth Bronfen and Misha Kavka. New York: Columbia University Press, 2001.

Karpf, Anne. *The War After*. London: Minerva, 1997.

Kellner, Tatana. *B-11226: Fifty Years of Silence*. Rosendale, New York, Women's Studio Workshop, 1994.

———. *71125: Fifty Years of Silence*. Rosendale, New York, Women's Studio Workshop, 1992.

Kestenberg, Judith. "A Metapsychological Assessment Based on an Analysis of a Survivor's Child." *Generations of the Holocaust*. Ed Martin S. Bergman and Milton E. Jucovy. New York: Basic Books, 1982. 137–58.

Liss, Andrea. *Trespassing through Shadows: Memory, Photography and the Holocaust*. Minneapolis: University of Minnesota Press, 1998.

Mitchell, Juliet. *Mad Men and Medusas: Reclaiming Hysteria*. New York: Basic Books, 2000.

Morrison, Toni. *Beloved*. New York: Knopf, 1987.

Sedgwick, Eve Kosofsky. *Epistemology of the Closet*. Berkeley: University of California Press, 1990.

Silverman, Kaja. *The Threshold of the Visible World*. New York: Routledge, 1996.

Spiegelman, Art. *Maus I: A Survivor's Tale: My Father Bleeds History*. New York: Pantheon, 1991.

Spivak, Gayatri. "Acting Bits/Identity Talk." *Identities*. Ed. Kwame Anthony Appiah and Henry Louis Gates. Chicago: University of Chicago Press, 1995. 147–80.

Van Alphen, Ernst. *Caught by History: Holocaust Effects in Contemporary Art, Literature, and Theory*. Palo Alto: Stanford University Press, 1997.

Wolin, Jeffrey A. *Written in Memory: Portraits of the Holocaust*. San Francisco: Chronicle Books, 1997.

Young, James. *The Art of Memory: Holocaust Memorials in History*. Munich: Prestel Verlag, 1994.

FOUR

Orphaned Memories, Foster-Writing, Phantom Pain: The *Fragments* Affair

Ross Chambers

> She wishes that the dead were not quite so dead. She also wishes that the dead were not quite so alive. She thought that dead people should feel more dead.
>
> —Lily Brett, *Too Many Men*

WHO'S THERE?

"Who's there?" is Bernardo's anxious question at the beginning of *Hamlet,* as he stands guard on the haunted heights of Elsinore. Of course it's a defining question for the play; perhaps too it's the question the condition of hauntedness regularly requires us to ask; certainly it's the question I'm led to formulate in response to the *Fragments* affair.

Commentators have mainly discussed the affair in two ways. It's seen first as a matter involving the perhaps fraudulent, more probably deluded, "borrowing" (Ganzfried) of the identity of Holocaust survivor, and hence—this being the second issue—as a problem in the ethics of authorship. Without denying the significance of these and other questions the affair raises, I would like to reframe the discussion and ask what it means for a culture to be haunted by a collective memory—the memory of painful events that few, if any, living members of the culture may have directly perpetrated or suffered from in their own persons. In particular I want to raise the issue of what it might mean for an individual to confuse the collective historical consciousness concerning outrageous events with painful personal memories; and to confuse them to the point of being *inhabited* (i.e., haunted) by the events *as though* he or she had actually lived through them. In short, I want to view the case of this text as symptomatic, but culturally symptomatic as much as personally so.

Fragments was published in 1995 under its original German title of *Bruchstücke* and rapidly translated into many other languages. The English language translation by Carol Brown Janeway appeared in 1996; it bears a subtitle that identifies the text generically as memoir, *Memoirs of a Wartime Childhood.* In all versions the author's name was given as Binjamin Wilkomirski, and indeed the text purports to consist of Wilkomirski's scattered and elusive memories of having been a small Jewish child in Nazi-occupied Latvia and Poland, including his internment in Majdanek and then apparently Auschwitz-Birkenau, before he was finally brought from Cracow to an orphanage in Switzerland at war's end, and eventually adopted by foster parents whose name he took.

Early readers, myself included, found in the book deeply moving personal testimony concerning an aspect of that atrocious historical period of which, for painfully obvious reasons, there is virtually no direct personal record: the experience of the infants and very young children who were caught up and brutally destroyed in the Nazi extermination machine. But some of the book's most powerful and moving passages are actually in the last third of the narrative, when the scene shifts from wartime Poland to Switzerland in the immediate postwar period. Having perfectly internalized the rules of survival appropriate to the Lager, the child Wilkomirski now finds himself in a terrifying new situation, more terrifying even than the extreme vulnerability of his situation in the camps, because it seems to him unreal and a pretense. He knows only the rules of survival that pertained in Auschwitz, but the world in which he moves both resembles and does not resemble the camp. Thus, his environment, reassuringly familiar to us, has become, for him, more frighteningly alien than the camp itself because it is the environment of aftermath: it continues the camp, but in unfamiliar guise.

These are passages to which I'll eventually return, because what they describe is a condition of hauntedness—the hauntedness of a placid and supposedly peaceful Switzerland to which, in the consciousness of the young Binjamin, Auschwitz and all the conditions of the *Endlösung* nevertheless remain fully and uncannily *relevant.* The Lager is present, actual and active—but spectrally so, because the continuity and connectedness between Switzerland and Poland that the relevance presupposes go unrecognized, and indeed are energetically denied, by virtually all, whether adults or children, who surround the child. Hence the child's sense of Switzerland's unreality. All survivors of extreme and traumatic events or experiences report a similar sense of dissociation from the supposedly normal life that surrounds them. But for Binjamin the sensation of normalcy's unreality is exacerbated because, precisely, he has never *known* this "normal" life that he is suddenly expected to recognize and embrace.

So, at least, *Fragments* could be read until 1998. In that year it was revealed that the book's author had the legal identity, not of Binjamin Wilkomirski, but of Bruno Dössekker, born in Biel (Switzerland) in 1941, the illegitimate child of a Swiss mother (see Ganzfried). Originally Bruno Grosjean, he had lived first in orphanages and foster care before taking the name of his foster parents and becoming Bruno Dössekker. He could not be identical with Wilkomirski. This bombshell provoked an immediate hue-and-cry, during which Dössekker has steadfastly—I'm tempted to say obstinately—clung to the claim that he is Binjamin Wilkomirski, a claim he grounds in the fragments of memory that inhabit his consciousness and in a distinction he had made in the afterword of *Fragments:* "Legally accredited truth is one thing—the truth of a life is another" (154). Dössekker, it seems, *trusts* his memories. He trusts them more than he trusts bureaucratic paperwork; and he trusts that *they* identify him as Binjamin Wilkomirski. It's fair to say that few now follow him in this belief. But also, few believe him to have been insincere or duplicitous in claiming the existential, if not legal, identity of Wilkomirski.

Whether or not the impersonation resulted from fraud or delusion, the scandal, of course, arose from the fact that the identity of Holocaust survivor had been successfully appropriated. Such a fact seriously challenged the historical and sometimes metaphysical uniqueness that is attributed by some to the events variously known as the Destruction, the Holocaust, the *Endlösung*. But the confusion about what it meant that Wilkomirski was Dössekker who is not Wilkomirski was compounded by the difficulties that now emerged concerning the book's actual genre. *Fragments* claimed to be memoir, but it could not now be regarded as autobiographical, since the memories are not Dössekker's but Wilkomirski's, who however apparently never existed and can't therefore be the book's author. The "autobiographical pact" (Lejeune) was violated. But on the other hand *Fragments* could not readily be regarded as historical fiction, in the manner of, say, Hersey's *The Wall* or Styron's *Sophie's Choice,* if only because the author (whether Dössekker or Wilkomirski) steadfastly continued to identify it as autobiography. No one has asked whether the existence of such a generic solecism might not be the sign of something more than a merely personal aberration, or whether the personal delusion might not be a cultural symptom, the evidence of a certain collective pathology. Such a pathology, I wish to suggest, might be the condition of a society subject to a troubled collective memory, and suffering from a haunted historical consciousness. To my mind it is as if the book functions, through a kind of lapsus or *Fehlleistung* on Dössekker's part, as a species of testimonial, but in a way and a sense different from the intention to testify that its deluded author has claimed. Not so much Dössekker's delusion as the hauntedness of a culture in which such a delusion is possible is what *Fragments* appears to bear witness to.

In the fall of 1999, following the advice of a professional historian (Stefan Mächler),[1] publishers began to withdraw *Fragments* from circulation, following the example of the original publisher, Suhrkamp. On November 2, Schocken Books announced that it was suspending publication in the United States. One may speculate about the pressures, legal, political, or otherwise, to which the publishers were yielding. If my hunch has some merit, a major, if probably unacknowledged, part of their motivation may lie in the desire characteristic of the living, when the dead are restless and specters roam, to *lay the ghost.* As a haunted text—the text of Bruno Dössekker, who is inhabited and indeed (it seems) possessed by Binjamin Wilkomirski—*Fragments* is evidence of a haunted society, in which an individual can mistake the collective consciousness of a painful past for a personal memory. As such, it makes a hauntedness that was easy to ignore more difficult to deny; the ghost must be laid. For if it is easy not to believe in ghosts, it is hard not to be troubled by them, and by the questions they raise. Acting as gate-keeper institutions for their various societies, the publishing houses have understandably—if regrettably—attempted to block the awkward questions *Fragments* raises, beginning with the question of haunted identity: Who's there?

Ghosts are not easily laid, however. The reason for this is that their presence signifies the sense the living have of an injustice that has gone unrepaired (and may indeed be irreparable). It always seems easier to lay the ghost than to repair the injustice—but "seems" is the operative word because ghosts ultimately refuse to lie down and be still, for the very reason that the consciousness of injustice, otherwise known as a sense of guilt, inhabits the living, not the dead. However much, like Lily Brett's character, we may think that the dead should feel less alive and act more dead, they remain restless because the living remain anxious, being prevented by guilt from completing the normal process of mourning that would lay them to rest. They keep returning, as *revenants*. Take the short item that appeared in the *New York Times* of November 3, 1999. Under the heading "Publisher Drops Holocaust Book," it announced the withdrawal of *Fragments* the previous day.[2] In the words of the *Times,* the book was withdrawn because of "evidence that the account was no more than a vivid fantasy." Do we think it was the fantastic character of the fantasy or its vividness that was judged to be at fault? For not surprisingly perhaps, but certainly very symptomatically, *Fragments* remains a "Holocaust book," to the *Times,* even as the headline reports its having been "dropped." And in the very sentence that announces Wilkomirski's fallacious existence (as "no more than" a vivid fantasy), a ghostly "Mr. Wilkomirski" walks. "The report concluded," says the *Times,* "that Mr. Wilkomirski had not been a Jewish orphan but a Swiss-born child named Bruno Dössekker." Here is evidence of the difficulty of laying ghosts.

True, it's the hasty prose of a sloppy journalist. But the paralogism, which is a bit like disbelieving in ghosts but being troubled by them, is startling. There is a stutter of sense here that can't be attributed to Dössekker's personal delusion. And what makes the sentence even more unsettling is not just that Wilkomirski survives as the subject of the clause that expunges him, but also that in surviving he is favored with an honorific "*Mr.* Wilkomirski," as if *he* were the adult, while Dössekker the putative author of the book and a grownup, becomes just Bruno, "a Swiss-born child." Each appears to have changed status with the other. Who then, one may ask, is being referred to as "the author" in the sentence that follows? "People with knowledge of the report said that when confronted with its findings, *the author* declared defiantly: 'I am Binjamin Wilkomirski.'" What matter who speaks? was a brash question much bandied about in theoretical circles in the 1960s; but the evidence of the *Fragments* affair is both that it *can* sometimes matter very much to whom speech is attributed, and that in haunted societies the attribution can be a somewhat rough-and-ready affair, given the difficulty of responding to the question of spectrality: Who's there? and the unwillingness of ghosts to submit to our desire and to be laid.

The *Fragments* affair is worth pondering, then, because it shows how the ghosts keep returning. A haunted society is not so much one that has

Publisher Drops Holocaust Book

Schocken Books suspended publication yesterday of "Fragments," a memoir about a Latvian Jewish orphan's early life in a Nazi camp. The publisher cited evidence that the account was no more than a vivid fantasy.

Questions about the authenticity of the book, written by Binjamin Wilkomirski, arose last year, and a historian's report prompted the book's German publisher, Suhrkamp Verlag, to announce last month that it was withdrawing all hardcover copies of the book from its stores.

The report concluded that Mr. Wilkomirski had not been a Jewish orphan but a Swiss-born child named Bruno Doessekker. People with knowledge of the report said that when confronted with its findings, the author declared defiantly, "I am Binjamin Wilkomirski."

Yesterday Carol Brown Janeway, Mr. Wilkomirski's American editor and a translator for Schocken Books, an imprint of Alfred A. Knopf and a subsidiary of Random House, said that evidence in the 137-page draft report "was sufficiently conclusive to require immediate action."

She said the book was published in the United States in October 1996 and had sold 17,000 copies in hardcover and 17,200 in paperback.

"Publisher Drops Holocaust Book," *New York Times,* November 3, 1999 (copyright © 2000 by the New York Times Co.; reprinted by permission) ghosts, the way a house might have mice, as one whose ghosts do not submit to being laid. The fact that *Fragments* has proved so unwelcome a visitant among us may have less to do, therefore, with the matters overtly discussed (the fungibility of identity, the ethics of authorship), which are the epiphenomena of hauntedness, than with the fact that the story of Dössekker's hauntedness asks questions about our own Wilkomirskis. After all, the most unequivocally genuine of Holocaust testimonies themselves frequently bear witness to their own utter inadequacy as testimonial. That is, they cannot report the full enormity of the Holocaust in such a way that this enormity might be, once and for all, recognized. Their testimony is haunting enough but it is itself also haunted; it testifies that there is no end to the business of laying our ghosts. Specters, as Derrida has said, are always plural; one reason for that is that they have specters of their own.

The Wilkomirskis who haunt authentic Holocaust testimonial are those for whom it knows it does not and cannot speak, but who insist on their right to "live," that is, on the injustice of their death. These are the shades of all those who, undergoing extermination, did not get a chance to testify, a category of people that was, so to speak, already recognized in the camps and came to be identified later, in the argot, with the fatalists or *Muselmänner* (cf. Levi's "sommersi" as opposed to the "salvati," and see Agamben).[3] In order to testify one must first survive—or one's story must survive. The nonsurvivors who haunt survivor testimony do so precisely because it is both surviving testimony and the testimony of survivors. It is the memory of the nonsurvivors that so-called survivor guilt acknowledges. And it is the category of the nonsurvivors that is poignantly figured in *Fragments* by the symbolic figure of the child—*in-fans,* not speaking—and represented in Dössekker's text as Binjamin Wilkomirski. A dubious figure who will not go away—a figure neither historical nor yet fictional, neither real nor imaginary, but symbolic—Binjamin stands for all the ghosts that inhabit a haunting testimonial text but do not—cannot—speak, with their own voice, within it.

My thesis, then, is that there are Wilkomirskis, or orphaned memories, who haunt the collective consciousness but *need a Dössekker*—a "host"— if they are to achieve some sort of vividness, some degree of discursive status within culture, and force our acknowledgment that they do indeed haunt us—an acknowledgment that will take the form, not of the laying of ghosts, but of anxiety over symptoms of their haunting: a "borrowed" identity, a generic conundrum, lapses in a journalist's hasty prose. When

Fragments was still understood to be an authentic text of Holocaust witness, the very implausibility of a small, unprotected, Jewish child's surviving the conditions of the extermination camps was sometimes cited as paradoxical evidence of the text's authenticity, or at least as evidence that did not disprove its authenticity. After all, the Holocaust itself was so improbable, and the most unlikely things were known to have happened. But now the same implausibility, along with some smaller historical and other inaccuracies, is held to prove the text's inauthenticity and, as an apparently unexamined consequence, its inability "therefore" to embody any form of truth: *Fragments,* that is, is "no more than a vivid fantasy." I submit rather that a "vivid fantasy" has truth as a cultural symptom, its very vividness testifying to its slightly uncanny quality, and that, in this case, its testimonial truth is quite directly conditioned on the very implausibility in historical terms of a child's having survived Auschwitz to tell the story of that survival. It is only through an anomaly of this kind—the anomaly of the symbolic—that what haunts our hauntedness can return, and in doing so, gain some sort of recognition of that hauntedness itself.

Inauthentic as *Fragments* doubtless is as an actual representation of a child's experience of Nazi persecution and the camps, it does force us to try to imagine what that experience must have been like for children; and in doing so it requires us, when more authentic survivor testimonies remind us, explicitly or not, that they too are haunted by orphaned memories—by the silenced voices of those who died—to realize with some anxiety that we can't so much as imagine the experience of all those whose very names—even the numbers—have not come down to us; to realize, that is, that we have therefore not adequately mourned them, and perhaps cannot do so. The more dead they are, as Brett says, the more uncomfortably alive they are capable of being, "to [us]." Quite paradoxically, then, it is the sense in which *Fragments* is an unlikely and problematic text of Holocaust testimonial that gives the book its agencing and presencing function—one that more genuine, more straightforwardly truthful, testimonies are precluded from subserving by virtue of their very honesty and authenticity. Their eyewitness scrupulousness is laudable, but it sets limits to the range of their testimony, limits that can be gotten around only through the possibility of less literal, symbolic praxes—including a parapraxis such as Dössekker's felicitous blunder (*Fehlleistung*). For parapraxes, too, are an "art de faire." Those who did not survive cannot give survivor testimony. Or they can, but only through language's unruly capacity to say more than we think it can, more than we may want it to do, more than we believe it ought to be allowed to do: its capacity, that is, to foster the orphaned.

ORPHANED MEMORY, FOSTER-WRITING

A central topological feature of Holocaust writing is its thematics of violent separation: the extermination of huge populations, the destruction of a culture, the brutal breakup of couples and family groups. Orphanages and foster care have little place in the story such writing tells; their prominence in *Fragments* is therefore noteworthy. It points to a thematics of continuity and survival—survival of violent separation, but survival in a mode significantly different from the already painful survival described by those witnesses (e.g., Wiesel, Levi, or Delbo) who emerged from the camps as young adults. It's not just that Wilkomirski survives as a young child, though. It's also that a survival that is institutionally marked as palliative, continuing to bear the traces of interruption, is a more dubious and troubled form of survival, more *assisted,* than that of others, deeply traumatized as they too may be. Such a survival is survival by relay, a highly mediated continuity that implies dependence on the intervention of another (or of others). It's a survival that's like the identity of Wilkomirski and Dössekker, claimed by Dössekker but now contested; a *fostered* survival, and one that therefore seems both fragile and artificial, even suspect.

There's a striking symmetry in *Fragments* between two orphanages, one in Cracow and one in Switzerland; the connecting train journey with Frau Grosz figures their relay. It's evident also that orphanages and foster care are the point of junction where the fragmentary narrative of Wilkomirski, as told in the book, grafts onto the biography of Dössekker, as it is now known from research. Elena Lappin cautiously suggests that Bruno Dössekker's early experiences of separation from his mother and subsequent life in the strict and probably unloving conditions of Swiss orphanages in the 1940s account for this grafting; they are the common ground on which Dössekker's deluded self-identification with Binjamin Wilkomirski, Holocaust survivor, actually rests. It seems a plausible hypothesis. Learning at school the history of the Holocaust, as he recounts in *Fragments,* he would have reinterpreted his personal experience of pain, by back-formation or *Nachträglichkeit* (another form of relay), as Holocaust memory. Assuming this psychological hypothesis, I want to suggest in turn that a further dynamics of relay is at work in the actual writing of

Fragments. I mean that in experiencing Wilkomirski's pain as his own, Dössekker the man transforms his personal sense of orphanhood into the experience of a "phantom" pain; and that his writing then functions as a mode of transmission for the painful Wilkomirski memories that derive from the collective memory but that he takes as his own, in such a way that they become phantom pain in the minds of his book's readers. This is to understand writing as itself the agent of a relay in the sense that it both records the evidence of a break, the damage done by the Holocaust, and produces a continuity, which is the survival, despite that break, of an orphaned memory, or the set of orphaned memories named Wilkomirski, in the form of a phantom pain experienced by readers. The agencing of that survival is the work of relay performed by Dössekker's writing as a fostering of the orphaned.

Foster-writing, then, fosters in the double sense of that word.[4] It's a surrogate, offering a form of hospitality or pseudo-home to that which is culturally homeless and agencing a phantom cultural existence for it. But thus it fosters, that is, encourages, the entry of the culturally homeless into culture, albeit in the uncanny form it owes to the highly mediated act of its presencing. Where once it was culturally ignored, like a waif, the haunt is recognized, in the form of pain. These, *Fragments* suggests, are the inevitable conditions of survival, contingent on the relay of writing, for a memory that culture would rather forget. So it is worth pointing out that the German title, *Bruchstücke,* broken pieces, is considerably more concrete than its translation as "Fragments" can convey; and that *Stücke* or items, was part of the Nazi administrative lingo, referring to the human victims of the extermination machine. The word "symbol" (throwing together) refers, for its part, to an ancient practice for identifying people long separated, each of whom held a fragment of an object—say a ring—broken into two or more parts. Phantom pain, the readerly effect of foster-writing, can be thought of, therefore, in a quite specific sense, as a bringing together of broken pieces: the symbolic re-membering of dismembered identities. What Dössekker understands, deludedly, as remembering in the literal sense is arguably true, I am suggesting—but in just such a symbolic sense.

The reason an orphaned memory haunts is that such a memory is both detached, like all memories, from its there-and-then context in the past and—more unusually—seemingly without attachment also in the here-and-now context of its present remembering. In discursive terms, the connection between the reference of the memory's statement and the circumstances of its utterance has been interrupted, except for the very fact of its being uttered (remembered), which seems to imply a connection per se. Thus the memory is received by the remembering subject, but as a kind of visitation. Phantom pain, properly speaking, refers to the neurophysiological phenomenon whereby people who have lost a limb experience a sensation of physical pain in the amputated extremity; but I use it here, by an extension of the metaphor, as a name for a certain capacity of moral hospitality—a capacity that Bruno Dössekker appears to have exercised in unusual measure. This is the capacity to experience the pain of another, or of others, as wholly or partly indistinguishable from a "remembered" pain of one's own.

Each phenomenon—orphaned memory and phantom pain—is a phenomenon of memory, then. But the effect of phantom pain is the converse of that of orphaned memory. Where orphaned memory is disconnected, except for the thread of its being remembered by the remembering subject, phantom pain is equally uncanny because it makes for a strong sense of connection and continuity, but of an unexpected kind, a connection between subjects—the subject of the remembered pain (say, Wilkomirski) and the subject of the remembering (say, Dössekker)—that are thought to be separate, because other. Memory-statement and memory-utterance are continuous with each other, they have the same object, but each has a different subject—a phenomenon that might be compared with identificatory reading. In each case, there is thus an experience of the anomalous co-presence of different contexts or categories that in normal circumstances (including normal memory) are not thought capable of coinciding: the there-and-then and the here-and-now in orphaned memory, in phantom pain I and not-I, self and other.

Gilles Deleuze would refer to each of these anomalous occurrences of dedifferentiation as a stammer, and describe it as a case of "disjunctive synthesis." I would add that they are disruptive of the workings of genre, whose seduction (Lyotard's word) consists in part of blinding us to the implications of, and aberrant possibilities inherent in, the split between statement and utterance that is constitutive of the discursive and characteristic, inter alia, of memory. In the case of autobiography, for example, or when I give legal testimony, it is assumed that I am *not* my other (unlike the evidence of phantom pain) and that (unlike the case of orphaned memory) there is an equivalence between the content of my memory and my remembering of it, such that (roughly speaking) my statements about then-and-there can be trusted in the here-and-now. Genre, in short, tends to exclude or diminish the possibility of haunting (as in orphaned memory) and of hauntedness (as in phantom pain). Thus it is the book's failure to conform to the conventions of genres such as these, as a consequence of its participation in the phenomena of orphaned memory and phantom pain, that has made *Fragments* an aberrant text, a ghost to be laid.

Foster-writing is the relay that transforms the orphaned memory experienced by the writing subject into a readerly experience of phantom pain—that is, transforms a hauntedness into a haunting. In that sense *Fragments* is readable, first, as a mimesis of orphaned memory, but second, as a mimesis that works to elicit reader involvement. This process helps make readerly subjectivity hospitable to phantom pain. In *Fragments,* as I'll suggest, the key tropes that, in combination, produce such an outcome, are asyndeton, in the form of a fragmented narrative, and hypotyposis (or vividness). Narrative fragmentation as the mimesis of orphaned memory merges first with a mimesis of phantom pain as the experience of hypotyposis—the experience of the child Binjamin in the orphanage, where Auschwitz is still more real than his actual surroundings. But by virtue of the reader-involving power of asyndeton, this latter mimesis also extends to an effect of utterance, such that the experience it describes, as Binjamin's phantom pain, becomes an effect of hypotyposis—that is, phantom pain—experienced by the reader. It is experienced, that is, on the *model* of the narrated experience, but as an *effect* of the narration. The relay produced by these figural means is thus a rhetorical shift or turn, from the referentiality of a fragmented narrative statement to an effect of address designed to make vividly co-present, to a readerly imagination nourished by its own personal memories of pain, the here-and-now of reading and the there-and-then of the pain named, inadequately, by the word Holocaust. In that way a haunted language of reference becomes a language that itself haunts: not just "about" pain, it also *hurts.*

The "paradox" of language is sometimes described (e.g., Becker 5, citing Ortega y Gasset) in terms of simultaneous deficit and excess: language does less than we want and more than we intend. That is, language is deficient with respect to reference—as statement—while as utterance it lends itself to effects of readability that appear unlimited because subject to infinite semiosis. Of course, here too genre intervenes to restrict these effects, limiting the range of interpretability of utterances and thus producing their referentiality as adequate in the way that genres like legal testimony and autobiography restrict the unreliability, the fantastic quality of memory. It's only when genre breaks down—a misunderstanding or differend arises, or genre conventions are flouted by being turned to unexpected and/or unwanted purposes, as is commonly the case in the practice of testimonial—that language users become uncomfortably aware of "aboutness" as lack and readability as embarrassingly plethoric. My point, of course, will be that foster-writing, as a generic solecism, turns these linguistic embarrassments to a certain rhetorical advantage, in ways that recall the dedifferentiating effects both of orphaned memory and of phantom pain.

As orphaned memory exacerbates the statement/utterance or remembered/remembering split, so foster-writing works to produce a simultaneous sense of severe referential inadequacy (the effect of fragmentation) and of hyperreadability (the effect of hypotyposis). But it does so—and this is the crucial point—in such a way as to align, in the mind of a reader, the object of referential lack and the object of interpretive excess—a combination that might be regarded as an exact definition of phantom pain. In foster-writing, then, questions like What is this statement *about?* and What does this act of utterance *mean?* begin to converge; they become nearly the same question. As a result the referential does not become less elusive but even more so because of its status as an (unstated) object of an act of phrasing (the status that, theoretically, it always has); and the outcome is that it thus comes to enjoy a kind of hallucinatory or hyper-reality, the effect of the "phantom." In orphaned memory the split between the there-and-then of reference and the here-and-now of utterance is uncanny because, as I've explained, memory brings together in an individual's psychic experience that which is known to be different; in phantom pain as it is produced through foster-writing the effect of strangeness arises because the different—that is, the referential pain of the other in the there-and-then and the object of my reading in the here-and now—becomes the same, the same pain, although now it is the difference between subjects (my reading, the other's experience) that persists. Relaying orphaned memory as phantom pain by means of the figural assemblage I'm about to describe, foster-writing combines the effects of both. Because the referential object and the object of my reading are dedifferentiated—the same object but not the same as each other—the distant referent (say Auschwitz, the Lager) and the immediate circumstances in which I read (say Ann Arbor, Michigan, in the year 2000), which I *know* to be vastly different, are crammed into a stammer. Reality becomes oddly dual.

With respect to a Swiss orphanage in the immediate postwar period, that experience of dedifferentiation or disjunctive synthesis is what, in

Fragments, Dössekker describes as having been Binjamin Wilkomirski's experience. And the trope that structures this account of Wilkomirski's phantom pain is the trope of vividness that is known technically as hypotyposis. The word hypotyposis seems to imply something like insufficient generalization, and so, on the one hand, fixation on striking detail. But also, on the other hand and by extension (from *typos,* a mark, character, representative trait, itself from a verb meaning to strike), insufficient generalization can be understood to refer to a failure sufficiently to categorize, that is, to a lack of attention to differences between kinds or a confusion of paradigms, and hence a disjunctive synthesis. Thus, as I'll argue, if the asyndeton that governs narrative fragmentation in the book is a trope of disconnectedness (etymologically a lack of binding together) that assumes the possibility of binding and continuity through reading, hypotyposis is a trope of binding that implies the separability and/or difference of the categories that it binds. It is the trope of vivid co-presence.

All the memories reported in *Fragments* are elusive, amputated, fragmented. It is those associated with Switzerland, that is, with orphanhood and foster care, that are also shot through with hauntedness, co-presence, and hypotyposis. In the narrative logic of the book it's obviously necessary for the child to leave the camp in Poland for that experience to subsist, hauntingly, in Switzerland. So the train journey, as I've mentioned, furnishes the relay between the two; and the two orphanages, one in Cracow, the other in Switzerland, underscore the symmetry, suggesting indeed that the whole book can be read as a meditation on transportation and transportability as that which connects the disconnected. But the crucial and determining moment of break in the narrative is not, therefore—as in most Holocaust narratives—the entry into the camp but rather the child's exit from the camp, when he quits his only reality and enters an outside world that for him does not exist, so that he is able to imagine his release from the Lager only in strictly Lager terms: it is "what the older children call 'the death walk'" (111). One can only leave the camp in order to die. Logically, therefore, his emergence from the camp coincides with his becoming a ghost, someone who lives—or seems to live—although really dead. Already in Poland he confides to his Cracow friend Mila: "Both of us were living among the living. Yet we didn't really belong with them—we were actually dead, on stolen leave, accidental survivors who got left behind in life" (82). This sense of his spectrality in the world outside the camp—the ghostliness that makes him an embodiment of orphaned memory—coincides absolutely, then, with his own hauntedâ€

ness: his consciousness that there is a reality of pain that lies behind in Auschwitz and has not been abolished by, but is more real than, the new, unfamiliar, not really credible and therefore doubly frightening world into which he has emerged. The two coexist, and their coexistence is the meaning of aftermath.

In Switzerland, then, it's not the long trip from Poland but a simple rail trip from the orphanage to his foster-home that instantly calls up the camp knowledge that to be put on a transport is to disappear, never to return. "'No, no transport, no—I won't go on any transport,' I screamed despairingly" (120). Food becomes an ordeal of anxiety *because* it is scarily abundant and varied. The garden is surrounded, like a camp, by a high fence that it is forbidden to climb. The cellar is a nightmare; it contains racks for storing fruit that resemble the stacked bunks in the barracks, and more frighteningly still, a furnace (German *Ofen*). "The oven door is smaller than usual, but it's big enough for children. I know, I've seen, they use children for heating too" (125). At school, a lesson about Wilhelm Tell—Swiss national hero—resonates with the phrase "heroes of the Third Reich": the teacher metamorphoses into a block-warden, and the image of Tell shooting the apple from his son's head becomes an SS man aiming at a child—bizarrely, however, since bullets are too precious to waste on children (132). On an excursion, a ski-lift becomes a "death machine," or rather *the* death machine itself, to which children are hooked and carried up the mountain, only to disappear, the hooks returning empty for more children (142). In short, "the camp's still here. Everything's still here" (125). And it's the camp that's real, everything else is deceit and trickery. And so later, on watching a documentary on the liberation of the camps: "Liberation—it's not true! . . . Nobody ever told me the war was over. / Nobody told me that the camp was over. Finally, definitively over" (148–49).

This derealization of the actual, the Swiss here-and-now, in favor of a much more real there-and-then is, of course, what motivates Dössekker's firm belief that his identity is that of Wilkomirski, not the ghostly identity now named Dössekker. It is also, for readers, a powerful ironizing device, vividly demonstrating the actual proximity of allegedly civilized existence to the barbaric, and denouncing civilization, therefore, as a pretense. But finally it is a device of hypotyposis that presences the world of the Lager, both in Switzerland and in the world in which one reads. Before it does this, however, it is only the *description* of a hypotyposis, that is, of an illusion—a form of flashback—that afflicts the traumatized consciousness of the young Wilkomirski. The illusion can be of interest to us, as readers, but we don't necessarily have to participate in it. What is it, then, that shifts the mimesis of Wilkomirski's phantom pain so that the description becomes a vehicle of phantom pain for readers?

This outcome arises, I propose, from the fact that the figure of hypotyposis in these passages is grafted onto the figure that informs the writing as a whole, which is that of fragmentation, a form of asyndeton. Fragmentation and hypotyposis have in common their concentration on detached details. Fragmented discourse obviously functions in this way as a mimesis of amputated, orphaned, free-floating memories, bereft of context; the text strings together these bits of memory in short chapters, following more an associative than a chronological order. Fragmented narrative thus allies itself readily with the feature of hypotyposis that consists of focusing on a detail (a fruit rack, a furnace, an image of Tell) that is amputated from its derealized context (that of peaceful Switzerland) and becomes what the fragments have been all along, for the reader: metonyms of the *univers concentrationnaire* (barrack bunks, a crematorium oven, an SS man anomalously wasting a bullet on a child), that is, of the *real*. In this way, the effect of hypotyposis described as Binjamin's experience merges into the response to fragmentation the reader has developed throughout the whole narrative, a response of involvement.

Asyndeton is a privileged figure of Holocaust witnessing, but it is also crucial to the genres of AIDS testimonial that I call dual autobiography and collective autobiography (or the farewell symphony). It's a figure that can take different forms. It is classically described as arising when syntactic connectives are strategically omitted (e.g., in the phrase "here today gone tomorrow"): a certain disconnectedness is mimed, but a continuity of sense is left to the audience to supply, and the audience does so. A similar compensatory response underlies the effectiveness of "suspended" sentences ("Do that again and I'll...") in which the meaning is interrupted on the assumption that it does not *have* to be spelled out. Similarly, the kind of narrative fragmentation that occurs in texts like *Fragments* that mime orphaned memory compels interpretive amplification on the part of readers; a "symbolic" reading supplies the missing pieces that form a context—here the context of the Holocaust—for the mere *Bruchstücke,* the broken bits, that are all the text is able to furnish, a little as when, in conversation, someone says: "You know what I'm saying?" By synecdoche, a "whole" is extrapolated from its scattered parts, from whose nature that of the whole (which does not have to be stated) is deduced. To do this, I need not have "known" the Holocaust in the sense of having been there, or in the way that a historian might know it; I need only to recognize its reality and *relate it to myself,* which presumably I do on the basis of personal experiences of pain that I remember. My response, to something that is phrased but not said, is one of anagnorisis—recognition as remembering, remembering as the negation of my previously supposed ignorance. It's an acknowledgment that I did not need for this thing to be spelled out, although I did need to be re-minded of it, for it to become real to me, real as it is to Binjamin Wilkomirski, hauntingly so. In the supposedly strange (that which, for me, is devoid of context) I recognize something deeply familiar (its context is mine).

Reading *Fragments,* then, and compensating in this way for its gaps, we draw on the cultural memory we've always had of the Holocaust, but in order to recognize now, thanks to our own memory of personal pain, the horror of the Holocaust that we had forgotten, denied, or ignored. We always knew, somehow, about the children, did we not? But now we remember them; and their pain is *realized,* by us, in the form of a phantom pain of our own. I intend both senses of the word "realized," for this is not only like young Binjamin's inability to forget Auschwitz in Switzerland; it's also not so different from what happens when Bruno Dössekker, a Swiss musician and instrument-maker, draws on collective memory and offers the hospitality of an identity to the probably imagined Binjamin Wilkomirski, orphaned like so many others in the Holocaust but whom Dössekker *recognizes* and takes in, recognizes as "himself." Few readers, I take it, will go so far as actually to exchange identities as Dössekker has done. But reading, for us, is like memory for him in that it mobilizes our capacity to foster the orphaned, and to give it the reality—the haunting reality—of a phantom pain of our own. As in the cruel ditty with which his schoolfellows taunt young Binjamin: "Der Bettelbub, der Bettelbub, / Er hat noch immer / Nicht genug," there's always a beggar-child in culture, whose demand goes unsatisfied ("er hat *noch immer* nicht genug") and whose haunting, therefore, can't be plumbed. It's an endlessly plural specter that can't be laid, but whom, at least, we can acknowledge and to whom we can respond, in the form of our anxiety and phantom pain.[5] Aftermath texts like *Fragments* are the agencing vehicles through which that response of recognition is solicited for culture's *Bettelbub.*

Given its legacy of trauma, such writing can't be literal, then. Relaying a severely deficient referentiality (the hauntedness of orphaned memory) by plethorically interpretive readability (the haunting quality of a phrasing of the unstatable that is productive of phantom pain), its mode is inevitably that of the symbolic. Its truth is neither the verifiable truth of the historical (which attempts to deal with the real) nor the unverifiable, if believable, truth of the fictional (which deals in the imaginary)—nor yet the combination of the two that would make it a historical fiction—but the recognizable truth that arises from the readability of the figural. In the thinking of young Binjamin Wilkomirski, "all mothers have to die once they've had children" (85), and orphanhood, therefore, is both universal and exactly synonymous with survival. Our inheritance from the dead is the very fact of their death, itself the consequence of our being born; and the question, therefore, is to understand the nature of this fatal orphanhood. *Fragments* furnishes at least three allegories of the crucial event that is the death of the mother and the birth of the orphan. One is the gaunt female cadaver, lying on a pile of cadavers in the camp, whose belly moves and "gives birth"—to a rat, which has been gnawing her insides.

> Other rats run startled out of the confusion of bodies, heading for open ground.
>   I saw it! I saw it! The dead women are giving birth to rats!
>   Rats!—they're the deadly enemies of the little children in the camp. . . .
> (86)

In this nightmare vision, orphanhood is nothing but disconnection, interruption, break: "Nothing connects to anything else any more" (87). The death of the mother is the death of the child; the vision is a figuration of the Real of the camps (the impossible in Lacan's lapidary definition).[6] But then, there is also Frau Grosz's disappearance as the train from Poland arrives in Switzerland, leaving the child in a "waiting room" that is the exact point of conjunction between the Wilkomirski narrative and the story of Bruno Dössekker (né Grosjean). Surely this is a figuration of the Lacanian Imaginary, an illusory solution whereby in orphanhood there is *no* break, but only identity—not an identity with the mother, however, but an identity constructed, somewhat desperately, out of abandonment, as absolute continuity between the Polish orphan and the Swiss orphan. It's as if, ultimately, *all* our orphanhoods were the *same* orphanhood, so that Binjamin's plaintive question: "Why am I always the one who's left behind?" (18) means that the one left behind is always *I*, the one with whom "I" identifies.

The third figuration of survival as inheritance is the episode in which Binjamin is surreptitiously taken through the camp to see his dying mother, who hands him a strange gift:

"What's this?" I asked the gray uniform as we reached my barracks. "That's bread," she said, and "You have to soften it in water, then you can eat it." Then she went away. (50)

The piece of dry, stale bread—a *Bruchstück,* or fragment—is a figure of orphaned memory, but also, as a fragment that joins the child to his mother even as it marks their separation, a symbol of the Symbolic, that is, of the register in which I've attempted to read *Fragments* and the category to which the representations of the Real and the Imaginary in the text themselves belong. Young Wilkomirski draws surprising sustenance from this, his sole inheritance from the lost mother, even as it shrinks to virtually nothing:

> I spent a long time chewing on the softened bread and then dunking it again into the little ration of water in my mug, and chewing again, over and over again, until the water was all used up and the crust had shrunk to a tiny little ball.
> Finally, all that remained was the indescribably delicious smell of bread on my fingers as I held them to my nose again and again. (50–51)

What we survivors have inherited from the dead is the order of the Symbolic; its signs are the inevitability of mediation, transportation, relay; all the evidence of aftermath that is hauntedness and haunting; co-presences that do not coincide, the "again and again" of the *Bettelbub* who never gets enough, orphaned memories and phantom pain. Perhaps that isn't much; but like the bread whose smell never quite leaves the fingers, it isn't quite nothing at all.

NOTES

1. Various implausibilities and errors have been noted in *Fragments* by historians of the Holocaust. Mächler focuses on the biography of Bruno Dössekker. His report is fair, sensitive, and exhaustive. It stops just short of accusing Dössekker of fraudulence, but predictably takes an either-or view of the truth-fiction dyad, and does not question conventional understandings of personal identity.

2. My thanks to David Caron for having drawn my attention to this item.

3. It's necessary to add, of course, that not being a Muselmann or a sommerso, in the camps, was a probably necessary but never sufficient condition of survival.

4. The corresponding German verb, *pflegen,* has a comparable double sense: it means to take care (*Pflegevater, Pflegemutter, Pflegekind,* foster-father, foster-mother, foster-child), but also to be wont (*ich pflege zu sagen,* I'm wont to say), thereby suggesting habituation and acculturation. Cognate with French *plier* and English "to

ply," *pflegen* refers to a frequentative action, which is a sememe common to both of its senses.

5. The peculiar aptness of this ditty from the point of view of testimonial—that is its haunting quality—derives from its half-rhyming of demand and satisfaction (*Bettelbub/genug*) and its intensification of the stock phrase "noch einmal" (once more) by substituting "immer" (always) for "einmal" (once). Janeway's translation is neat, but obscures the point by transforming the song into specifically anti-semitic doggerel: "Beggar kid, beggar kid. / There's never enough for the yid" (138). Lea Marcou, the French translator, tries an effect of antiphrasis, a common figure in French (here: "jamais trop" for "toujours pas assez"): "Le petit mendigot, le petit mendigot. / Il en a jamais trop, / le petit mendigot" (135). Perhaps: "The beggar-kid, the beggar-waif. / Can't never get enuf, / The beggar waif"?

6. I thank Aaron Nathan for showing me the relevance of the Lacanian catego-ries to testimonial in general and aftermath writing in particular. See his unpub-lished paper on *La vita è bella* (*Life is Beautiful*), "Lacan/Benigni."

WORKS CITED

Agamben, Giorgio. *Remnants of Auschwitz: The Witness and the Archive.* Trans. Daniel Heller-Roazen. New York: Zone, 1999.

Becker, Alton. *Beyond Translation: Essays toward a Modern Philology.* Ann Arbor: University of Michigan Press, 1995.

Brett, Lily. *Too Many Men.* Sydney: Pan McMillan (Picador), 1999.

Deleuze, Gilles. *Essays Critical and Clinical.* 1993. Trans. Daniel W. Smith and Mi-chael A. Greco. Minneapolis: University of Minnesota Press, 1997.

Ganzfried, Daniel. "Die Geliehene Holocaust-Biographie." *Weltwoche,* Aug. 27 and Sept. 3, 1998.

Lacan, Jacques. *Ecrits: A Selection.* Trans. Alan Sheridan. New York: Norton, 1977 [1966].

Lappin, Elena. "The Man With Two Heads." *Granta* 66. 1999.

Lejeune, Philippe. *On Autobiography.* 1975. Trans. Kathleen Leary. Minneapolis: University of Minnesota Press, 1989.

Lyotard, Jean-François. *The Differend: Phrases in Dispute.* 1983. Minneapolis: University of Minnesota Press, 1988.

Maechler, Stefan. *The Wilkomirski Affair: A Study in Biographcal Truth.* Trans. John E. Woods. New York: Schocken, 2001.

Nathan, Aaron. "Lacan/Benigni." Unpublished essay, University of California, Berkeley, 1999.

FIVE

Prosopopoeia and Holocaust Poetry in English: The Case of Sylvia Plath

Susan Gubar

Exploitation, larceny, masochism, sensationalism: the terms of opprobri-um hurled against Sylvia Plath's use of Holocaust material generally ac-cord with George Steiner's distress at any writer boasting "the right to put on this death-rig" (305). In 1962, the same year Plath wrote "Daddy" and "Lady Lazarus," Adorno qualified his famous injunction against the bar-barism of composing poetry after Auschwitz; however, her appropriation of the voices of the casualties still seems outrageous to those who point out the lack of any reasonable affinity or parallelism between Plath's in-dividual suffering and mass murder. These readers wonder, how dare she presume to imagine herself as one of the victims, to arrogate the otherness of the deceased through a projection that might be said to profane the memory of people exterminated by the Nazis? To honor the dead, Elie Wiesel has cautioned, the living must comprehend that "no one has the right to speak on their behalf" (194). Plath's non-Jewishness as well as her lack of a personal stake in the disaster made her speaking on behalf of the victims appear like a desecration. Yet, hardly anomalous, Plath's adoption of the voices of the imagined, absent dead—her deployment of the rhe-torical figure of prosopopoeia—surfaced in some of the most powerful poems about the Shoah composed by literary women and men with quite divergent relationships to the calamity. The impersonation of an absent speaker or a personification: prosopopoeia allowed those poets searching to find a language for the staggering horror of what had happened to speak as, for, with, and about the casualties in verse that has been either ignored or disparaged for too long.

If, as Tadeusz Rozewicz supposes in "Posthumous Rehabilitation," the dead who "see our snouts," "read our books," and "scrutinize our lectures" cannot or will not exonerate the guilt of the living ("the dead will not rehabilitate us"), postwar poets who confronted Western civilization's guilt over the catastrophic genocide of the Final Solution sometimes attempted an admittedly nugatory but nevertheless shocking rehabilitation of the dead (Schiff 170). Because the victims of the Holocaust did not have a cemetery, such writers ground their art in exactly the conviction that Elie Wiesel deduces from this fact, namely that the living must be their cemeteries. In the hard want of the bodies and of graves to mark their demise, the poet writes from the perspective of corpses deprived of coffins, either directly before or directly after they were murdered, speaking words eerily evocative of the epitaphs carved on ancient gravestones. Such a shocking reanimation of the dead cannot be equated with the traditional elegist's attempt to bring a particularly cherished person back into living memory, to assert the dead person's immortality, or to envision some union with the dead in a place elsewhere.[1] Nor does it form the only (or even the major) poetic response to the Shoah. But that the authors who manipulate prosopopoeia summon the posthumous voice to conceive of subjectivity enduring beyond the concentration camp means that the anguish of the Shoah does not, will not dissipate. Perhaps the inexorable vacancy, the vacuity, of the anonymous and numerous victims made this project urgent, licensed it, despite its unnerving presumption; or perhaps historical proximity to irreparable and stunning slaughter plunged some writers into an awareness of the impotence of the normative languages at their disposal.

So many of "the testimonies which bore the traces of *here*'s and *now*'s" were destroyed, Jean-François Lyotard once explained, that "the monopoly over history granted to the cognitive regimen of phrases" has been broken by the Shoah. The poet may therefore feel the need to step in (where Lyotard would have the historian venture forth) "by lending his or her ear to what is not presentable under the rules of knowledge" (57). Massive in its proportions, yet concealed at the time and denied later, the wrong suffered by millions of defenseless noncombatants marked for persecution and extirpation cannot be signified in extant words. Therefore "idioms which do not yet exist" need to be forged to prove that "the silence imposed on knowledge does not impose the silence of forgetting" but instead "a feeling" or a constellation of feelings (13, 56).[2] In *The Differend,* Lyotard outlines the sinister logic of a revisionist who would sanction amnesia: "in order for a place to be identified as a gas chamber, the only eyewitness I will accept would be a victim of this gas chamber; now . . . there is no victim that is not dead; otherwise, this gas chamber would not be what he or she claims it to be. There is, therefore, no gas chamber" (3–4). Grappling with the consequences of what Dori Laub has described as an atrocity perpetrated without witnesses (80), Lyotard's effort to combat repression issues in his belief that "The shades of those to whom had been refused not only life but the expression of the wrong done them by the Final Solution continue to wander in their indeterminacy" (56). A retort to Holocaust deniers, the adopted voices of the dead express the wrong done to one-third of the world's Jewish population. Several decades before Terrence Des Pres's 1988 defense of Holocaust poetry, Sylvia Plath substantiated Des Pres's assertion that the imagination confronted by negation "automatically starts asserting itself"; along with such contemporaries as Irena Klepfisz, Randall Jarrell, Charles Simic, Adrienne Rich, and Michael Hamburger, Plath implicitly agreed with Des Pres that "We cannot *not* imagine" (228).

At the risk of usurping those killed in the Holocaust, British and American writers who summon up the audacity to write in English from the perspective of the immolated tap the techniques of some of the most important poems composed in Yiddish, German, Hebrew, and Russian. With its chorus of prisoners ingesting "black milk" ("we drink it and drink it"), Paul Celan's "Death Fugue" can stand for a number of unsettling works that have definitively entered the Holocaust canon (Schiff 39–40). In the less frequently taught Holocaust verse written in English, prosopopoeia has been put to a range of purposes characterized by varying degrees of distance between poets and their vulnerable personae. At one extreme, the trope generates a haunting surrogate embroiled in the fate to which empathic writers suspect they would have been consigned if they had been born at the wrong place, in the wrong time. At the other extreme, it results in a critique of the lure of empathy, exposing it as a ruse shaped by spurious mechanisms of identification. On both ends of this spectrum stand Sylvia Plath's most famous works, yet her impudent project of "posthumous rehabilitation" has met with disparagement from critics protesting the equation she constructed between a sense of her own traumatized womanhood and Jewish vulnerability in the Shoah, an analogy that is thought to reduce Jewish suffering to instrumentality.

Such derogations depend upon reading Jewishness as a mere figure of verse "really" about womanhood; however, a reversal of the usual interpretive approach can attend to the uses to which Plath's poems put femininity as a mere figure of verse "really" about the psychological repercussions of Auschwitz on literature and Jewish identity. I propose this shift not to supplant psychosexual approaches to Plath's three most sustained deployments of Holocaust matter but to supplement them. Like a number of poets in her generation and not unlike Adorno, Plath viewed the Shoah as a test case for poetry and, indeed, for the imagination as a vehicle for conveying what it means for the incomprehensible to occur. Given the force of its Holocaust imagery, "Getting There" expresses Plath's horrified compassion for captive shades being hurtled by the onrushing fatality of history toward an irrevocable, incomprehensible death sentence that later observers only know as a hiatus where evidence ought to exist.

"How far is it? / How far is it now?" the poem begins and the first stanza locates its speaker in a train traveling through Russia. The proud "gods" of the willful steel engine Krupp know its destination, while this anonymous prisoner drags her body "through the straw of the boxcars" thinking of bribery, of a letter, of a fire, of bread. At the end of the first stanza, which is dedicated to an inexorable driving propulsion toward what the speaker dreads, the train stops where nurses and the wounded appear:

> Legs, arms, piled outside
> The tend of unending cries-
> A hospital of dolls.
> And the men, what is left of the men
> Pumped ahead by these pistons, this blood
> Into the next mile,
> The next hour-
> Dynasty of broken arrows! (248)

The train pumping ahead on its pistons, the blood pumped ahead in its pistons, the plummeting forward of the poem's short lines and their multiple gerunds issue only in a furor of a future, as the poem evokes the furious pace of the Nazis, recalled by eye-witnesses: "'Out! Out! Everyone! Fast! Fast!' *The Germans were always in such a hurry*" (Leitner 30). This is not the autobiographical Plath writing in *The Bell Jar* about women being reduced to the passive place from which phallic arrows shoot off or in "Ariel" about her personal desire to become an arrow flying suicidally into the red eye of morning; however, the poet's persistent identification does seep into the "I" perceiving the collective emasculation of a "Dynasty of broken arrows" and "dragging" her body through the Russia she has "to get across."[3]

In the second stanza, which also begins "How far is it?," the horror of the boxcar has been supplemented by the horror of a forced march. With red, thick mud slipping beneath her feet, the speaker experiences the earth as "Adam's side," out of which she rises in agony. Steaming, breathing, "its teeth / Ready to roll, like a devil's," the train metamorphoses into a screaming animal, as Plath-Eve confronts a series of "obstacles" amid the thunder and fire of guns, including "The body of this woman," whose "Charred skirts and deathmask" might signify her own double dying (249).[4] Simultaneously at the trainstop, on the march, in the cattle car, Plath's persona seeks some silent stasis, but her wish to bury the wounded and count the dead remains stymied in the subjunctive. The end of the poem, sometimes read as a hopeful attempt to imagine rebirth,[5] sounds more disturbing in the context of the Shoah:

> The carriages rock, they are cradles.
> And I, stepping from this skin
> Of old bandages, boredoms, old faces
> Step to you from the black car of Lethe,
> Pure as a baby. (249)

At the conclusion to which the poem flies, Plath-Eve arrives at Hades, where forgetfulness courses. Unable to retain a sense of herself or her past—she is stripped of her possessions, her clothing, her previous life, her identity—she too enters the "tent of unending cries." The Final Solution toward which all events rush transforms Plath's victim into a being as innocent but also as naked and defenseless as an infant. Unlike Whitman's "Out of the Cradle Endlessly Rocking," where the endlessly rocking cradle of waves and poetic meters consoles by weaving death into life, the rocking cradles of the train's carriages plunge toward the inconceivable "There" not of birth but of oblivion.

Blatantly disturbing in its revision of the "rocking cradles" of Yeats's "Second Coming" as well, Plath's "Getting There" sutures the gap between poet and persona through an empathic identification related to what motivates Irena Klepfisz, Randall Jarrell, Charles Simic, Adrienne Rich, and Michael Hamburger in a number of poems that have gone for the most part unread and unanthologized. Like these other poets' work, Plath's verse inevitably displays the blatantly unrealistic rhetoric of prosopopoeia: readers know that the author has merely simulated the personification of the dead. For even those writers who strenuously decrease their distance from the "deathmask" disclose their grating awareness of the inescapable inauthenticity at the core of their oxymoronic undertaking. Bestowing presence onto the absent dead, "*prosopon-poiein*," Paul de Man's analysis explains, "means to *give* a face and therefore implies that the original face can be missing or nonexistent" in an optative fabrication that stresses its own illusory nature (57). The disjunction between "deathmask" and ventriloquist bears witness to contemporary poets' efforts to confront the flimsy insubstantiality of the visionary company they keep. In addition, of course, the English language itself marks not merely British and American writers' remoteness from the catastrophe, but also the fictionality of their impersonations because English was one of the few Western languages not generally spoken by prisoners inside the boxcars, camps, gas chambers, and mass graves that supply the settings of Holocaust verse.

Whereas Plath's "Getting There" provisionally elides the gap between the poet's personal self and the posthumous voice, her more famous deployments of prosopopoeia dramatize the linguistic discontinuity between Auschwitz and poetry by foregrounding the distance between victim and poet, by questioning the possibility of "heteropathic memory," an "identification-at-a-distance" that Kaja Silverman defines as a method of aligning (without interiorizing) the "not-me" with the "me" (185). Despite the barrage of criticism directed against her, perhaps no poet has been more scathingly critical of the figure of prosopopoeia than Plath. Even as she exploited the trope in the Holocaust context, Plath emphasized her awareness that imaginative identification with the victims could constitute either a life-threatening trap for the poet or a sinister trip for the poet's readers, as "Daddy" and "Lady Lazarus" demonstrate.

Imbued by Plath with a definitively postwar perspective on her own deployment of the voice of the victims ("I think I *may well be* a Jew" [emphasis mine]), "Daddy" puts into play not an assumed identification but instead a consideration of what it might mean and in a manner better sustained than that of one of its sources; Anne Sexton's probably influential line from "My Friend, My Friend" is "I think it would be better to be a Jew" (Cam 223–26). A more self-consciously fictive and qualified identification than John Berryman's effort to see himself as an "imaginary Jew," Plath's illuminates the psychological scenarios which most critics examine, but also her brilliant insights into a debilitating sexual politics at work in fascist anti-Semitism.[6] For, by highlighting the precariousness of her own identification with the Jews of Nazi Germany, Plath asks us to consider the dynamics of German-Jews' vicarious identification with their exterminators. From this perspective, "Daddy" reads less like a confessional elegy about Plath's grief and anger at the loss of her father, more like a depiction of Jewish melancholia—the primitive, suicidal grieving Freud associated with loss over a love object perceived as part of the self—and thus a meditation on an attachment to Germany in particular, to Western civilization in general that many European Jews found not only inevitable but galling as well.

Although numerous readers have noted that Plath anathematizes Nazism as patriarchalism pure and simple, they have failed to understand how the dependencies of a damaged and damaging femininity shape her analysis of genocide. A "bag full of God," a "Ghastly statue," an "Aryan" blue-eyed "Panzer-man" with a "neat mustache," Daddy deploys all the regalia of the fascist father against those robbed of selfhood, citizenship, and language, for the speaker's stuttering tongue is "stuck in a barb wire snare. / Ich, ich, ich, ich, / I could hardly speak." The daughter confronts a symbolic order in which the relationship between the fragile "ich" and the overpowering national and linguistic authority of Daddy frustrates any autonomous self-definition. That, as Jacqueline Rose points out, the English "you do not do" can be heard as the German "you *du* not *du*" (226) heightens awareness of the daughter's vulnerable and blurred ego boundaries, the European Jew's conflicted but nevertheless adoring address, her ardent responsiveness to the lethally proximate society that constructed her. Standing "at the blackboard," the fascist represents the irrational power of rationality, of the arts and the sciences, of culture in the "Fatherland." According to Plath, the Jews chuffed off "to Dachau, Auschwitz, Belsen" suffered the horror of impending extermination along with a crippling consciousness of complicity, if only the collusion of those doomed by a long history of intimacy to love and respect a force dead set against them.

For, through a rhetorical strategy itself implicated in the calculus of colonization, the poem dares to confront the daughter-speaker's induction into revering Daddy and his charismatic power: "Every woman adores a Fascist, / The boot in the face, the brute / Brute heart of a brute like you" (223). The daughter's subsequent decision to make and marry "a model" of Daddy (224) suggests how difficult it may be for a consciousness captivated by the inimical source which shaped it to escape self-destructive forms of thralldom that refigure bonds saturated with the only pattern of attachment known, lexicons of emotion devised by the dead Daddy. Vampiric, the phantom father and his constructed surrogate, the husband who loves "the rack and the screw," have drained the speaker of her creative talents, her currency, her autonomy. Depleted, the daughter rages against her appalled feelings of radical insufficiency, which bespeak a blurring of boundaries between Jewishness and Germanness that many German-Jews lamented before, during, and after the Shoah.

Since this tiny percentage of the German population played a relatively important role in business, finance, journalism, medicine, law, and the arts in the twenties and thirties, many German-Jews felt shocked at the betrayal of a culture to which they had vowed what Saul Friedlander calls "ever-renewed and ever-unrequited love" (*Nazi Germany* 78). When Leo Baeck, the famous Berlin Rabbi, sat down to pay his electric bill moments before the SS dragged him off to Theresienstadt, Hyam Maccoby thinks his act exemplified not passivity but instead many Jews' inability to believe that "this Germany, *which they loved, felt obligations toward, . . . felt gratitude toward*" could have dedicated itself to their annihilation (Rosenbaum 335; emphasis mine). The forfeiture of a beloved language and a revered homeland, the loss of a citizenship that had signified and certified professional status and security: such grief reeks of the narcissistic wound Plath's daughterly speaker suffers after she tries to commit suicide, only to find herself instead "pulled . . . out of the sack" and stuck together "with glue."

As the Mother Goose rhymes on "you," "*du*," "Jew," "glue," "screw," "gobbledygoo," "shoe" accumulate, the poem goose-steps toward the concluding "I'm finally through" that proclaims a victory over the spectral afterlife of the fascist, but only at the cost of the daughter's own life. At the very moment Plath declares she is "through" with her father, the final line intimates that she herself is also and thereby "through." No longer supported by the fragile hyphen between German and Jew, the outraged daughter knows her "gipsy ancestress" and her "Taroc pack" only confirm her status as a pariah, even decades after the catastrophic engagement with Daddy. Plath's scandalizing feminization of Europe's Jews suggests just how appalling, how shameful would seem, *would be* the emasculation of often intensely patriarchal communities. Just as Plath's speaker asks herself who she can possibly be without Daddy, European Jewish men and women might well have asked themselves who they could possibly be after the Shoah definitively estranged them from their fathers' lands, their mother tongue, their neighbors' customs, their compatriots' heritage, or so the ghastly number of postwar suicides of survi-vors-who-did-not-survive intimates. Without in any way conflating the different motives and circumstances of Walter Benjamin, Paul Celan, Pri-mo Levi, Peter Szondi, Jean Améry, Bruno Bettelheim, Jerzy Kosinsky, Piotr Rawicz, Tadeusz Boroswki, and Andrzej Munk, this frightful list of suicides attests to the devastating on-goingness of the Shoah.

If identification with the victims who could not disidentify with their tormentors constitutes the trap of prosopopoeia in "Daddy," the trope functions as a trip in "Lady Lazarus." What does it mean to think of the imperiled Jews as fetishized "masters of un-mastery," a phrase Maurice Blanchot used to approach the complex subject of Holocaust-related sui-cides (70)? The wronged speaker here can only liberate herself from "Herr Doktor" or "Herr Enemy" by wresting the power of persecution from him and turning it against herself. We know that the ongoingness of the tor-ments of the Shoah perpetuated postwar suicides, but did those casualties mutate into mystic scapegoats whose envied status as paradigmatic vic-tims would in turn generate ersatz survivor-celebrities? This is one way to grasp the shock of "Lady Lazarus," for the narcissistic and masochistic speaker has become obsessed with dying, relates to it as "a call." With her skin "Bright as a Nazi lampshade," her foot "A paperweight," and her face "featureless, fine / Jew linen," Lady Lazarus puts her damage on theatri-cal display through her scandalous suicide artistry (244). Have Jews been made to perform the *Trauerspiel* for a "peanut-crunching crowd" at the movies and on TV, like the striptease entertainer through whom Plath speaks? Does Lady Lazarus's "charge" at making death feel "real" and at "the theatrical / . . . / Comeback" anticipate a contemporary theatricaliza-tion of the Holocaust? Certainly, her vengeful warning that "there is a charge / For the hearing of my heart" evokes the charge—the cheap thrill and the financial price and the emotional cost—of installations, novels, testimonials, college courses, museums, and critical essays dedicated to the six million.

Because the commodification of Lady Lazarus's exhibitionism issues in spectators paying "For a word or a touch / Or a bit of blood / . . . / Or a piece of my hair or my clothes," her bragging about her expertise at the art of dying—"I do it so it feels *like* hell. / I do it so it *feels* real" (245; em-phasis mine)—seems to adumbrate the notorious celebrity of a writer like Benjamin Wilkomirski, whose gruesome bestseller *Fragments* (about a child's experiences in the camps) was praised as "free of literary artifice of any kind" before it was judged to be a fraud.[7] When Daniel Ganzfried ar-

gued about Wilkomirski's defenders, "These people talking about suicide
will *suggest* it to him" ("Some of his supporters would love him dead because then it looks like proof that he's Wilkomirski" [Gourevitch 66]), his
remarks gloss Plath's suicide-performer pandering to her audience as well
as Blanchot's caution about the contamination of the very idea of the
genuine (upon which Plath's work broods): "If there is, among all words,
one that is inauthentic, then surely it is the word 'authentic'" (60). To the
extent that the impresario of Plath's stage, "Herr God" or "Herr Lucifer,"
has reduced Lady Lazarus from a person to an "opus" or a "valuable," the
poem hints that even reverential post-Shoah remembrances may be
defiled by the Nazi perpetrators, that prosopopoeia will not enable the
poet to transcend the tarnished uses to which the past has been, can be,
will be put. In the voice of a denizen of disaster, Plath mocks the frisson
stimulated by the cultural industry she herself helped to spawn.[8]

Revolted by her own dehumanization, Lady Lazarus then imagines
triumphing over the murderous Nazis by turning vengeful herself, if only
in the incendiary afterlife conferred by the oven:

> Ash, ash—
> You poke and stir.
> Flesh, bone, there is nothing there—
> A cake of soap,
> A wedding ring,
> A gold filling.
> Herr God. Herr Lucifer
> Beware
> Beware.
> Out of the ash
> I rise with my red hair
> And I eat men like air.

As it feeds on "men like air"—predatory psychic dictators but also
perhaps men turned to smoke—the red rage rising out of the ashes only
fuels self-combustion, debunking the idea of transcendence or rebirth at
the end of the poem. With its ironic echoing of the conclusion of Coleridge's "Kubla Khan"—"Beware, beware, his flashing eyes, his floating
hair"—"Lady Lazarus" repudiates Romantic wonder at the power of the
artist, replacing the magical "pleasure dome" of his artifice with the de-
tritus to which the Jewish people were reduced, in a speech act that
amounts to a caustic assessment of the aesthetic sell-out, the disaster-

imposter luminary: "there is nothing there—."[9] That no consensus exists among contemporary historians over whether the Nazis made cakes of soap out of their victims (though they certainly did "manufacture" hair and skin, rings and fillings and bones) drives home the bitter irony that propels the poem, namely that imaginative approaches to the Shoah may distort, rather than safeguard, the dreadful but shredded historical record. Reenactments of the calamity, including her own, are indicted, even as Plath issues a warning that they will take their toll.

Has the figure of prosopopoeia, so seductive for poets of Plath's generation, outlived its functions as the Holocaust recedes into a past that will soon have been witnessed by no one alive to provide firsthand testimony of its atrocities? Or will the imperatives of what Marianne Hirsch calls "postmemory" imbue this rhetorical strategy—which insists on returning to the unbearable rupture of suffering—with newfound resonance once the Shoah can no longer be personally recalled? Given the passage of time as well as the flood of depictions of the catastrophe, the very vacuity of the buried alive, incinerated, unburied, dismembered bodies that licensed the personifications of prosopopoeia may make verse epitaphs seem shoddily inadequate. Plath's taunting sneer—"I turn and burn. / Do not think I underestimate your great concern" (246)—chronologically preceded the highly profitable entertainment industry the Holocaust business has so recently become; however, besides forecasting it, "Lady Lazarus" offers up a chilling warning about the hectic hype of a hyper-identification, a fetishization of suffering, with which the figure of prosopopoeia flirts. Indeed, Plath's verse uncannily stages the bases for accusations of exploitation, larceny, masochism, and sensationalism that would increasingly accrue around Holocaust remembrance. In addition, her impersonation of the real victims invariably generates awareness of the spurious representation put in the place of the absence of evidence. Calling attention to what Geoffrey Hartman and Jean Baudrillard term our propensity to adopt a "necrospective," poems deploying prosopopoeia draw us closer to an event that is simultaneously distanced by their debased status as merely simulated and recycled image-substitutions (Hartman 45).

Today, in accord with scholars who stress the exceptionality of the Shoah,[10] creative writers may choose to emphasize the opacity of the disaster, as Jorie Graham does, rather than freight it with voices of their own devising. For we have become exceptionally sensitive to the political and moral problems posed by a trope like prosopopoeia, quandaries articulated by one of the poets who has employed it herself: "The living, writers

especially, are terrible projectionists," Adrienne Rich has declared, adding "I hate the way they use the dead" (113). Anne Michaels calls the effort "to smuggle language / from the mouths of the dying / and the dead"
a "suicide mission" because what is rescued cannot be "the old language
at all; / only the alphabet the same" and because "language of a victim
only reveals / the one who named him" (115). Yet, addressing the aetiol-
ogy and ethics of prosopopoeia in earlier Holocaust verse, Graham's "Annunciation with a Bullet in It" exposes both the injuries and the urgen-
cies of using the dead and does so by returning to Lyotard's central issue,
splicing it with eye-witness testimony taken from Isabella Leitner's *Fragments of Isabella: A Memoir of Auschwitz*. As forecast by its title and its occasional setting (someone has shot the poet's dying dog, with whom she
sits throughout the night), the poem concentrates on shocking moments
of inexplicable violence.

In particular, sections 5 through 12 of "Annunciation with a Bullet in
It" consist of reprinted passages from Leitner's account of her deportation
("Anyone not up at four a.m. will get a *Kugel*"), the strength she gains in
the camps from her three sisters ("*Cipi, Chicha, Rachel, Isabella.* We seem
to be alive"), their touching of a newborn baby ("before she is wrapped
in / the piece of paper / and handed over to the Blockelteste—"), her fear
of carrying a dead body ("the *Oberscharffuhrer* will choose me, I know he
will") (Graham, *Dream* 66–77): all these quotations, sprinkled with foreign
words and prefaced by the phrases "Then, she said," do not resemble the
language employed by Plath so much as the more modestly documentary works of such poets as Charles Reznikoff and Barbara Helfgott Hyett,
both of whom limited themselves to affixing line breaks to (and deleting
what they viewed as extraneous details from) the oral testimonials they
recorded and then published. But in Graham's poem, the documentary
source is immediately followed by another quotation ("Said the angel"),
this one expressing the sinister logic of the cynic Lyotard paraphrased in
The Differend, a revisionist who has "analyzed thousands of documents"
and "tirelessly pursued specialists":

> I have tried in vain to find a single former deportee
> capable of proving to me that he had really seen
>   with his own eyes
> a gas chamber
>   TIRELESSLY
> (wingprint in dust) (smoke) the

only acceptable proof that it was used to kill
  is that one died from it—
(tirelessly)—
  but if one is dead one cannot testify
that it is
  on account of such a chamber-
  there is, therefore, no gas chamber. (72–73)

When history consists of "a rip where evidence exists" or a "stammer between invisibles, / The soft jingling of a chain" (75, 73), can any documentation be found to meet the perverse objections raised by Lyotard's Holocaust denier? To Graham's consternation, what cannot be "seen" in her complex meditation threatens to degenerate into the equivocations of the word *"seem,"* turning the "plaintiff" into a "victim" who cannot find the means to prove the damages incurred (75, 73). Although Isabella Leitner's incorporated testimony focuses, like Walter Benjamin's Angel of History, on a single catastrophe rather than the "chain of events" we observe from a distance, the words of her Auschwitz memoir jingle against those of Lyotard's malignant "angel" in a sequence that recalls Graham's earlier definition of history as *"the creature, the x,"* a beast "on a chain, licking its bone": "it is on a chain / . . . / that hisses as it moves with the moving x, / link by link with the turning x / (the gnawing now Europe burning)."[11]

A retort to Lyotard's revisionist, the adopted voice of one of Leitner's family members at the conclusion of the poem—whose emphatic lie here ("I really really am not hungry" [77]) bespeaks her loving offer of a piece of bread—testifies to her survival in Leitner's and Graham's memory, but only as "A stammer between invisibles" because we know nothing of her fate, nor that of the other two sisters in the concentration camp with her. Indeed, in *Fragments of Isabella* Leitner herself has no definitive knowledge of one sister's destiny ("Cipi, Cipi, where are you?"), though she may have been compelled to undertake the death march to Bergen-Belsen; possibly she survived the British liberation (84). That annunciation, with its promise of an emancipating enunciation, has been riddled by such absences accords with Cynthia Ozick's protest against any "search for spots of goodness, for redemptive meaning" in the Shoah (279). At the same time, Graham's poem explains why some of her precursors felt compelled to go beyond testimonial evidence, to occupy the "rip where evidence exists," to communicate a "stammer between invisibles." Despite the indubitable fact that the inanimate dead cannot possibly attest to what or who murdered them, imaginatively inhabiting the genocidal hole in annunciation means disproving the logic of revisionists. Bloodless, even the words of survivors or photographs of the victims only generate after-the-fact narrativizing that *"the creature, the x"* gnaws, "making stories like small smacking / . . . / sounds, / whole long stories which are its gentle gnawing" (*Dream* 146). "How," Graham asks in another poem, "can the scream rise up out of its grave of matter?":

> The war is gone. The reason gone. The body gone. Its
> reason gone. The name the face the personal
>   identity and yet here
> is a pain that will not diminish. (*Materialism* 100)

As if inspired by Walter Benjamin's Angel of History, in a passage which Graham quotes elsewhere in *Materialism* (the book in which "Annunciation with a Bullet in It" appears), Plath and her peers "would like to stay, awaken the dead," though their stutters and caesuras, their foreignisms and fragments prove they know full well that the not-said, the unheard, the unsayable have been buffeted in the storm of time irresistibly propelling them away from the pile of debris growing skyward (*Materialism* 55). Through their invention of the voices of the dead and dying as well as their sometimes explicit, sometimes implicit acknowledgment of the futility of their task, American and British writers provide images that testify to the feelings of an event as well as its incomprehensibility—or its limited comprehensibility as a piece of a larger phenomenon that itself still defies understanding. "The past can be seized only as an image which flashes up at the instant when it can be recognized and is never seen again," Benjamin declared; "every image of the past that is not recognized by the present as one of its own concerns threatens to disappear irretrievably" (255). By generating unreal images of a past partially obliterated from history, the figure of prosopopoeia enabled poets of Plath's generation to fulfill Benjamin's definition of the most adroit historian: "Only that historian will have the gift of fanning the spark of hope in the past who is firmly convinced that *even the dead* will not be safe from the enemy if he wins. And this enemy has not ceased to be victorious" (255).

NOTES

This essay is excerpted from a longer version published in *Yale Journal of Criticism* 14.1 (2001): 191–215. © 2001 by The Johns Hopkins University Press. Reprinted by permission of The Johns Hopkins University Press. It could not have been written without the support of a Rockefeller Fellowship in the spring of 1999 and the staff as well as the other Fellows at the Virginia Foundation for the Humanities. Early and late in the formulation of this subject, the generous help of Jahan Ramazani shaped my thinking. I am also grateful for the critical insights of Linda Charnes, Donald Gray, Geoffrey Hartman, Anna Meek, Nancy K. Miller, and Alvin Rosenfeld.

1. A number of critics—including Schenck, Sachs, and Ramazani—examine laments composed by a bereft friend or relative grieving over loss and seeking (sometimes hopelessly) consolation; even those elegies skeptical about solace are formally different from poems exploiting prosopopoeia.

2. Related meditations on the "silence imposed on knowledge" are offered by Shoshana Felman and Dori Laub.

3. On Plath's use of the arrow in fiction and verse, see Gilbert (251).

4. The last phrase in quotes comes from Alvin Rosenfeld's book of that name.

5. According to Linda Bundtzen, "The train's carriages are transformed into the mother's cradles, rocking the dead and wounded toward resurrection" (250) as the speaker becomes "a mother-god, raising the dead, her body the divine vehicle for human salvation from history" (251).

6. On Berryman, see Flanzbaum. For an excellent approach to "Daddy" and "Lady Lazarus" in terms of Plath's "agonistic mourning" (263), see Ramazani (276–82, 285–88).

7. The quote comes from a blurb on the book by Jonathan Kozol, but many other reviewers could be quoted in their praise of the authenticity of *Fragments*. In "The Memory Thief," Gourevitch also discusses Jerzy Kosinsky as an impostor.

8. See Friedlander, who views the "frisson" of the Holocaust entertainment industry as a product of "the meeting of kitsch and death" in *Reflections of Nazism* (25).

9. See the discussion in Gilbert and Gubar of Plath's use of a ghostly iambic pentameter in this closing allusion to Coleridge (290).

10. See Lanzmann's influential attack on efforts to explain the Holocaust or understand the perpetrators (200–220); many agree with him that, as Friedlander puts it in *Memory, History, and the Extermination of the Jews of Europe*, "the 'Final Solution,' as a result of its apparent historical exceptionality, could well be inaccessible to all attempts at a significant representation and interpretation" (113).

11. The phrase "chain of events" comes from a passage in Walter Benjamin's description of the angel of history that Graham quotes in "On Description," *Materialism* (55). The "creature x" appears in Jorie Graham, "History" (*Dream* 145 and 147).

WORKS CITED

Benjamin, Walter. *Illuminations*. Ed. Hannah Arendt. New York: Schocken, 1969.

Blanchot, Maurice. *The Writing of the Disaster*. Trans. Ann Smock. Lincoln: University of Nebraska Press, 1995.

Bundtzen, Linda. *Plath's Incarnations: Woman and the Creative Process*. Ann Arbor: University of Michigan Press, 1983.

Cam, Heather. "'Daddy': Sylvia Plath's Debt to Anne Sexton." *Sexton: Selected Criticism.* Ed. Diana Hume George. Urbana: University of Illinois Press, 1988. 223–26.

de Man, Paul. *The Rhetoric of Romanticism.* New York: Columbia University Press, 1984.

Des Pres, Terrence. *Praises and Dispraises: Poetry and Politics, the Twentieth Century.* New York: Viking, 1988.

Felman, Shoshana, and Dori Laub. *Testimony: Crises of Witnessing in Literature, Psychoanalysis and History.* New York: Routledge, 1992.

Flanzbaum, Helene. "The Imaginary Jew and the American Poet." *The Americanization of the Holocaust.* Ed. Flanzbaum. Baltimore: Johns Hopkins University Press, 1999. 18–32.

Friedlander, Saul. *Memory, History, and the Extermination of the Jews of Europe.* Bloomington: Indiana University Press, 1993.

———. *Nazi Germany and the Jews.* Volume 1, *The Persecution, 1933–1939.* New York: Harper Collins, 1997.

———. *Reflections of Nazism: An Essay on Kitsch and Death.* Trans. Thomas Weyr. Bloomington: Indiana University Press, 1993.

Gilbert, Sandra M. "A Fine, White Flying Myth: The Life/Work of Sylvia Plath." *Shakespeare's Sisters: Feminist Essays on Women Poets.* Ed. Sandra M. Gilbert and Susan Gubar. Bloomington: Indiana University Press, 1979. 245–60.

Gilbert, Sandra M., and Susan Gubar. *Letters from the Front.* New Haven: Yale University Press, 1994.

Gourevitch, Philip. "The Memory Thief." *New Yorker* June 14, 1999: 48–68.

Graham, Jorie. *The Dream of the Unified Field: Selected Poems 1974–1994.* Hopewell, N.J.: Ecco Press, 1995.

———. *Materialism.* Hopewell, N.J.: Ecco Press, 1993.

Hartman, Geoffrey H. *The Longest Shadow: In the Aftermath of the Holocaust.* Bloomington: Indiana University Press, 1996.

Hirsch, Marianne. *Family Frames: Photography, Narrative, and Postmemory.* Cambridge, Mass.: Harvard University Press, 1997.

Hyett, Barbara Helfgott. *In Evidence: Poems of the Liberation of Nazi Concentration Camps.* Pittsburgh: University of Pittsburgh Press, 1986.

Lanzmann, Claude. "The Obscenity of Understanding." *Trauma: Explorations in Memory.* Ed. Cathy Caruth. Baltimore: Johns Hopkins University Press, 1995. 200–220.

Laub, Dori. See Shoshana Felman.

Leitner, Isabella. *Fragments of Isabella: A Memoir of Auschwitz.* New York: Dell, 1979.

Lyotard, Jean-François. *The Differend: Phrases in Dispute.* Trans. Georges Van Den Abbeele. Minneapolis: University of Minnesota Press, 1988.

Michaels, Anne. *The Weight of Oranges/Miner's Pond.* Toronto: McClelland and Stewart, 1997.

Ozick, Cynthia. Comments in "Round Table Discussion." *Writing and the Holocaust.* Ed. Berel Lang. New York: Holmes and Meier, 1988. 277–84.

Plath, Sylvia. *The Collected Poems.* Ed. Ted Hughes. New York: Harper and Row, 1981.

Ramazani, Jahan. *Poetry of Mourning: The Modern Elegy from Hardy to Heaney.* Chicago: University of Chicago Press, 1994.

Reznikoff, Charles. *Holocaust.* Los Angeles: Black Sparrow Press, 1975.

Rich, Adrienne. *Sources. Adrienne Rich's Poetry and Prose.* Ed. Barbara Charlesworth Gelpi and Albert Gelpi. New York: W. W. Norton Critical Edition, 1993. 101–14.

Rose, Jacqueline. *The Haunting of Sylvia Plath.* Cambridge, Mass.: Harvard University Press, 1992.

Rosenbaum, Ron. *Explaining Hitler: The Search for the Origins of Evil.* New York: Harper Collins, 1999.

Rosenfeld, Alvin. *A Double Dying: Reflections on Holocaust Literature.* Bloomington: Indiana University Press, 1980.

Sachs, Peter M. *English Elegy: Readings in the Genre from Spenser to Yeats.* Baltimore: Johns Hopkins University Press, 1985.

Schenck, Celeste. *Mourning and Panegyric: The Poetics of Pastoral Ceremony.* University Park: Pennsylvania State University Press, 1988.

Schiff, Hilda. *Holocaust Poetry.* New York: St. Martin's, 1995.

Silverman, Kaja. *Threshold of the Visible World.* New York: Routledge, 1996.

Steiner, George. "In Extremis." *The Cambridge Mind.* Ed. Eric Homberger, William Janeway, and Simon Schama. London: Jonathan Cape, 1969. 303–7.

Wiesel, Elie. *From the Kingdom of Memory: Reminiscences.* New York: Summit Books, 1990.

PART THREE

Testimony and the Making of Community

SIX

Holocaust Testimony, National Memory

Orly Lubin

In June of 1943, a memorial service was held at kibbutz Yagur for Tossia Altman and Zivia Lubetkin, the young Polish Zionists who led the Warsaw Ghetto uprising in April and were assumed to be dead in its wake. Although the two women were "not granted success in rescuing the surviving remnant," as Mair Ya'ari of the Hashomer Hatzair movement declared, they "did save our dignity," and for that, they were "already legends." Other eulogists followed Ya'ari's logic to honor the dead women who lived on in the living collective. "Zivia-Tossia, these are not names," said Emma Levin-Talmi, a leading educator. "They symbolize battalions and flocks of rebels. They are a symbol." "Zivia," another eulogist intoned, "the name has become an insignia, a symbol and a flag" (Shalev 209–10).

But it was soon discovered that if Tossia and Zivia survived the uprising symbolically, they survived it in the physical sense as well. Tossia Altman escaped her supposed death only to die soon after—she was killed one month later in a fire at the celluloid factory where she hid (Shalev 194)—but Zivia Lubetkin lived to emigrate to Palestine, where she founded a kibbutz with other survivors. Although Tossia and Zivia met dramatically different fates, their narratives serve similar functions in the symbolic history of the nation. The Zionist collective assumed ownership of their stories and used their bodies as symbols of the uprising, of resistance and force. This purpose is fundamentally different from that of their male counterparts, who entered the collective memory as heroic personas, re-membered for the specificity of their deeds. Lubetkin's companion Antek Zuckerman, for example, is remembered as the head of the uprising; K. Tzetnik is remembered as an author, and as the witness who fainted on the stand while testifying at the Eichmann trial in 1961.[1] Surrendering this kind of specificity, the stories of Tossia and Zivia were subsumed into the nation's, and remembered only in symbolic terms.

Lubetkin's testimonies worked to sustain the memory of the Holo-caust, but they also represented a new Zionist ethos. In that ideological framework, they served at least three narratives. First, they supported the linear Zionist meta-narrative that traced the people's progress from the diaspora to redemption in Zion. Second, they absolved the guilt of Jews who lived in Palestine during the war by reassuring them that someone else had "stood in" for them when they failed to act on behalf of their brethren in Europe. Third and most important, they "proved" the exis-tence of a "New Jew." Unlike the diasporic one, this New Jew was a fighter who protected herself and others; she was Western, secular, and socialist (thus excluding Orthodox Jews, Jews from Muslim countries, and the bourgeoisie).[2] Lubetkin fit this description perfectly, especially in light of Benedict Anderson's thesis that nations describe themselves in the femi-nized terms of kinship and home (Anderson 7, 143). As a woman, Lubet-kin was well suited to symbolize the imagined community of Israel.

Her testimonies served this purpose through multiple layers of visu-al, physical, and semantic mediation. A documentary film made some fifty years later shows Lubetkin's sister recalling that Zivia's arrival on the shores of Tel Aviv was "like something from another world. You stand at the port and there on the boat you see her alive and life-size and even laughing, and I've boarded the ship and of course you hug, cry. You don't speak. Not a word. You don't ask. . . . You're struck speechless until the excitement subsides. And then we got off and of course she wasn't mine right away."[3] Upon her arrival, Lubetkin was immediately summoned to Yagur, where the Kibbutz Hameuchad movement held its convention. She was scheduled to bear witness on the site of her premature eulogy, where her resurrection would symbolize the new life of the Jewish nation. As she described the ghetto, the expulsions, and, most important, the events of the uprising, she was to describe how the rebels withstood their conditions, and how they fought against them.

But Lubetkin did not go directly to Yagur. The leaders of the Kibbutz Hameuchad movement took her to Bet Oren, where she gave her testimony first in private. In the documentary, Yoske Rabinovitz reported that he and Tabenkin, two of the leaders of the movement, sat with Lubetkin for "two nights and three days, part of the time in the wood and part of the time in the room. She told us—in tears, with pauses, in Yiddish, in Hebrew, in silences—what was in her heart. The story was unimaginably tragic. There was nothing in it of heroism, no glory, but it was as if she herself was bearing the entire six million."

Reflecting on the difference between Lubetkin's first testimony and her second, the documentary's narrator says that, "two days later at the convention at Yagur, Zivia's tears dried up." She rewarded her comrades' efforts to unify her fragmented past into a narrative that would unite the members of its audience. Seemingly risen from the dead, she offered her story to the nation's history. From the details of alleyways and bunkers, she built a city out of language; from specific acts of self-assertion, she constructed historical meaning. This act of construction was recapitulated in her miraculous "resurrection," which gave the dead a physical presence, suggesting that they participated symbolically in the national effort at Yagur.

This affirmation was desperately needed. Before Lubetkin spoke, other orators expressed their hope that she would explain the behavior of Jews during the war. "We were tortured by the question: Why did the Jews act this way," one reflected. "This way of annihilation without resistance bore into us and ate away at us: For haven't we turned over a new leaf in the history of Israel? Haven't we created a new, different kind of Jew? . . . In the depths of our souls burnt the anticipation for news of a rebellion and an uprising in the Diaspora. Therefore, we urgently await this testimony, the tidings of this testimony, the word of active reaction."[4]

Zivia Lubetkin complied with her listeners' demands. Relinquishing the first-person grammatical form, she translated her personal experience into a collective narrative. That act of translation is captured and repeated on the thirty-five seconds of film—visuals with no audio—which are all that remain of the convention's documentary. Edited to serve the movement's purpose, the film begins with Lubketkin facing the camera and the audience standing behind her; wearing a pinafore and shot from below, she speaks to the void, her head moving slightly. The camera seems to prefer the audience to the speaker as it then pans to a long shot of the crowd standing outside the tent, smiling. For a few seconds, the entire screen is filled with people, and then the camera pans away, framing them against the stark, surrounding landscape. This movement from figure to ground represents a movement from the individual to the collective, and at the same time, it represents a movement from the old Jew to the new one who is "local born," settling the land that the Zionist ethos holds to be abandoned. In the end, the camera unites Lubetkin's listeners by severing them from her and from the terror of her testimony.

As it is recorded, Lubetkin's speech deviates from the generic conventions of testimony. It does not seem to reach for catharsis, or to perform the labor of mourning, or to inscribe material traces of the truth that must be told, much as it defies telling (Felman and Laub 57–63; Friedlander 1–21). It does not strive to generate an historical truth or to represent a life experience, even with the two additional sections that formed the autobiographical book *In the Days of Destruction and Revolt.* It does not reflect the constitution of the single subject through the act of writing, as Georges Gusdorf suggests that autobiography does (Gusdorf 28–48). Rather, refusing to present herself primarily as a survivor of trauma, Lubetkin constructs herself as a symbol of the New Jew, as evidence of the new nation.

Dori Laub shows that the listeners of a survivor's testimony assume a position that is both essential and perilous.[5] Following a "journey fraught with dangers," the listener must "be unobtrusively yet imminently present, active, in the lead," so that "when the flow of fragments falters, the listener has to enhance them and induce their free expression" (Felman and Laub 71–72). Lubetkin rehearses her testimony to prepare it for its imperiled listener, who, as Laub writes, "comes to partially experience trauma in himself" (Felman and Laub 57). But Lubetkin allows her listeners to do more than enable the testimony; she allows them to mold it, to determine its narrative form and its symbolic use. Making herself subservient to the group, she tells a story that they need to hear. She aims to offer a testimony that will not rupture her audience's psyches but will, on the contrary, gather them together into a coherent, collective whole.

According to the movement's journal, Zivia began her testimony by posing four questions, which are stricken from the book (*Mibifnim* 1–8). "How did it happen," Zivia asked rhetorically, "that an entire people, millions of Jews went to the slaughter? What was the fate of our movement and its members? How did we work in the movement? What was the source of the strength we needed for the stand we took?" These are the same questions that her listeners raised before her arrival, and Lubetkin offers only factual answers; she does not provide the far-reaching explanations that her audience evidently wanted. She does, however, suggest that they might do what she does not. At the beginning of her speech, she expresses her wish "to tell, to speak simply, and you will put together the picture yourselves" (*Mibifnim* 5). Subsequent speakers reminded the audience that Lubetkin had put her narrative in their hands, to do with it what they would. "Zivia said," one speaker chided, "I shall tell so that you shall hear and so that you shall know, and so that you shall judge and so that you shall learn" (*Mibifnim* 5). Another speaker took this didactic move one step farther, aiming to control the audience's interpretation of the events that Lubetkin reported. The Jews who led the uprising demonstrated courage and self-determination, the speaker argued, and "they could not have done otherwise. They walked a hundred paths until they reached the clear understanding that there was no other way. And how did they find the strength?—Man was not alone, an individual; these were groups, kibbutzim, collectives" (*Mibifnim* 5). With this retrospection, the speakers turned Lubetkin's autobiographical narrative into a Zionist allegory.

Testimony is a duty fulfilled to the community of listeners, but as Shoshana Felman writes, it is also a declaration that this duty is unfulfillable. Ruz'ka Korchak acknowledged both of these functions in the testimonies she gave. To the executive committee of Hakibbutz Ha'artzi, she said that "what I tell you will not be a report. It will be a greeting, greetings from the other side" (Tuvin, Dror, and Rav 87); at the Women Workers' Council one month later, she said that "one thing was always clear to us: that we wouldn't be understood. . . . Human beings are incapable of understanding what took place there. . . . You already know a lot about the genocide and its form. What it was like, you'll never understand anyway" (101). Like Chayka Grossman, Korchak addressed this paradox by collecting her memories of the war into an autobiographical book that is highly detailed. Working on a local level, both Grossman and Korchak document history almost hour-by-hour, describing who said what to whom, and who met whom under what circumstances. But while these women survivors avoid focusing on the self in their testimonies the better to serve the collective's needs, they serve the self as well. By testifying about an extreme event, they gain entrance into the national narrative as full participants. Their testimonies, therefore, simultaneously constitute "the self" autobiographically and submerge it in collective history.[6]

But it is not only the combination of gender, genre, and national demands that enables "I" to accede to "we." It is also the extreme event that these women witness and try to represent in testimonial language. Dori Laub distinguishes Buber's loss of the "thou" from the survivors' loss of the "I": for the Jewish people, he reflects, "there was no longer an other to which one could say 'Thou' in the hope of being heard, of being recognized as a subject, of being answered. The historical reality of the Holocaust became, thus, a reality which relinquished philosophically the very possibility of address, the possibility of appealing, or of turning to, another. But when one cannot turn to a 'you' one cannot say 'thou' even to oneself. . . . This loss of the capacity to be a witness to oneself and thus to witness from the inside is perhaps the true meaning of annihilation" (Felman and Laub 82). Thus, the Holocaust is what Laub calls "an event without a witness" (Felman and Laub 80–81). Even when she testifies to the events of the uprising, the witness cannot be "a witness to herself," because she is not an "I." She is something else.

To protect that version of herself, she entrusts it to the collective to which she belongs. Zivia Lubetkin had no interest in the "I"—neither in its uniqueness, nor in its relations with the others. "I'll never forget," she began in one of the extremely rare instances when she used the first person; "I'll never forget the night when the whole ghetto went up in flames on every side. I rushed out of my hiding place at night and behold it was alight like daylight. This great light aroused such wonder." The testimonial subject disappears into the disaster she witnesses. Lubetkin becomes even less present as her testimony continues. In the transcription of the oral testimony she still gives a first-person account, but now she describes what she has heard rather than what she has seen, and in the book version that subjective account moves even further toward objectivity. "Surrounding me" was "a burst of blazing flames, the din of falling buildings, breaking windows, pillars of smoke rose sky high, and the fire spreads and gnaws away, spread and gnaws away" (Lubetkin, *In the Days of Destruction and Revolt* 141). The first person disappears into a self that is disembodied, attributing its eyes and its ears to everybody.

At the moment of testimony, however, a chasm opens up between the "individual I" and the symbol: the "I" refuses to accede to its collective purpose in a moment when the creation of the symbol is briefly postponed. It is a moment like that of Zivia Lubetkin's testimony at the Eichmann trial in 1961, when her body is put on display.[7] A woman who exists as a national symbol appears, briefly, as an actual person. But this appearance of the corporeal "I" must be repeated endlessly—hence, the repetition of annual rituals, in which the witnesses repeat their testimonies to audiences in schools, public centers, and on TV. Ruz'ka Korchak offered her testimony to the executive committee of Hakibbutz Ha'hartzi and again at the Women Workers' Council; Zivia Lubetkin repeated hers at Bet Oren and then, again, before the convention at Yagur. This repetition works through a duality that is characteristic of the testimonial act: the duality between the symbol and the corporeal body. Both a symbolic effort of mourning and an actual act of violence, testimony is inherently dual. At the same time as it represents its speaker's experience with violence, it enacts violence against its listeners. It forces the knowledge of trauma upon them, which traumatizes them as well. In this way, it doubles with every telling; it is at once the story of an individual and a contribution to a memory that is collective.

The filmed sequences of Lubetkin's testimony demonstrate this duality. Moving swiftly from Lubetkin to the listeners who left the tent where she spoke, the camera allows the retreating listeners to override the witness, to control her testimony and its interpretation. But even as the camera locates Lubetkin within a single, symbolic frame, it also allows her to escape it by helping her to create a testimonial site. Even as her corporeal body disappears into the national landscape, it also provides a locus for all of the locations she describes. Once "there" in Warsaw, it is now "here" in Yagur, where it defies immediate symbolization. As it becomes a visual object, it betrays its testimonial role: it does not testify to her specificity, but rather, to her symbolic function.

The extremes that Lubetkin represents are determined by the symbolic distance between Warsaw and Eretz-Israel. As she represents the Warsaw Ghetto and its surroundings in terms of the Zionist narrative, she creates a continuum from the dying diaspora to the site of Zion. She links the bodies that perished in Europe to the laboring ones that occupy the newly captured—and supposedly deserted—territories. Emphasizing the newness of the land and its people, she brings continuity to the national narrative she helps create; speaking from one site about another that is lost, she knits the two in one body that occupied both. Her corporeality dissolves in the heroism of "there" and its origin "here," in Zionist ideology. Relegating the distant diaspora to history, this ideology locates the present in Eretz-Israel. It associates the site of the past with (feminine) passivity and erases the female body.[8] Like diasporic sites, the female body no longer exists except in memory, in testimony that is unspeakable. The principal problem of Lubetkin's testimony is not the struggle to create a female voice; it is the struggle to find the site from which she can speak. As she constitutes that site, she becomes a full participant in a history that typically excluded women. Using the dualities of testimony, she creates a dual presence in the nation's meta-narrative: both as a symbol and an active member of the community. However, at the same time, she resists assuming a strictly allegorical status, as the image of the female body has historically done. She retains her individual specificity not through the autobiographical tale, but through the materiality of her body—by insisting upon its relationship to the site, binding its presence to the place where it appears.

Using her body as a voice for thousands, Lubetkin represented people who were without a place, without a site. Continually displaced, her body was removed again and again—in the false reports of her death, in her concealment at Bet Oren, and in the movement of the camera, away from her body to the body of the collective. Distanced from public life through her own actions and the actions of others, she was finally buried at Lochamei Hageta'ot in the north, away from the national leaders' cemeteries. Yet the repressed body repeatedly returned: it rose from the dead, bore witness at Yagur, testified at the Eichmann trial. All the while, it remained a symbol, addressing the national order not as a voice and a body, but rather as a myth, a flag. Undermining the unity of this symbol, Lubetkin divides her history into "there" and "here," Warsaw and the kibbutz—and as she represented each site, she divided it yet again. "Here" is comprised of Bet Oren and Yagur, of Yagur and Lochamei Hageta'ot—and the speaker of her story is also fragmentary. The speaker shifted from alleyway to alleyway, crossed to the Aryan side of the ghetto wall through a hole and back into the ghetto through the sewer pipes. The unity of her narrative is continually shattered by the rebels' lack of control over the events, by the arbitrariness of life and death, by the individual names that make up the collective. It is also disrupted by the singularity of each individual body that was burned, tortured, starved to death, gassed inside the headquarters' bunker, wounded on the Aryan side. The unity of the city decomposed as the roofs caved in, as the hidden escape shafts of the bunker were sealed, as the sewage pipes filled up with gas. All of these things fragmented the site, rendering it unsuitable to house a unified narrative or a unified territory.

This fragmentary movement between one place and another prevents the reification of "the other," for as the "other" changes with every movement, "otherness" changes, too. Zivia Lubetkin inhabited the status of the "other"—as a Jew, a woman, and most important, as a diasporic immigrant coming from "there." But at the same time, her testimony creates other "others"—Germans, Poles, Polish collaborators, Jewish traitors, Jews who did not perceive the gravity of the situation, and Jews in Palestine who divided all the pioneering movements after the war. She does not demonize the others she creates, however, because to do so would jeopardize her entry into the national narrative. She avoids the definitive determination of her otherness by avoiding the crystallization of a foreign, hostile otherness, as well; she moves incessantly, shifting from one place to another.

Without solid ground beneath her feet, Lubetkin constructs herself in movement. In this way, she resists the construction of Zion as a fixed site from which to speak. The Zionist meta-narrative constitutes itself vis-à-vis the Palestinian "other," which erases other forms of difference (women, Arab Jews—Jews from Muslim countries—diasporic Jews). Lubetkin's narrative, in contrast, represents many others, even the body of the refugee, which appears both "there" and "here"—"there" as erased speech, and "here" erased into "human dust," as the refugees were called.

The human body reappears in Lubetkin's testimony when the site disappears—when the ghetto burns. She describes the fighters coming out of the bunker at 18 Mila Street "looking horrible—creatures covered in filth and sand, weak and shivering as if not of this world. Someone faints and another breathes with difficulty. Yehuda Wangrover, of Hashomer Hatzair, takes rattling, strangled breaths, and Tossia Altman lies there wounded in her head and leg. We're surrounded by broken pieces of people" (Lubetkin, *In the Days of Destruction and Revolt* 160).

In this geography, the new site of testimony is constructed as the site of the Jewish people's resurrection and also the place where the body accedes to the collective. But where does that collective belong? Does it belong "there," where the events in the testimony happened, or "here," where the people listen to the testimony, where formerly they refused to hear? Given these two choices, Lubetkin selects a third: a new site, which she helps constitute. She joined Antek Zuckerman and other core groups of survivors to create the Museum of Heroism and founded the kibbutz of Lochamei Hageta'ot. They did not constitute their site through testimony, to reflect the hopes of the nation; rather, they built a museum at the site the nation needed to occupy. "You see," Ruz'ka wrote, "today I live the past, and the present and future are vague. I always thought that when you came we would found a kibbutz, our kibbutz, that would reflect everything we went through" (Tuvin, Dror, and Rav 128). An alternative national site, the survivors' site belonged to the nation only in its kibbutz structure and its territorial holding. It remained as liminal as the location of Lubetkin's testimony, which exists between "here" and "there."

Through a series of performative acts on stage, Lubetkin constitutes a self that shifts from the Warsaw Ghetto to the convention, the kibbutz, the courthouse, and the museum. With this shifting self, she strives to become part of the national narrative without "othering" her Palestinian neighbors through the occupation of territory.

The conditions of testimony allow Lubetkin to transform herself into a symbol, but they also enable her to maintain some notion of her body and how it occupies a specific space. She enters the national discourse through a paradox: she constitutes an "I" by submerging it in the collective. Both integral to the nation and indelibly severed from it, Lubetkin's testimony reconciles the injured individual and the newly formed collective. She gives up the specificity of her experience so that she can symbolize the heroism and rebirth of her nation—and as a symbol, she can actively participate in the creation of her nation's narrative.

NOTES

I thank Rela Mezali for translating this essay into English and Gloria Fisk for her careful editing.

1. "Katzetnik" is Yehiel Dinur's literary name. Dinur (then Feiner) wrote his first novel in a British army camp near Naples, Italy, after his release from Auschwitz. "I sat down to write, and did not get up for almost two and a half weeks," he recalls. "I gave the manuscript to a soldier, to pass it on to Eretz-Israel. The soldier [...] bent his head towards me and whispered: 'the name of the writer?!' Them who went to the crematorium, they wrote this book! Write down their name. Katzetnik" (qtd. in Segev).

2. The nation's need for those three narratives to represent a fighter symbolically continued through the Eichmann trial. Until then, the Holocaust was represented exclusively through heroism; only following the trial did the victims' stories gain national legitimacy. For a discussion of the evolution of the national narrative, see Felman, "Theaters of Justice." The trial, she contends, narrates "a story at the same time of the victims' suffering and of the victims' recovery of language. . . . The newly acquired semantic and historical authority of this revolutionary story [for the first time] create what we know today as the Holocaust: a theme of international discussion and of world conversation designating the experience of the victims and referring to the crime against the Jewish people independently from the political and military story of the Second World War" (Felman 201, 234).

3. *Zivia Lubetkin: A Life,* documentary film; script, Rivka Yogev and Ayelet Heller; executive producer, Shelly Sadot; producers, Gidon Ganeni and Amit Breuer, 1998.

4. *Mibifnim* 1–8. This text precedes the chapter entitled "The Last Days of the Warsaw Ghetto Uprising," published in the periodical of the General Histadrut

[Labor Union] of Hebrew Workers in Eretz-Yisrael and Hakibbitz Hameuchad Publishing, Ein Charod, 1946. This introduction is absent from *In the Days of Death and Rebellion,* which also contains this chapter, in combination with the testimony (published in installments in the daily *Davar,* during and after the convention, and again in the "Proceedings of the 15th Convention of Hakibbutz Hameuchad at Yagur," under the title "The Last Guards on the Wall") and with Lubetkin's text published in the *Dror Book* of 1947.

5. On the place, the function, and the effect of the listener in the process of the witness's attaining consciousness, and especially the effect of the testimony on the listener, see particularly Dori Laub (Felman and Laub 57–75).

6. This double function recalls the Latin American *testimonio,* which, Mary Beth Tierny-Tello argues, "seems to promise an authentic representation of the subaltern's voice in Latin America: previously silenced voices, given access to the written word by sympathetic scribes, have the opportunity to make their particular and collective plights (which may include poverty, exploitation, imprisonment, or genocide) known to a wide reading public and possibly to garner that public's support and solidarity" (Tierny-Tello 79). *Testimonio,* Arturo Arias notes, is a "collective, communal account of a person's life" (76). The similarities between the *testimonio* and the case of women bearing witness of the Holocaust within the national Zionist context are even stronger when one remembers that "*testimonio* constitutes an affirmation of the individual self in a collective mode" (Beverley 97). Like Lubetkin's testimony, *testimonio* springs from "a desire to impose oneself on an institution of power, such as literature, from the position of the excluded or the marginal" (Beverley 96).

7. In the documentary film on Lubetkin, her sister tells of a conversation between them: "During the Eichmann trial she came to consult me about which dress to wear to the trial, and I was beside myself—how could it even occur to her to ask such a thing, why should she care at all? And she said, 'Look I'll be standing for thousands behind me, and I need to be correct.'" Being on display necessitates "being correct," when "correct" is a perfect adherence to the demands of the spectators.

8. On the erasure of gender in the Holocaust, and then also in Claude Lanzmann's *Shoah,* see Marianne Hirsch and Leo Spitzer, "Gendered Translations: Claude Lanzmann's *Shoah*" (Cooke 3–19) Hirsch and Spitzer argue that "in the elaborate 'final solution' devised by the Nazis during the early 1940s, all victims were to be stripped of difference and rendered powerless. The Holocaust victims were thus to be 'degendered' by the process of persecution and extermination" (3). Although Lanzmann similarly treats gender as "irrelevant to the death machinery," they continue, "traces of gender difference are nonetheless reinscribed in his film" (5–6).

WORKS CITED

Anderson, Benedict. *Imagined Communities: Reflections of the Origin and Spread of Nationalism.* 1983. London: Verso, 1991.

Arias, Arturo. "Authoring Ethnicized Subjects: Rigoberta Menchú and the Performative Production of the Subaltern Self." *PMLA* 116.1 (Jan. 2001): 75–88.

Barthes, Roland. *On Racine.* 1960. Trans. Richard Howard. New York: Hill and Wang, 1964.

Beverley, John. "The Margin at the Center: On *Testimonio* (Testimonial Narrative)." *De/Colonizing the Subject: The Politics of Gender in Women's Autobiography.* Ed. Sidonie Smith and Julia Watson. Minneapolis: University of Minnesota Press, 1992. 91–114.

Cooke, Miriam, and Angela Woollacott, eds. *Gendering War Talk.* Princeton: Princeton University Press, 1993.

Felman, Shoshana. "Theaters of Justice: Arendt in Jerusalem, the Eichmann Trial, and the Redefinition of Legal Meaning in the Wake of the Holocaust." *Critical Inquiry* 27.2 (2001): 201–38. Also in *Theoretical Inquiries in Law* 1.2 (July 2000): 465–507.

Felman, Shoshana, and Dori Laub. *Testimony: Crises of Witnessing in Literature, Psychoanalysis, and History.* New York: Routledge, 1992.

Friedlander, Saul, ed. *Probing the Limits of Representation: Nazism and the "Final Solution."* Cambridge, Mass.: Harvard University Press, 1992.

Grossman, Chayka. *The People of the Underground.* Merchavia, Israel: Moreshet and Sifriat Poalim, 1965 (Hebrew).

Gusdorf, Georges. "Conditions and Limits of Autobiography." *Autobiography: Essays Theoretical and Critical.* Ed. James Olney. Princeton: Princeton University Press, 1980. 28–48.

Korchak, Reizl (Ruz'ka). *Flames in Ash.* Merchavia, Israel: Moreshet and Sifriat Poalim, 1965 (Hebrew).

Lubetkin, Zivia. *In the Days of Destruction and Revolt.* Lohamei Hageta'ot, Israel: Ghetto Fighters House Ltd. and Hakibbutz Hameuchad Publishing, 1980 (Hebrew).

Mibifnim. 12.1 (Nov. 1946) (Hebrew).

Segev, Tom. "Katzetnik's 'Trip.'" *Koteret Rashit* May 27, 1987 (Hebrew).

Shalev, Ziva. *Tossia: Tossia Altman: From Leadership in Ha'shomer Hatza'ir to Command of the Jewish Combat Organization.* Tel Aviv: Moreshet, Bet Edut in Memory of Mordechai Anilevitch; Tel Aviv University—Department of Jewish History, 1992 (Hebrew).

Stanford Friedman, Susan. "Women's Autobiographical Selves: Theory and Practice." *The Private Self: Theory and Practice of Women's Autobiographical Writings.* Ed. Shari Benstock. Chapel Hill: University of North Carolina Press, 1988. 34–62.

Tierny-Tello, Mary Beth. "Testimony, Ethics, and the Aesthetic in 'Diamela Eltit.'" *PMLA* 114.1 (January 1999): 78–96.

Tuvin, Yehuda, Levy Dror, and Yossef Rav, eds. *Ruzka Korchak-Marle: The Personality and Philosophy of Life of a Fighter.* Tel Aviv: Moreshet and Sifriat Poalim, 1988 (Hebrew).

SEVEN

Unbearable Witness:
Toward a Politics of Listening

Wendy Hui Kyong Chun

On Wednesday, December 6, 1989, around 5:00 P.M., Marc Lepine (né Gamil Roderigue Gharbi), dressed in hunting garb, entered a classroom in the École Polytechnique. Disturbing a presentation by Eric Chavarie, he waved a .22-caliber rifle and ordered the men and women into opposite corners of the classroom. Thinking it was a joke arranged to relieve the tedium of the last hour of the term, no one moved. A single gunshot persuaded them otherwise. Next, Lepine ordered the men to leave. Alone with the women, he stated, "I am here to fight against feminism, that is why I am here." Nathalie Provost, a twenty-three-year-old mechanical engineering student, argued, "Look, we are just women studying engineering, not necessarily feminists ready to march on the streets to shout we are against men, just students intent on leading a normal life." Lepine responded, "You're women, you're going to be engineers. You're all a bunch of feminists. I hate feminists." He then opened fire, killing six women—and closing the discussion. After leaving the classroom, Lepine stalked through the halls of the school saying, "I want the women." Lepine killed himself at approximately 5:35 P.M., his gun still loaded and the police not yet in sight. The total death count: fourteen women and Marc Lepine.

And then the discussion reopened.

A variety of discussions followed, from the successful campaign to make December 6 a day of commemoration for all female victims of male violence to the heated media exchange between feminists and postfeminist "survivors" (women, usually in male-dominated fields, who identified themselves as rugged beyond-feminist "daughters" of feminism). This conflict reveals that if feminism makes the sovereign subject its goal, it can end with postfeminism. That is, it can produce postfeminists, who, confronted with systemic discrimination not redressable by "equal rights," employ antifeminist individualism in order to turn a blind eye to their own vulnerabilities. This strategy renders many postfeminists incapable of acknowledging and addressing any injury, since such an acknowledgement is tantamount to admitting failure. And this conflation of vulnerability with failure, combined with the traumatic nature of the massacre, waylaid an ethical encounter between feminist and postfeminist "witnesses." Like most traumatic events, the massacre invoked testimony not only from its survivors (the most vocal of whom, ironically, called for an end to the testimony), but also from those who were never physically present, who seemed to be testifying belatedly to a prior event or who were called to testify because of the proximity of the event. Although non-eyewitness testimony cannot and should not be dismissed as irrelevant, it is also essential that this testimony not take the place of, or inadvertently re-wound, those mainly silent eye-witnesses: it is essential that they identify with, rather than as, those eye-witnesses, while at the same time listening to and trying to respond to them. In order to avoid a hostile or sentimentalizing encounter between all "witnesses" to the massacre, I will argue that we need a politics of listening as a necessary complement to a politics of speaking. Feminism has often concentrated on consciousness raising, on producing speech that breaks one's silence and inaugurates one as a feminist. The question of how to listen and respond to these testimonials has been largely unaddressed, since the question of listening in general tends to be under-theorized and under-valued: more often than not, we assume we know how to listen. The aftermath of the Montreal Massacre demonstrates the disastrous consequences of such a dangerous assumption, whose result was in fact a missed encounter between witnesses and those who might have heard.

• • •

The unexpected horror of this "American-style carnage" (Pelletier 33) shocked most Canadians and defied them to make sense of the worst one-day massacre in Canadian history. To those whose complacency had been shattered, it was imperative that some lesson be extracted from the events of December 6, 1989. In response, the Montreal police launched an investigation, centered on the life of Marc Lepine: the day after, the police released a brief biography that described Lepine as "an intelligent but deeply troubled young man with no known psychiatric history" and alluded to a suicide note found on his body, which blamed feminists for his life's misery (Malarek and Aubin A1). The authorities, however, soon aborted their investigation. On December 11, the chief coroner, Jean Grennier, told the press that he preferred not to call for a public inquiry since an inquiry "would mean more pain and suffering for the families." The coroner did say that he would call for a public inquiry if he felt the public was not being properly informed (Malarek, "More Massacre" A14). The next day, the Montreal police refused to answer reporters' questions and stated that they "will provide any further pertinent information when it becomes available" (Malarek, "Police Refusal" A18). For the sake of those who had suffered most, the authorities argued, discussion must be closed —again.

The authorities, however, did not consult the families in question: the following June, nine of the fourteen families would join the National Action Committee on the Status of Women (NAC) in calling for a public inquiry into the massacre ("Demanding Answers" 17). As the police psychologists would later explain, the authorities had closed down the investigation because they feared that continuing it would unleash an unstoppable flow of antifeminist violence ("Police Won't" A16). They interpreted retelling not only as re-enacting the violence against the bereaved families, but also as propagating violence by calling others to identify with and act as Lepine. Thus, while they were claiming that the massacre was an isolated and incomprehensible event that no amount of investigation would ever render comprehensible, they were also assuming that the desire to kill feminists was already present in segments of the general public. For their own safety, female reporters and newscasters were advised not to dwell on the matter. To the surprise of the authorities, it was not male antifeminism that refused to be contained; it was female testimony. Testimony by women who identified with or as his victims flooded the media; vigils were held in almost every city; and anniversaries were and still are commemorated.

After the Montreal police refused to hold an inquest, it appeared that the crisis of truth and evidence resulting from the massacre would be addressed publicly only through the media. Without a privileged juridical space that demarcated eyewitnesses from commentators or expert witnesses, the victims, experts, and the police would offer their testimony—that is, *"vow to tell,* to *promise* and *produce* one's own speech as material evidence for truth"—only in the glare of publicity (Felman and Laub 5). Within the first week after the murders there were three narratives competing for the public's support: that the massacre was an isolated, incomprehensible act of a madman; that it was a case of child abuse reproducing its violence in a disturbed young man; that it was a crime against women and, as such, representative of Canadian misogyny. All these narratives treated Lepine as key to understanding the massacre.

The first narrative, of Lepine as a Mad Killer, coincided with the Montreal police interpretation. According to this explanation, the killings could not be politically motivated, since an insane subject could not act rationally and thus politically. The fact that all of Lepine's victims were female was incidental: it was unfortunate that these particular young women died, but any group could have been targeted. Particularly frightening about the massacre in light of this interpretation was that Lepine had no prior history of insanity so that his insanity could only be determined, after the fact, by his murderous act. Nonetheless, there were lessons to be learned: mass murder is not only an American problem; stiffen gun control laws; and invest in police psychology so that dangerously insane but apparently normal people cannot get gun permits.

The second interpretation also portrayed Lepine as insane, but as an insane victim. Numerous articles describing the childhood of Marc Lepine, citing the testimony of child psychologists, argued that his Algerian father's physical abusiveness combined with his steady diet of war movies had shaped him into an antifeminist mass murderer. As a victim of abuse, it was argued, Lepine could not help but repeat the violence around him. Once again, any larger responsibility for the Montreal Massacre disappeared, for, as the product of an aberrant family, Lepine represented the possible ramifications of "cultural differences" and the potential for violence lurking within all abused children. Again, the specificity of his victims vanished, since any group could have been targeted. Particularly frightening about the massacre in light of this interpretation was that Lepine had undergone therapy as a young boy after his parents' divorce precisely to prevent the repetition of violence. Nonetheless, there were lessons to be learned: treat children as the "final frontier"; keep old war movies away from young children; teach them that violence is not to be tolerated; and stiffen gun control laws, just in case.

The last interpretation, produced and supported by most feminists, argued that Lepine's actions were comprehensible and reprehensible. Feminist analysts, such as Francine Pelletier, emphasized the premeditated nature of the massacre in order to downplay the significance of Lepine's insanity: "He was crazy when he started shooting but it was a cold, rational and calculated act on his part" (Lamey A1). Accordingly, the Montreal Massacre became representative of the violence inherent in patriarchal society and was a spectacular instance of the routine killing of women by men. The violence of the massacre was also not limited to these fourteen deaths, since, as Nicole Brossard argued, "each woman cried over having been symbolically put to death" (Brossard 31). Particularly tragic to feminists was the innocence and youthful potential of the victims, for, instead of killing prominent feminists, Lepine had killed "fourteen of our bright and shining daughters . . . [who] were doing things that we, their mothers, [had] only dreamed of" (Cameron 161).

Essential to the gradual acceptance and dominance of the last narrative was the publication of Lepine's suicide letter nearly one year after the event. Working against the wishes of the police psychologists and some of the survivors, Francine Pelletier, who had been sent a copy of it anonymously, made the note, which named her as an intended victim, public. She argued that "publishing the note makes Lepine's motive impossible to ignore. . . . unlike the police and the psychologists, I don't believe it is dangerous to have a window inside Marc Lepine's head. Personally, I think it is dangerous not to, to continue pretending the Polytechnique (massacre) had nothing to do with anything but the insanity of Marc Lepine" (Lamey A1, A4). By privileging the written *intentions* of Lepine, feminists treated him as their star witness:

> Would you note that if I commit suicide today 89-12-06 it is not for economic reasons (for I have waited until I exhausted all my financial means, even refusing jobs) but for political reasons. Because I have decided to send the feminists, who have always ruined my life, to their Maker. . . .
>
> Even if the Mad Killer epithet will be attributed to me by the media, I consider myself a rational erudite that only the Grim Reaper has forced to take extreme acts. For why persevere to exist if it is only to please the government. Being rather backward-looking by nature (except for science), the feminists have always enraged me. They want to keep the advantages of women (e.g. cheaper insurance, extended maternity leave preceded by a preventive leave etc.) while seizing for themselves those of men.
>
> Sorry for this too brief letter.

Marc Lepine
[The letter is followed by the nineteen-name list, with a note at the bottom.]
    Nearly died today. The lack of time (because I started too late) has allowed these radical feminists to survive.
    Alea Jacta Est. (Malette and Chalouh 180–81)

Lepine's list of the nineteen intended if not actual victims legitimated Pelletier's and other Québecois feminists' claims to testify on behalf of, and as, victims of Lepine. They could no longer be accused of taking the massacre personally, because they had been personally implicated by Lepine. Because of his "testimony" or adjudication, their interpretation of the event could no longer be construed as self-serving, as "outside" the events of December 6, 1989, since only an *accident* prevented them from being Lepine's victims; only an accident made these other women Lepine's target. Because they linked this event to other acts of violence endemic to a patriarchal society, the public outpouring of testimony by women who had been abused by men—or who felt vulnerable to male violence—became essential to establishing the massacre's historical and national significance. Final (?) lessons learned: never again; don't be silent about violence against women; mourn, then look into society and yourself; question your misogyny; and don't forget.

Accepting Lepine's actions as representative of violence against women has brought much-needed attention to the question. In a "Post-Montreal-Massacre" Canada, violence against women emerged as a category in the Canadian News Index. It was a new, comprehensive, gendered name for abuse that was formerly hidden under the label domestic violence, or undifferentiated from violence in general, or pinned to an identity category such as battered women. To this day, Canadian articles about violence against women, sexual harassment, and antifeminism refer directly or indirectly to the Montreal Massacre. The massacre also caused many engineering societies, albeit reluctantly, to abolish more offensive practices such as strippers at Iron Ring Stag parties; mascots called "The Rigid Tool" (University of Waterloo); and racist and sexist jokes published in society newspapers (University of Calgary and University of British Columbia). Lastly, the massacre motivated more women to enter engineering and also motivated universities and government to provide incentive programs for these women.

I believe these changes have been positive, yet I also believe there are dangers in allowing this narrative to explain fully the Montreal Massacre. Making the massacre representative of all violence against women flattened the differences among domestic violence, the violence of the massacre, and "the fear with which every woman must live." This narrative, however unintentionally, privileged fear of violence as *the* issue that unites women and defines women as women. Moreover, by privileging the perpetrator's testimony, the feminist interpretation thus unwittingly undercut the significance of the testimonies of Lepine's actual victims. This exposed and widened fault lines between certain older feminists and younger women—usually women in male-dominated fields—who resented the older feminists' commentary and their imposition and usurpation of "victim" status. By insisting on "don't forget" and the need to publicize the event, feminists also kept certain unwilling eyewitnesses in the public's eye, calling into question exactly what we were not to forget. Lastly, this interpretation encouraged and was encouraged by paternal men who took the blame for the massacre and for "the fear with which every woman must live." For these reasons we should not, and cannot, rest in our reading of the Montreal Massacre.

WILL THE REAL VICTIM PLEASE STAND UP

Is the witness the one who *sees,* the one who *undergoes,* or the one who *propagates,* the accident to which he bears witness?

—Barbara Johnson

The media in reporting resistance to feminist testimony did not focus on angry male responses but rather on the testimony of certain female survivors and engineering students, such as Nathalie Provost, the young woman who had tried to reason with Lepine.[1] In response to the letter's publication, Provost chided feminists for losing sight of the true victims' needs: "Those of us who survived are strong and solid. We grew tremendously. Now, we need our peace. We need serenity" (Peritz A1). Provost's plea for peace was not necessarily a rejection of the feminists' interpretation, but rather a rejection of their testimony, and indeed of any testimony other than hers. After all, Provost—the first female survivor to talk to the press—speaking from her hospital bed, had defined public recounting of the massacre as morbid: "You know what has happened. I am not going to dwell on it. It has been a nightmare. I have talked it over with my friends. I don't intend to do it in public. It was horrible; to dwell on the details now would be morbid" (Buchignani A1). Provost, finding it impossible both to speak and not to speak, emphasized the importance of taking leave, of leaving the event.[2]

Although refusing to re-narrate the events, Provost did have two messages she wanted to disseminate. First, she wanted "to tell [others] . . . that there was nothing that could have saved her friends, to tell others who survived and perhaps herself that there should be no guilt" (Kastor B1). No one could have prevented the massacre: "He had decided to do what he did. When you plan to do a movie, every scene is set down. He knew how it would happen, I think. I tried to talk to him. It didn't change a second. I am sure that if people had tried to get him [i.e., if the men had not left the classroom], it might have been worse. Maybe he would have shot everyone. Maybe he would have gone on shooting. It is terrible now, but I am happy it wasn't worse" (Kastor B1). Provost's first message attempted to alleviate guilt for possible complicity with Lepine and for surviving (although the statement "it might have been worse" leaves open the possibility that it might have been better as well). It also created something to be grateful for—a bright side to the tragedy. It cast the events of December 6, 1989, as something that she and others *survived,* rather than as an event that simply killed her peers.

Provost's second message urged reporters to "use the power of information to explain to men that women are equal to them. I am as much a human being as if I were a man; I deserve as much respect, and I have the right to have my life the way I want it" (Buchignani A1). Not willing to interrogate why men are privileged examples of human beings, nor to consider the ways one's "right" to have one's life the way one wants is always compromised, Provost demanded that the media stop their investigation and direct their efforts "to explain *to men* that women are equal to them" (emphasis mine). Her second message, then, directed at men in general, implies that she, like the feminists, linked the massacre to broader societal attitudes.

Provost did offer a tentative narration and explanation of the event to the American press. In an interview with Elizabeth Kastor of the *Washington Post,* she offered the following account: "There were two crimes. The first one was something like a thief who comes into my house—the first crime was that. Everyone felt that. There's another crime, which was a guy attacking girls. I felt a bit like it was a rape. Maybe it's a strong word, but I feel a bit like that, and I have talked to friends who have had that experience and they felt as I do" (B1). Provost herself linked the Montreal Massacre with violence against women and identified with rape victims, which implies that she was upset by the fact, rather than content of, feminist testimony. Provost's angry insistence that her views and experiences stand as the lone legitimate source of information or noninformation was, perhaps, a response to the fact that she had been "twice injured"—once in front of Lepine's gun, again in front of the media's relentless coverage. In both situations, she had lost control.

Provost was not alone in calling for silence. On the second anniversary of the massacre, the Polytechnique was the only major Canadian engineering school not to hold a commemorative service for the fourteen dead women. On the first anniversary of the massacre, the school's director, André Bazergui, sent letters to several news outlets asking them to use restraint in their coverage: "Let's forget about this guy. This guy was completely crazy. By talking about him . . . you are just encouraging more crazy people to act like him" (Lalonde, "Students' Silence" A5). This "you" is not only aimed at the media, who played an active role in the propagation and resolution of the massacre; it is also aimed at the feminists, who were perceived as needlessly propagating the massacre for their own purposes. Although Bazergui phrases his comment as a call for restraint for their own safety, he positions feminists as aggressors whose talk *encourages* massacres. Similarly, many students at the Polytechnique focused on the similarities between feminist arguments and Marc Lepine's. According to Bazergui, the students refused to rally publicly behind the feminist cause because they were uncomfortable using the "crazy logic" of Marc Lepine: "The girls and guys don't want to be separated like they were in the class by Lepine. They don't want to get into the crazy logic of Marc Lepine. They are saying, 'This happened to us as a community and we want to stick together'" (Lalonde, "Students' Silence" A5). Since the crime began with the students separating themselves into different corners of the room, any admission of gender difference became inseparable from this "complicitous" action. Some students, like Bazergui, sympathized with Lepine by blaming the feminists for the murders. As Heidi Rathjen, a graduate of civil engineering, commented later:

> Feminists got a really bad rap out of what happened at the Polytechnique. I mean, people were telling them to shut up before they had even begun to say anything. There was a mass denial of what had happened at the Polytechnique, and *part of that denial was to blame feminists for what had happened.*

You have to understand, though, that immediately following the massacre, the entire Polytechnique was not thinking about male-female issues.

We were in intense mourning. These were our friends and classmates that had died and we just couldn't take on the social implications. It was impossible to see the big picture. Incomprehensible. ("For Many Women, Mourning Is Not Enough " A1; emphasis mine)

Incapable of taking on the social implications of their tragedy, the students construed Lepine and the fourteen dead women as casualties of feminism. Thus, if the feminists depended on the motives of Lepine to validate their interpretation of the event and to combat his "crazy logic," the students, still in shock, re-enacted his logic by blaming feminism for causing the massacre.

CUTTING THE APRON STRINGS

Yes, yes, in theory, in my head, I am a feminist. But in my guts, basically, no. I don't need—I won't say I don't need it because I did need it, and if I had been born 50 years ago, I would have done the same as my mother. I just don't feel it.

—Nathalie Provost

After the feminist testimony had persuaded the general public to read the event as representative of violence against women, Provost and her peers reframed their objections in terms of a generational dispute. Opposing the older feminists' portrayal of universal female victimhood, these younger women refused to accept the role of feminist heroines/victims and refused to limit December 6, 1989, to the *deaths* of their peers. Taking up the rhetoric about their being "bright and shining daughters," they established themselves as the legitimate offspring of sixties radical feminism who were "*living* the feminist principle"—and, as a natural evolution—disposing of their "mothers'" adversarial methods (Rathjen, qtd. in "For Many Women, Mourning Is Not Enough" A1; emphasis mine).

In the French-language film *Au-delà du six décembre,* Nathalie Provost and Catherine Fol (another Polytechnique graduate) responded to the feminists by discrediting not the validity but the relevance of their victimhood. According to Fol: "The debate articulates itself differently now than it did 30 years ago. Because we are different, a new generation. Feminists cleared the road for us and we say thank you. But we are on that road right now. We grew up on it. We have a different way of looking at it, a different way of working for feminism" (Lalonde, "I Am Not" B1). Since "the debate articulates itself differently now," the older feminists are caught in a time warp, mistakenly applying old methods to a new situation they have "cleared the road" for but cannot understand. Provost and Fol insist that the Montreal Massacre was an accident on the new road of feminism and, as such, could not be rendered comprehensible as a normal occurrence. Thus, even surviving the massacre did not involve them in "women's struggles": "When feminists talk about women's struggles, I don't find myself in that. I don't want women's struggles—not in my personal life, not in my professional life, not with my boyfriend. Women's struggles have nothing to do with me. . . . The massacre opened a lot of wounds for many women. We, in our 20s, we don't have those wounds" (Fol, qtd. in Zerbisias A1).

Fol can allow that the massacre may have been traumatic to others, but not to us, "in our 20s," because the massacre merely reopened old wounds. The "we, in our 20s" construction allows Fol to conflate her own experiences with Provost's, though one could indeed argue that she was unwounded, since she had graduated from the Polytechnique eighteen months prior to the shootings. By concentrating on the "reopened wounds" of the older feminists, she renders the pain these women feel as strangely incongruous with the actual event, and turns a blind eye to the ways in which other bodies—including Provost's—were wounded. Such a construction dismisses testimony by Sylvie Gagnon, who was wounded in the shooting. In the English-language film *After the Montreal Massacre,* Gagnon states that she is "emotionally frozen . . . living in horror. I have lost the capacity to interpret what happened. It was too huge, too unfair, too sick" (Quill F3). Such a construction of the survivor as unwounded also denies the pain that other men and women associated with the Polytechnique claim "will always be there" ("Pain of Lepine's" A2). Lastly, such a construction unfairly blames the victim. As Fol so succinctly puts it: "in my life, I don't have these problems because of my comportment, as an individual. Men who are sexist are not sexist with me" (Conlogue C2). Fol, then, can choose not to be involved in women's struggles because *men heed her.* Through this gesture to disidentify as victims of the shootings, Fol and Provost now become outsiders to the Montreal Massacre. They become spectators to an unusual traumatic event and reassure themselves that this wounding, which actually happened to at least one of them, could not happen to them, thus admitting finally that they do not own the event, but *also denying that the event owns them.*

In opposition to (and emerging from the loins of) the older, battle-scarred feminists, the new woman arises, whole and impenetrable. She is the victim who cannot be victimized, the woman who cannot be wounded. To Fol, Provost exemplifies this new (non)victim: "Of course, Nathalie Provost is a victim of violence. What people didn't seem to like about her was that her reaction to it was one of strength. She would not play a role of weakness. She would not define her life in terms of what this madman had done" (Conlogue C2). Arguably, Provost's response was one of strength.[3] She refused to go along with the script; she argued the terms; she refused to be Marc Lepine's feminist; and later, she refused to be the innocent victim whom others could commemorate with a white ribbon. Despite this, she did not resist his categorizations: she did not question his formula that "feminists equal women who hate men." She preserved Lepine in his self-appointed role of judge/vigilante and accepted her role as the woman on trial, trying to explain away the presence of women in the classroom to a man with the adjudicative power of a gun.[4] Before the barrel of the semiautomatic, she tried to explain to Marc Lepine that it was a case of mistaken identity. And she would do it again: "If Marc Lepine were in front of me tomorrow morning I would say the same damn thing. It's true that I don't *feel* like a feminist. I *feel* like any guy does in his life. I feel that way, period, with all the doors open in front of me. And if someone who is sick tries to close it, well I'll open it, damn it" (Lalonde, "I Am Not" B1; emphasis mine).

Here is the key to the (non)victim: *feeling* like a guy, with the complete confidence of having assumed the male subject position. Tellingly, there are only two positions in this world: feeling like a guy or feeling like a feminist. Feeling like a woman is not even an option or possibility, or, to put it differently, being a woman is limited to either feeling like a guy or a feminist. Moreover, for Provost, Marc Lepine is someone sick who *tries* to close doors (by killing women) and she *opens* doors (by surviving). In this "just like a guy" world, agency and control are highlighted to such a degree that vulnerability cannot even be narrated; thus, survival is narrated as winning, and winning is crucial.[5]

Provost's willingness to repeat the event may be linked to her desire to relive her survival, but, by desiring to repeat the event as it happened, Provost must continue to explain that she is no different from a man, that she is no feminist and that Lepine should not shoot her. This repetition and escape of the event is evident in the very name of the film *Au-delà du six décembre*. It is "beyond" the sixth of December, and thus the leaving and surviving of the event, but it is also beyond *every* sixth of December, rather than December 6, 1989. It is a beyond that repeats itself every year. As an annual event, this film resonates with feminist attempts to commemorate December 6, but re-inscribes December 6 as a day of surviving, rather than mourning. Given the emphasis that Provost puts on surviving, on agency and on feeling, it should be no surprise that Provost repeatedly insists that her survival is her way of "winning" over Lepine. Upon receiving an award for female engineering students (set up by the funeral home that handled the funerals of Lepine's victims) Provost repeats, "for me, it [the award] is a way of saying to Marc Lepine that women will continue to be present and active in the fields of science and engineering . . . because I lived through the shooting, it is important to me that he doesn't win" (Moore A1).

Repeating the events of December 6, 1989, however, is not the most efficacious way to fight violence. Telling Lepine that they were "just women in engineering," "just students intent on leading a normal life," did not stop him from pulling the trigger, nor did it stop pro-Lepine graffiti in other engineering schools.[6] Refusing to be hailed as a feminist did not stop the hail of the bullets. As Provost herself remarked after the massacre, her challenge "didn't change a second." Unfortunately, deciding that one is not going to be a victim does not prevent violence. Even women who believe fully in male-defined "merit" and who add their voices to the lobby against affirmative action and special scholarships for women are still threatening to some, are still, according to those who sympathized with Lepine, "instigating" violence. Lepine felt threatened by their very "I feel just like a guy" position. He wrote down the names of famous, vocal feminists to whom he had no access, but he hunted down the women who were personally threatening to him—women who were succeeding in a profession at which he had failed to even enter. Lepine saw them as subjects, hailed them as feminists, in order to blame them as the "cause" of his misery. Lepine did not see these women as victims, nor as battle-scarred. He agreed with their view that they have agency and that they hold responsibility for their own actions: Lepine claimed to be appointed by the Grim Reaper to punish these women and to make them take responsibility for their disruptive activity. Nathalie Provost's position does not oppose Marc Lepine's. In fact, it eerily repeats his view.

Thus, feminism can produce a postfeminism virtually indistinguishable from antifeminism if it ends at claiming the rights of man, whatever those rights may be. Postfeminism's denial of systemic violence and the female body as always at risk is not simply a repudiation of ideology and sentimentality, but also a survival strategy: a survival strategy that conflates "feeling empowered" and "being empowered." By claiming to be equal at all costs, these women attempt to level the playing field, or, at the very least, synchronize themselves with the emphasis on "meritocracy" within these male-dominated fields. What was devastating about the massacre was that the postfeminism failed. Lepine should have put down his gun after Provost denied being a feminist, denied being different from a male engineer. And so, in response to this contradiction between "feeling like a guy" and being a woman, these women insist on a fantasy body—the victim that cannot be victimized.

The impossibility of control that trauma exemplifies is traumatic to postfeminists. According to Caruth, traumatic experience cannot be treated as one's possession since it tends to possess the one who has survived it (*Trauma* 4–5). Because of this, trauma moves the subject position from that of screenwriter to that of a screen. Postfeminism as an ideology, however, makes seeing oneself as screen inadmissible and impossible. It renders "out of control" events beyond the experienceable. Provost and other immediate survivors of the massacre seemed caught in a trap, unable to acknowledge their wounds not only because of the belatedness of traumatic experience, but also because of their hypostatization of choice. Because the crime of Lepine was interpreted as the denial of their right to have their life the way they want it, the only way to fight back was by reclaiming this right while at the same time conceding the larger argument. Because of the need to construct an autonomous ever-present subject, postfeminists construed feminists as the cause of their distress, just as Lepine constructed feminists as the cause of his life's sufferings. In this world of freely acting subjects, responsibility had to be attributed to someone for the postfeminists' media (mis)representation, for the untethering of event and context. The question we must ask is: how has this been construed by young women such as Heidi Rathjen as "living the feminist principle," and by older feminists such as Stevie Cameron as fulfilling their mothers' dreams?

By taking for granted the impact of violence on all women and "women's experience," feminism stumbled in the aftermath of the Montreal Massacre. This is not to say that feminism sunk irretrievably, for many women in engineering devastated by the failure of the postfeminist defense, such as myself, turned to feminism—especially to strands of feminism that called into question the freely choosing subject—for strategies to cope with and analyze our precarious position. This is to say that if feminism sentimentalizes victims while at the same time reifying the putative normal male subject, it has, and will, produce a situation where women who have "made it" must deny the discrimination they see in order to keep their precarious hold on the male subject position. In order to move "living the feminist principle" away from postfeminism, we must keep insisting that subjectivity is always compromised, that a fantasmatic identification with a wholly impenetrable and fully "in control" subject is not possible. This means that feminists—that we—must produce strategies for dealing with violence that do not allow for blindness or appropriation, for supermen or infants, so that we may deal with experiences outside our control rather than simply re-narrating them in the first person over and over again.

TOWARD A POLITICS OF LISTENING

Now, more than ten years after the massacre, the question I am still asking is: how could a difficult yet nonhostile encounter between feminists and postfeminist survivors have taken place? How will such an engagement take place? I do believe that such an encounter is still necessary, especially since the impact of the murders has not yet been dispelled; the murders return every year. Indeed, Provost's accusations against feminists can be understood as a cry for such an ethical engagement. But before such an encounter can take place, we need to ask: how is an ethical engagement in the context of a traumatic event possible, given that so many women identified *as* victims of Lepine? How can an ethical encounter take place given that the events in Montreal became construed as a "national trauma"? The murders in Montreal defied comprehension and shocked a substantial percentage of the Canadian population. One year after the murders, headlines proclaimed: "Canadians haunted by Montreal's Ghosts," "A Year after the Trauma, the Answers and Insights Still Go Begging," "Scars, Fear, the Legacy of Montreal Massacre." Commentators such as Judy Rebrick, president of the NAC, proclaimed that "in some way, all of us have been touched by it [the Montreal Massacre]" (qtd. in Peritz A16). Although these statements are both extreme and banal, the murders did affect far more people than those present at the Polytechnique on December 6, 1989. To call it a national trauma, however, erases the differences between the woman in the classroom and the man watching the events unfold on the television.

Many women who were not present at the Polytechnique identified themselves as victims and, in their mourning, many conflated the identities of Lepine's victims with other women. As Paula Sypnowich put it: "I do not wish to understate the tragedy of the deaths of those fourteen women. But I mourn their deaths as I do the deaths of relatively anonymous women who are raped and murdered, or as I would if Lepine had gunned down fourteen strippers, bag ladies, or secretaries instead of fourteen aspiring engineers. And I'll end up heartsick again when misogyny is no longer 'topical,' and the media once again address women's issues only through articles on daycare subsidies and debate over who does the dishes" (130). This move to mourn the murders in Montreal in the context of other violent acts, this move to make the act of mourning the link between disparate violent events, enabled many women to respond to the Montreal massacre. However, such a linkage can also deny the singularity of the event. According to Dori Laub, "trauma is . . . an event that has no beginning, no ending, no before, no during and no after. This absence of categories that define it lends it a quality of 'otherness,' a salience, a timelessness and a ubiquity that puts it outside the range of associatively linked experiences, outside the range of comprehension, of recounting and of mastery" (Felman and Laub 69). To those, such as Provost, who saw the event unfold and yet could still not view it as "other," this mourning did violence to the event and to themselves. In the aftermath of the Montreal Massacre, the line between identifying with and identifying as was often (involuntarily) breached, partly due to the belatedness of traumatic experience, partly due to Lepine's separation between intended and actual victims, partly due to the fact that one does not need to be present in order to feel threatened by an event. Even if one is working through another event, identifying as the victim rather than with her poses the possibility of violating the eyewitness. "Outsider" testimony can easily substitute for eyewitness testimony.

The conflict between responding to and identifying with eyewitness experiences is one of the most important challenges to theories of trauma. Since traumatic events are experienced only in conjunction with another event, traumatic events will *necessarily* produce conflicting testimonies. Testimony is both an enabling and disabling violence; it is both voluntary and involuntary. The intertwining of experience that trauma demands means that testifying is not enough: we must also respond and listen to others' testimony so that the self does not take the place of the other. Even if, as Laura Brown controversially argues, trauma is not unusual and we need to include "as traumatic stressors all of those everyday, repetitive, interpersonal events that are so often the sources of psychic pain for women" (108), there are still unusual traumatic events such as the Montreal Massacre. Although I agree with Brown that admitting the immanence of trauma will help dispel the illusion that we are invulnerable, I question the assumption that "acknowledging we might be next" is the best way to link together gender-based trauma. If we "acknowledge we might be next," we are forced to assume that our experiences can or will be the same. We avoid confronting experiences and selves as other and risk looking only at ourselves and our own possibilities. As the aftermath of the Montreal Massacre makes clear, arguing via experiential analogy—making certain experiences representative of others—can and will lead to conflict.

Instead of relying on analogy or substitution, we should link traumatic events via citation, by arguing that the force of the traumatic event comes partly from its citation of other such events. By doing so, we can link events together, yet insist on the singularity of each one. Iteration alters, yet a citation gains force only because it "repeats" or refers to other events. If we view such events as citations, we can discuss larger social implications in ways that shift the focus away from the perpetrator's inner psychology or intentions. Rather, we can discuss the community that the perpetrator joins with his or her actions. Butler, commenting on the force of the racial slur, argues:

> The racial slur is always cited from elsewhere, and in the speaking of it, one chimes in with a chorus of racists, producing at that moment the linguistic occasion for an imagined relation to an historically transmitted community of racists. In this sense, racist speech does not originate with the subject, even if it requires the subject for its efficacy, as it surely does. Indeed, racist speech could not act as racist speech if it were not a *citation of itself;* only because we already know its force from prior instances do we know it to be so offensive now, and we brace ourselves against its future invocations. The iterability of hate speech is effectively dissimulated by the "subject" who speaks the speech of hate. (80)

In terms of the Montreal Massacre, Lepine's actions reached beyond his immediate victims because, in his address and actions, he cited other events and called others to respond to them as such. Lepine's actions also linked him with an historically transmitted community of misogynists and this link to a larger community made his actions to some degree comprehensible. Again, this link does not make his actions completely understandable. It does, however, offer us a larger political goal: to destroy the community made possible by such citations (in terms of Butler's example "an historically transmitted community of racists"). Citation also offers us a way to think about the community established by the act of testifying. Through this speech act, one links oneself with others who have also testified and thus testimony cannot be construed as an individual act that does not involve others. Lastly, since every citation is also an appropriation, it foregrounds the possible violence of citation.

Sylvie Gagnon's moving testimony in *After the Montreal Massacre* attests to the traumatic experience as citation. Filmed one year after the massacre, Gagnon speaks of her experiences in the cafeteria of the Polytechnique on December 6, 1989—the day she completed all the requirements for her engineering degree. Lepine entered the cafeteria and began shooting the women. After a bullet grazed her head, Gagnon lay on the floor playing dead but refused to faint, in order to see what was happening. As Lepine walked between Gagnon and another woman who lay beside her, he shot the other woman point blank. After he passed by, she ran from the Polytechnique to a friend's home in order to transmit her story. To help both herself and her friend believe that the events she witnessed were real, they watched the news coverage on television.

Like Provost, Gagnon was soon angry at the interpretations propagated through the media. However, rather than railing against feminists for having usurped her tragedy, she argued that media analysts had tried to turn her tragedy into an "isolated event," and had sought to explain her tragedy in the terms of Lepine's life-story. For her, this event was linked to "all the little sadnesses" and abuse that she, and other women, had suffered through their entire lives, to all those daily episodes "too small" to be registered. According to Gagnon, women's testimonies exploded after the Montreal massacre because the murders "recalled" all these other little sadnesses. Importantly, Gagnon states that she does not know Lepine and she does not want to know Lepine—to her Lepine is death. Unlike other feminists, she refused to link her interpretation to his intentions. Rather, the event's significance stemmed from its ability to *re-call* other women's sadnesses. Gagnon was also able to testify because she was not a postfeminist. As she put it, the murders did not teach her anything, but rather made her feel with her nerves and her body what she had always known in her head. For this reason, she was able to "already know its force from prior instances." Arguably, she was able to speak because of her "other" little sadnesses, and her "other" little sadnesses opened her to the pain of other women.

If Gagnon's feminism and history prepared her for the murders, the feminists' emphasis on fact-finding and on disseminating their testimony foreclosed the possibility of listening to the survivors' testimonies. It reduced the massacre to a question of knowledge about Lepine. Those who pinned their interpretations of the Montreal Massacre on knowledge of Lepine left little space for survivors' stories as anything other than corroborating testimony. Because of this, there was little opportunity for witnesses to testify *together* to a truth inaccessible to anyone alone. By this, I do not mean to imply that simple cooperation between witnesses is sufficient, nor that consensus should be the goal, nor that we must simply respect the survivor's desire for silence and stop testifying. Instead, I am suggesting a politics and practice of listening as a necessary complement to a politics of testifying. I am suggesting a politics that does not valorize the act of speaking in and of itself: a politics that listens to a person's speech or silence and then grapples with the question of how to respond to it. In other words, I am suggesting a politics that begins, rather than ends with, the speaking subject, that begins with the other who addresses us with her speech or silence.

Gagnon was able to testify because she externalized the event through a sympathetic interview with Gerry Rogers, a former nun and advocate against violence. Through this interview, Gagnon turns to television—the same medium that initially corroborated her testimony—to externalize and validate it. Through this interview, Gagnon speaks, validates, and transmits the story, from a position of enabling vulnerability. She presents a narrative that refuses the position of either superman or child. Although she talks about her childhood dreams and her belief, prior to Lepine's actions, that the world was hers, she does not insist on returning to these dreams and beliefs. Rather, she says that she is a different person now, that such an event changes a person, and that slowly she is dealing with the pain and the trauma, that it gets better every day.

Through a politics of listening, both testimony and an historical understanding of December 6, 1989, emerges. A politics of listening, as Laub describes it, is a contract that emphasizes recognizing and meeting "'the gaping, vertiginous black hole' of the experience of the trauma" (Felman and Laub 64). Such a contract acknowledges that, by listening, we become implicated in the traumatic event, but that we are still separate human beings:

> The listener to trauma comes to be a participant and co-owner of the traumatic event: through his very listening, he comes to partially experience trauma in himself. The relation of the victim to the event of the trau-

ma, therefore, impacts on the relation of the listener to it, and the latter comes to feel the bewilderment, injury, confusion, dread and conflicts that the trauma victim feels. He has to address all these, if he is to carry out his function as a listener, and if trauma is to emerge, so that its henceforth impossible witnessing can indeed take place. . . . The listener has to feel the victim's victories, defeats and silences, know them from within, so that they can assume the form of testimony.

The listener, however, is also a separate human being and will experience hazards and struggles of his own, while carrying out his function of a witness to the trauma witness. While overlapping, to a degree, with the experience of the victim, he nonetheless does not become the victim—he preserves his own separate place, position and perspective; a battleground for forces raging in himself, to which he has to pay attention and respect if he is to properly carry out his task. (58)

The important task in listening, then, is to feel the victim's victories, defeats, and silences, know them from within, while at the same time acknowledging that one is not the victim, so that the victim can testify, so that the truth can be reached together. In this model, distance must be maintained between listener and speaker. The listener must remember that as she feels the victim's victories, defeats, and silences, she is also re-experiencing her own and involuntarily relating them to her own life. She must constantly ask, "what is being elided in my identifications with the speaker?" The goal is not to cure either the listener or the speaker but rather to respond and listen so that survival is possible.

Such a contract is based on *lack* of comprehension. As Caruth, in her reading of the dialogue between the French women and Japanese man in *Hiroshima mon amour,* argues, "their ability to speak and to listen in their passionate encounter does not rely . . . on what they simply know of one another, but on what they do not fully know in their traumatic pasts." That is, "what we see and hear, in *Hiroshima mon amour,* resonates beyond what we can know and understand; but it is in the event of this incomprehension and in our departure from sense and understanding that our own witnessing may indeed begin to take place" ("Unclaimed Experience" 56). By emphasizing gaps in understanding, in refusing interpretations that reduce traumatic events to factors we can know, we may begin the encounter that may help us finally to say together, "au-delà du six décembre dix-neuf quatre-vingt neuf." This would mean acknowledging Lepine as a necessary but not sufficient cause of the massacre, that the key to the massacre lies not in "knowing" Lepine, but rather in what we cannot know—and yet must still try to know—about the experiences of women such as Nathalie Provost and Sylvie Gagnon. It would mean acknowledging that our experiences diverge in ways that we can never fully understand, and that, just because an event causes us pain or causes us to speak, it does not mean that we can feel another's pain. Sympathetic identification is the beginning of a difficult process of listening. This contract of listening must be accompanied by a relentless critique of the ways in which the belief in and desire for a sovereign subject undermine systemic changes to society and undermine feminism. It must be accompanied by a politics that understands acts of violence not as "representative of" or "substitutable for" each other, but by a politics that sees these acts as forceful because they recall other events, because they open the self to others. Such a contract of listening would allow for history. Perhaps with these strategies in hand we may finally encounter each other without recriminations and hostility, but also without sentimentality and identity as appropriation of the same.

NOTES

This essay is excerpted from a longer version published in *differences* 11.1 (Spring 1999): 112–49. Reprinted by permission of Indiana University Press. The quotation from Barbara Johnson that forms the first epigraph appeared in Felman and Laub 23. The quotation from Nathalie Provost that forms the second epigraph appeared in Lalonde, "I Am Not a Feminist" B1.

    1. See Johnson C12.
    2. On the appointment to bear witness, Felman and Laub 3.
    3. See Marcus.
    4. This resonates with the classic woman-on-trial image that Jennifer Wicke discusses in "Postmodern Identities and the Politics of the (Legal) Subject."
    5. See Provost's message in Kastor B1.
    6. See Greenhill.

WORKS CITED

After the Montreal Massacre. Dir. Gerry Rogers. National Film Board of Canada, 1990.
Au-delà du six décembre. Dir. Catherine Fol. National Film Board of Canada, 1991.
Brossard, Nicole. "The Killer Was No Young Man." Malette and Chalouh 31–33.
Brown, Laura S. "Not Outside the Range: One Feminist Perspective on Psychic Trauma." Caruth, *Trauma* 100–12.
Buchignani, Walter. "Victim Tried to Reason with Killer." *Montreal Gazette* Dec. 9, 1989: A1+.
Butler, Judith. *Excitable Speech.* London: Routledge, 1997.

Butler, Judith, and Joan W. Scott, eds. *Feminists Theorize the Political.* New York: Routledge, 1992.

Cameron, Stevie. "Our Daughters, Ourselves." Malette and Chalouh 159–61.

Canadian Committee on Women in Engineering. *More Than Just Numbers: Report of the Canadian Committee on Women in Engineering.* Apr. 1992.

Caruth, Cathy. *Unclaimed Experience: Trauma, Narrative, and History.* Baltimore: Johns Hopkins University Press, 1996.

———, ed. *Trauma: Explorations in Memory.* Baltimore: Johns Hopkins University Press, 1995.

Chun, Wendy Hui Kyong. "Unbearable Witness: Toward a Politics of Listening." *differences* 11.1 (Spring 1999): 112–49.

Conlogue, Ray. "Different Views of Montreal Massacre." *Globe and Mail* Dec. 4, 1991: C2.

"Demanding Answers." *Maclean's* June 11, 1990: 17.

Felman, Shoshana, and Dori Laub. *Testimony: Crises of Witnessing in Literature, Psychoanalysis, and History.* New York: Routledge, 1992.

"For Many Women, Mourning Is Not Enough." *Montreal Gazette* Dec. 6, 1990: A1.

Greenhill, Pauline. "A Good Start: A Graffiti Interpretation of the Montreal Massacre." *Atlantis* 17.2: 106–18.

Hedges, Elaine, and Shelley Fisher Fishkin, eds. *Listening to Silences: New Essays in Feminist Criticism.* New York: Oxford University Press, 1994.

Johnson, Anthony. "Mood Varies among Engineers at U of C: Some Resent Use of Murder for Political Purposes." *Calgary Herald* Dec. 6, 1991: C12.

Kastor, Elizabeth. "In Montreal, a Survivor Heals after the Horror: 23-year-old Student Tried to Reason with Killer." *Washington Post* Dec. 11, 1989: B1.

Lacelle, Nicole. "The Political Is Personal." Malette and Chalouh 28–30.

Lalonde, Michelle. "A Year after the Trauma, the Answers and Insights Still Go Begging." *Globe and Mail* Dec. 4, 1990: A5.

———. "I Am Not a Feminist." *Montreal Gazette* Nov. 30, 1991: B1.

———. "Students' Silence Part of Debate Over Killings." *Globe and Mail* Dec. 4, 1990: A5.

Lamey, Mary. "Lepine Rampage Was a 'Cold, Rational Act,' Pelletier Says." *Montreal Gazette* Nov. 25, 1990: A1+.

Malarek, Victor. "More Massacre Details to Be Released by Police, but an Inquiry Ruled Out." *Globe and Mail* Dec. 12, 1989: A14.

———. "Police Refusal to Answer Questions Leaves Lots of Loose Ends in Killings." *Globe and Mail* Dec. 13, 1989: A18.

Malarek, Victor, and Benoit Aubin. "Killer's Letter Blames Feminists: Man Very Intelligent, But Deeply Troubled." *Globe and Mail* Dec. 8, 1989, A1.

Malette, Louise, and Marie Chalouh. *The Montreal Massacre.* Trans. Marlene Wildeman. Charlottetown, Prince Edward Island: Gynergy Press, 1991.

Marcus, Sharon. "Fighting Bodies, Fighting Words: A Theory and Politics of Rape Prevention." Butler and Scott 385–403.

Moore, Lynn. "A Victory Over a Madman: Women Honored for Work after Polytechnique Massacre." *Montreal Gazette* Sept. 11, 1990: A1+.

"Pain of Lepine's 14 Killings Lives On, College Witness Says." *Toronto Star* Dec. 7, 1990: A2.

Pelletier, Francine. "They Shoot Horses, Don't They?" Malette and Chalouh 33–36.

Peritz, Ingrid. "Scars, Fear, the Legacy of Montreal Massacre." *Vancouver Sun* Nov. 30, 1990: A1+.

Poirier, Patricia. "Canadians Haunted by Montreal's Ghost." *Globe and Mail* Dec. 6, 1990: A1.

"Police Won't Confirm Authenticity. Paper Gets 'Photocopy' of Lepine's Suicide Note." *Toronto Star* Nov. 25, 1990: A16.

Quill, Greg. "Witness Can't Forget Lepine." *Toronto Star* Nov. 27, 1990: F3.

Sypnowich, Paula. "An Incitement to Violence." Malette and Chalouh 128–30.

Wicke, Jennifer. "Postmodern Identities and the Politics of the (Legal) Subject." *Boundary 2* 19.2 (1992): 20–33.

Zerbisias, Antonia. "Massacre Survivor at Heart of Controversy." *Toronto Star* Dec. 6, 1991: A1+.

EIGHT

Testimony and the Subjects of AIDS Memoirs

Jason Tougaw

Before they died, David B. Feinberg, Paul Monette, David Wojnarowicz, Hervé Guibert, Reinaldo Arenas, Michael Callen, and John Preston published autobiographies, memoirs, diaries, and personal essays about life with AIDS—testimonies about the epidemic widely circulated throughout the 1980s and early 1990s. Their autobiographical acts did not keep them alive. In fact, the pages of their books read like a roll call of the deceased, a litany of proper names to replace young men, members of their community of readers, dead from AIDS—among them, Monette's lover, Roger Horwitz, and Guibert's friend and mentor, Michel Foucault. These are memoirists with divergent approaches to writing, but they consistently foreground writing as an alternative to silence, evoking Act Up's famous slogan, Silence = Death. They also share an ambivalence about their own projects, a simultaneous devotion to and skepticism about the value of AIDS writing as a combatant to the collective trauma of the epidemic.

Monette has produced the largest body of AIDS memoirs, including four books in all. *Borrowed Time: An AIDS Memoir* finds Monette still healthy and his lover, Roger Horwitz, dying; *Love Alone* is the generic reconstruction of the same story in poetry; *Becoming a Man: Half a Life Story* chronicles Monette's gay life before and after AIDS; and *The Last Watch of the Night* is a series of resigned but still angry essays. Callen, in *Living with AIDS,* and Preston, in *Winter's Light: Reflections of a Yankee Queer,* have also compiled collections of essays which chronicle the progress of their illnesses. Along with his loosely autobiographical novel, *Eighty-Sixed,* Feinberg's essay collection, *Queer and Loathing: Rants and Raves of a Raging AIDS Clone,* treats AIDS sardonically, alternating between black humor and despair. Wojnarowicz, in *Close to the Knives: A Memoir of Disintegration* and *Memories That Smell Like Gasoline* (a graphic novel); Guibert, in *To the Friend That Did Not Save My Life;* and Arenas, in *Before Night Falls* (a memoir about persecution under Castro in Cuba and life with AIDS in the U.S.) all use techniques of the novel, with chilling effects, to convey the horror and immediacy of their trauma. Even these works manage to give very clear indications of parallels between stages of the disease and narrative development, their fragmentation reflecting the authors' own ravaged communities and traumatized psyches.

Silence = Death has been *the* emblem of western AIDS activism at least since 1987, demanding political action—Act Up style—in the face of widespread apathy. As a metaphor, Act Up's slogan is a product of the first decade of AIDS discourse, emphasizing research and education, the generation and dissemination of information—hard facts about the epidemic that could save lives. AIDS memoirs are written as alternatives to silence, to combat the terrifying effects of the epidemic. As testimonies, these memoirs are engaged in the autobiographical act of bearing witness to a collective trauma: speaking for a group of people who have shared a traumatic experience. In *Queer and Loathing,* Feinberg, with typically confrontational Act Up style, echoes the testimonial concerns of many AIDS memoirs: "Okay, if I wait eight to ten years for good science to approve a drug, I'll be dead. That's simple enough, isn't it? It's tough being politically active from six feet under. If I remain silent in the face of this epidemic and the government's unwillingness to act effectively, then I'm just as well dead. SILENCE = DEATH, get it?" (7). They have been a crucial form of AIDS activism from the start. In the period between the mid-1980s and the mid-1990s, AIDS had begun to be understood but was still a more or less absolute death sentence; it was ravaging the globe—most devastatingly in Africa—but was still linked in the western cultural imagination to gay men in urban centers. The testimonies of gay men during this period were speech acts meant to sway government policy, rally AIDS communities, and make sense of an epidemic which defies explanation.

In their urgency, AIDS testimonies often read like instructions: how to diagnose, how to choose a doctor, how to find the right drugs, how to stay alive longer. The culmination of several years' AIDS writing, Michael Callen's *Surviving AIDS* is the most explicit example of a "how to" testimonial. As its title suggests, Callen's memoir outlines his own list of AIDS symptoms, his maneuvers through medical bureaucracies, and his quest for treatments. To bear witness, or testify, for Callen, Feinberg, and most AIDS memoirists means publicizing the private experience of illness, turning memoirs into self-help books that help create and maintain an AIDS community able to foster the health of its constituents. Feinberg's refrain, "If I remain silent . . . then I'm just as well dead," suggests that testimony, like a speech act, produces tangible effects, helping to keep the writer alive.[1] The suggestion is made through what it presupposes, that not remaining silent will help keep the writer alive. But Silence = Death is a metaphor, not a cure. It cannot promise that the alternative to the silence it vilifies—speaking, shouting, writing, Acting Up—will deliver health and life to people with AIDS. Feinberg has died since the publication of his memoir and so have too many other People with AIDS (PWAs) who wrote to stave off death, whose testimonies chronicle, in minutiae, the progress of their own bodies' decay and the radical changes AIDS thrusts onto a life story.

Testimony, though necessary, hasn't cured AIDS. By the mid-1990s, the death toll had forced some shifts in the understandings of the epidemic, its bodily effects, the social questions it raises, and the search for solutions it hastens. "Hard facts" are still in short supply, and even new therapies may prolong lives (and, very often, suffering), but they don't save them. Not yet. Silence = Death, as a metaphorical model for AIDS discourse (research, education, activism, testimony), spins its own signifiers at a rapid rate, proliferating multiple and often inscrutable meanings. The flip side of Silence = Death, in Act Up's heyday, was Action = Life, but "action"—in-your-face demonstrations, political lobbying, inexorable memorializing—is difficult to sustain when the new research demanded seems fruitless, when the *actors* are dying at an incomprehensible rate. People continue to become infected, suffer, protest, lobby, educate, testify, and die. As Lee Edelman has pointed out, "action" for AIDS activists has largely meant the "production of discourse," but neither the forms of discourse nor its intended effects can be captured by a political slogan, no matter how powerful (299). Antonyms for silence include writing, activism, research, medicine, visual arts, and any other intervention into the standard, homophobic responses to AIDS. None of them, however, is able to cure AIDS. Silence = Death appears to offer a tidy formula for the decimation of a catastrophic plague. The implication is that if we speak, write, and act, we can defeat the epidemic. However, the discourses instigated by the trope as a call to arms almost always defy the apparent simplicity of a metaphor that takes the form of an equation. AIDS memoirs are constructed by the slogan at every turn, but as narratives they complicate and even repudiate its claims.

Because silence still means certain death—because AIDS defies explanation and because it is traumatic—testimony continues despite ambivalence and uncertainty. The narratives of AIDS testimonies are fueled by a tension between two conflicting but viscerally felt drives: toward survival and death. These narratives would not exist if death did not seem imminent for their authors, nor would they be written if their authors did not see writing as a vehicle for survival. In *Winter's Light,* John Preston synthesizes many of the common aims of AIDS testimony:

> The purpose of AIDS writing now is to get it all down. Andrew Holleran says the purpose of the writer in the time of AIDS is to bear witness. Sarah Schulman makes the case that we cannot allow ourselves to be separated from what's happening by being seduced into an observer status. To live in a time of AIDS and to understand what is going on is to know that writing must be accompanied by action. Writing is not what our teachers told us, something that stands alone.
>
> To be a writer in a time of AIDS is to be a truth teller. The truth is more horrible than anything people want to hear. . . . The truth is devastating. The truth can't be contained in a pleasantly structured short story that will satisfy the readers of a literary magazine.
>
> We have to *get it all down.* (113)

Preston's narrative is a self-conscious call to arms, but he doesn't see writing as a speech act. One step removed, writing compels readers to act by condemning "observer status" and urging them to take "action" to avoid silence. He wants "to get it all down" so that the writing can act on his behalf if, or when, he dies. AIDS memoirs are written with the explicit goal of "getting it all down" while the writers are still alive and still physically and intellectually sound enough to write. However, in the years before protease inhibitors autobiographical writing about AIDS is suspicious of its own most common trope. Before 1996, most people with AIDS could not hope to live to be cured. Preston's assessment of AIDS writing teeters on the brink between the common trope, Silence = Death, and the increasingly common observation that the "truth" about AIDS is "devastating" precisely because the alternatives to silence ("action," discourse, testimony) *still* haven't been able to ward off death.

That devastating truth confronts writers bearing witness and their audiences with a familiar problem of testimony: what to do when politics confronts aesthetics, when "the truth can't be contained in a pleasantly structured short story that will satisfy the readers of a literary magazine." To avoid silence, Preston's testimony requires a narrative structure to ensure its own transmission from writer to audience. A testimony can never "get it *all* down." It must manipulate the pleasure of the text, the ruses of narrative, to ensure a warm reception. One method is to shift the focus away from narrative and onto the construction of a community—readers, writers, and their characters linked through the text. Testimony is littered with proper names, signifiers of community, like those of AIDS writers Andrew Holleran and Sarah Schulman, like Roger Horwitz and Michel Foucault, but despite their "realness," they are also characters in a narrative, characters who often fail to live to see the publication of the books in which they appear.

Writers of book-length testimonials about their lives with AIDS tend to begin defiantly, even hopefully, to testify with the aim of making sense of and warding off the virus. However, as their authors become increasingly ill, the drive toward an integrated self shifts toward a relational subjectivity, one with a different understanding of the Silence = Death model of AIDS writing. These writers, by the ends of their narratives (which very often coincide with the near-end of their lives), come to see writing ambivalently, as a *speech act* capable of transforming, but not prolonging, lives. Testimony, as a speech act, requires a community of readers whose intersubjective relations are structured by and through the text. This intersubjectivity enables the testimony to produce its desired effects, which can range from memorializing to inciting political revolution.

This intersubjectivity is analogous to the relation between teller and listener that Dori Laub has outlined as the enabling condition of Holocaust testimony. Laub makes at least two points which apply to AIDS testimony as well as Holocaust testimony: "The traumatic event, although real, took place outside the parameters of 'normal' reality, such as causality, sequence, place and time. The trauma is thus an event that has no beginning, no ending, no before, no during and no after. This absence of categories that define it lends it a quality of 'otherness,' a salience, a timelessness and a ubiquity that puts it outside the range of associatively linked experiences, outside the range of comprehension, of recounting and of mastery" (Felman and Laub 69). AIDS does not "transport" most of its "victims" to literal concentration camps, but it does radically transform their "ordinary" or domestic lives, which, at least for gay men, already stray from the norm. Trauma, by definition, defies "parameters of 'normal' reality" and is therefore incomprehensible, needing testimony to frame it, to put it *inside* "the range of associatively linked experiences," *inside* "the range of comprehension, of recounting and of mastery." It does so by insisting on reader-identification with the experience of fatal disease, by insisting that readers measure their mortality against that of the author, by insisting that readers acknowledge their own risk for HIV infection. The vicissitudes of trauma, Preston insists, are complex and not easily rendered in narrative form because trauma defies narrative and social conventions. The conventions and norms of ordinary life foreclose the possibility of trauma by framing it outside the culture's epistemological possibilities. Testimony, however, provides trauma with its missing narrative (beginnings, endings, befores, durings, and afters), with conventions all its own to organize and explain what defies social conventions, what twentieth-century "enlightened," humanist subjects—even after the Holocaust—still cannot imagine. The "community" formed from collective trauma is configured by and through psychic and epistemological ruptures whose effects are radically altered subjectivities and often permanent uncertainty in the face of the most ordinary of details.

To be effective as testimony, the narrativization of trauma, however, must alter the speaking subject's relation to an audience, and by extension, it must also alter social relations in general, opening up the possibility for the culture to accommodate the trauma that compels the testimony. In Laub's words, "Bearing witness to trauma is, in fact, a process that includes the listener. For the testimonial process to take place, there needs to be a bonding, the intimate and total presence of an *other*—in the position of one who hears. Testimonies are not monologues; they cannot take place in solitude. The witnesses are talking *to somebody:* to somebody they have been waiting for for a long time" (70–71). In AIDS testimony, HIV, AIDS, and the trauma they produce link gay men through "the intimate and total presence" of each other. The signifiers of AIDS in and on our bodies, like the signifiers of homosexuality, rely on connotation and endless proliferation. Even the "AIDS Test" is more accurately a test for the presence of HIV antibodies. It can detect the virus only through inference, through the connotative signaling of HIV's presence, which itself does not even directly "cause" the multiple symptoms that constitute AIDS. Because they are detected through inference, "signs" of AIDS can be detected everywhere, even in their absence. One result is that gay men tend to see evidence of our own "risk" in others.

The subjects of AIDS testimony, its writers and characters, "read" their bodies in relation to others, looking for signs of infection, debilitation, and decay. Their own interpretations of the prolific signifiers of AIDS help create a model of *relational subjectivity*. They see themselves as products of multiple relations, mostly within the AIDS communities their memoirs are so concerned with maintaining. The virus travels between us because our bodies (like our psyches) are permeable, and the bodily infection spreads, signifying both corporeal and psychic connections between us. Not surprisingly, the exegesis of risk in AIDS memoirs often employs tropes of eyes and mirrors as the sites of recognition, the places where relational subjectivities are reflected. What I'm calling "the exegesis of risk" is crucial to the construction of these narratives, shifting the trope of Silence = Death onto more realistic, if less hopeful, grounds—grounds on which testimony, as a speech act, is revealed not to save lives but to establish new kinds of psychological and social relations appropriate to life at the epicenter of an epidemic. The construction of relational subjectivities, borne out of trauma, marks AIDS testimony's deviation from the standard autobiographical models, in which singular subjects are formed by the narrative and are generally "complete" by the end of the book.

It is on page 7 of *Queer and Loathing* that David Feinberg insists, "If I remain silent . . . I'm just as well dead." Silence = Death is *the* trope for AIDS testimony which just might give him his chance to restore his own singular subjectivity, but by page 214 his model shifts. The shift, not surprisingly, coincides with his declining health, because of which he has invested in an IV (and its unwieldy apparatus) to avoid hospitalization for treatments he can receive at home:

> My very best friend in the entire world, John Palmer Weir, Jr., to whom my entire writing output is dedicated, came over to sit through the second pentamidine, which was a total of only forty-five minutes of drip. I always used to watch the needles; now I just avert my eyes. But John Weir was making a conscious effort to show me that nothing human offended him; he wanted to show me it was okay. I knew it was okay. I asked him, but *noooooooo,* he had to stare in shock and horror and revulsion as Manny the nurse stuck me, and Manny wasn't that used to doing this sort of thing in the home environment because even though I have excellent veins—indeed, I've entered them in competitions and always gotten at least hon-

orable mention—he was used to hospitals, Manny said, where the patient can be tied down with straps or something or other, and he stabbed me and I bled and John's eyes turned to saucers, and even though I didn't want to look it was as if his eyes were reflecting what was going on, which I didn't want to know; one could see the depth of the sorrow and the pity; it was like watching a twenty-hour movie about the Holocaust in his eyes. Manny tells me that he had a wonderful time skiing in Colorado last winter, and I stifle the impulse to tell him how politically incorrect it is of him to travel to Colorado: Hasn't he heard of the boycott? What about the political ramifications? Because he is the one sticking the needle into me.

Afterward John Weir admitted it wasn't particularly pleasant watching me get sticked. (214–15)

Feinberg is very ill by this point in his narrative. His body has become increasingly less autonomous, relying more and more on drugs, blood tests, and medical machinery. Despite Feinberg's decision to "avert his eyes," he is confronted with the "shock and horror" and "the depth of the sorrow" in his own sick self. He sees his own subjectivity, transformed by AIDS, constituted in the eyes of his friend. The subject of testimony needs an audience to be effective. Through the exegesis of Feinberg's body and the trauma it induces, he and Weir recognize their subjectivities as constructions produced out of corporeal and psychic ruptures, ruptures in the isolated bodies and selves promised by traditional autobiography. Along with the reader, they participate in the exegesis of risk, viewing their bodies and psyches in relation to AIDS, to each other, to the prophylactics used as "protection" against each other's infections, to AIDS drugs, medical devices, activism itself, and any other body "at risk" for AIDS. In scenes like this, AIDS writers, characters in their narratives, and readers, taken as a collective, become subjects in a *community of risk*—each necessary to the other's survival, but each a source of "shock and horror" as well.

Note the similarity between Feinberg's reading of his own trauma in John Weir's eyes and the following passage from Hervé Guibert's *To the Friend Who Did Not Save My Life:*

My blood, unmasked, everywhere and forever (except in the unlikely event of miracle-working transfusions), naked around the clock, when I'm walking in the street, taking public transportation, the constant target of an arrow aimed at me wherever I go. Does it show in my eyes? I don't worry so much anymore about keeping my gaze human as I do about acquiring one that is too human, like the look you see in the eyes of the concentration camp inmates in the documentary *Night and Fog.*

> I felt death approaching in the mirror, gazing back at me from my own reflection, long before it had truly arrived to stay. Was I already throwing this death into other people's faces whenever I looked into their eyes? (6–7)

Like Feinberg, Guibert locates the signification of infection in the eyes; uses Holocaust documentary as a reference point to contextualize his trauma, with the screen functioning like the eyes to reflect a trauma which cannot be seen in the original; and associates AIDS with a tension between the inhumane and the "too human" gaze. Guibert's trope of his eyes and "the mirror" reveals the inverse of Feinberg's relational subjectivity. Gay men, via AIDS, exist in relation to each other as a community of risk *and* as a potential source of infection that threatens the world at large. By "throwing this death into other people's faces" and worrying, "Does it show in my eyes?" Guibert constructs a subjectivity that threatens to "infect" more conventional social (and narrative) relations. That is the double bind of bearing witness to AIDS, of creating testimony in an effort to carve out a space in the culture that can accommodate the trauma of AIDS. The testifying subject reveals his position in a community under siege and his position as the bearer of a story no one wants to hear, a carrier of a virus that conjures people's worst fears. Testimony, when it comes to AIDS, creates panic because it suggests the vulnerability and interdependence of bodies and psyches in relation to each other; in fact, it relies on these for its narrative construction. The "subjects" of AIDS memoirs—their writers, their casts of characters, and their readers—rely on that interdependence to forge community relations in which it is possible to live and die with AIDS.

Silence = Death posits a speaking or writing subject whose agency, by sheer force of will, can put an end to an epidemic; as a trope it implies a conventional model of stable, autonomous subjectivity, the kind more often found in traditional autobiography. Silence = Death assumes an untroubled relationship between discourse and social change. As a motivating force and a trope, however, Silence = Death tends to give way to resignation by the ends of most AIDS memoirs. As writers become increasingly sick, it becomes clear that "the intervention of voice" alone will not save lives. As that realization sets in, a relational model of subjectivity becomes more dominant.

The subjects of AIDS memoirs are subjects in crisis, and the trauma of the epidemic renders the intersubjective relations within AIDS communities more immediately visible. The "depth and the sorrow" of AIDS is unavoidable; we see our trauma in each other. This new subject of writing, who does not believe the promise of a happy ending, or even a just one, has multiple effects: It ensures the transmission of the testimony from writer to audience; it produces narrative conventions outside traditional autobiographical models for writing the self; it positions members of this community in relations of identification and risk; it constructs an AIDS community (writer, characters, audience) tailored to the experience of gay men; it threatens, through the violation of conventional boundaries between Self and Other (both literally, through bodily exchange, and figuratively, through total psychic identification), to *infect* the culture at large; it charts new social relations, in which AIDS is no longer incomprehensible but a full-fledged social problem, with a language and structure that can "accommodate" people with AIDS.

Despite its power as a speech act, testimony can also exacerbate trauma. For AIDS memoirists, the tensions between the need to tell and the trauma of doing so—or the simultaneous narrative drive toward staying alive and coming to terms with imminent death—give way, in the end, to resignation, and very often, to an abandonment of writing. But such resignation does not diminish the memoirs' power as speech acts. If to testify is to speak for a collective in order to heal the wounds of the survivors of trauma, if it is a speech act endeavoring, despite the very real and severe risks of speaking, to establish a community of such survivors and to disseminate their stories with the intention of preventing the recurrence of the historical conditions of their trauma, then AIDS testimony is unique. It speaks for a collective but cannot eliminate the conditions which have prompted the testimony, and when those conditions exist in the present of the narrative and not the past, the writing itself is a reminder of the grim circumstances which have produced it. That is not to say that AIDS testimony is ineffective; on the contrary, AIDS testimony has reconfigured gay discourse and gay communities in the face of this epidemic.

Because of its rampant yet elusive signifiers, HIV links everyone, each person's body, via its infectious path and creates radical divides between people infected and others who are not. Throughout *Queer and Loathing*, Feinberg writes himself simultaneously as both a commonplace, the potential AIDS patient in all of us, and a pariah, disavowed and abject:

> I think of much as I contemplate the tiles on the bathroom floor.
> What is the thin line between normal health and HIV? Is this diarrhea that bizarre? Is this something I could have if I were HIV-negative? Am I violent-

ly ill, or is it all my imagination, the mental amplification of minor symptoms and ailments to the resonant frequency of insanity? It is getting harder and harder to distinguish between common ailments and pathology.

What separates me from everyone else? Low T-cells? It's just a number. The seventeen thousand and one warts on my hands? I can always wear gloves. An insane fear of death? That's completely normal. The runs? Who doesn't have the runs once in a while? An occasional allergic reaction capable of immobilizing me for a week? I have one friend who gets hives when he eats seafood, and another who has asthma. A ream of prescriptions for monthly doctors' visits? Maybe I'm just a hypochondriac. Fatigue? Is there anyone in New York City who doesn't have at least a mild case of fatigue? (230)

Because any single symptom is both alarming and dismissible, whether a gay man is "negative" or "positive," his post-AIDS body always "separates him from everyone else," links him to every other gay man, "separates" him from people outside "risk groups," and links him, via his potentially infectious status, to people outside risk groups. Diarrhea, T-cell levels, warts, allergies, and fatigue do not necessarily signify trauma in other contexts, but AIDS has invested them with multiple meanings. Because those meanings are inscrutable, however, relying as they do on connotation and inference, they both do and do not signify AIDS. They create a community of men who are always, at once, ordinary *and* pariahs. Such overdetermination has forced gay men to revise our assessments of our bodies. They are at once liberating and dangerous. We have maintained our communities, but those communities are both life-sustaining and life-threatening.

As members of *communities of risk* we cannot escape ambivalence. We are obsessed with AIDS because it determines our social positions, in relation to each other and to the culture as a whole. Wojnarowicz's *Close to the Knives: A Memoir of Disintegration* is nothing if not ambivalent. He hates and loves AIDS and writes of the AIDS community as both revolutionary and doomed: "A month ago someone called from out of state to inform me that a guy I knew from ten years ago had died. I'd had a fight with this guy and thought he was an asshole up until the moment when I'd heard he was ill. He then became perfectly human in my eyes. I'd been comforted seeing him on the street since then; something about his being alive and occupying the same space meant that my life was not threatened by the virus. Now he's dead and I feel more vulnerable, like I'm standing on a conveyor belt leading into an enormous killing machine" (166–67). The sight of other PWAs surviving is comforting; it can mean that our lives "are not threatened by the virus." However, repeatedly, the PWAs defy our hopes. They die and leave us "standing on a conveyor belt leading into an enormous killing machine." Testimony can have a similar effect, warding off vulnerability as its narrative unfolds and revealing a person living and surviving AIDS. But inevitably, as Wojnarowicz's subtitle points out, AIDS testimonies become "memoirs of disintegration." In Wojnarowicz's words,

> The social landscape I have grown to be comforted by is being exploded and is disappearing. There are dozens of faces I hardly know but who have become familiar over time; I have been reassured by the fact that those people are somewhere walking the face of the earth, pushing air around and *thinking*. Each one of them is a receptacle for some belief or projection of the beliefs and each one of them carries a piece of myself; and in the last month each time I pick up the phone it is to learn that another of them has died. Piece by piece the landscape is eroding and in its place I am building a monument made of fragments of love and hate, sadness and feelings of murder. This monument serves as a shrine where innocence is slowly having its belly slit open, its heart removed, its eyes plucked out, its tongue severed, its fingers broken, its legs torn off. (165–66)

Testimony doesn't write us out of vulnerability, but it can link us as a community living with risk. Wojnarowicz's memoir is a "monument made of fragments of love and hate, sadness and feelings of murder." It is testimony, proof of a PWA "pushing air around and *thinking*." As a speech act it signifies the existence of people living with AIDS, an existence generally met with silence. By representing himself as a writer and addressing a community of readers, Wojnarowicz is tending the "social landscape." Since AIDS writing constructs the subjects of its community as relational, and, as Wojnarowicz puts it, each member "carries a piece of myself," then pieces of every gay man are dying every day because as AIDS memoirists observe again and again, "each time I pick up the phone it is to learn another of them has died."

Testimony, then, as a speech act, a way of constituting AIDS communities, must constantly re-envision itself and adapt to the vicissitudes of trauma. Benefiting from the lessons of feminism, Paul Monette, in *Becoming a Man: Half a Life Story*, suggests that AIDS has politicized the private story of every gay man's life: "every memoir is now a kind of manifesto, as we piece together the tale of the tribe. Our stories have died with us long enough. We mean to leave behind some map, some key, for the gay and lesbian people who follow—that they may not drown in the lies, in the hate that pools and foams like pus on the carcass of America" (2). Memoirs become manifestos when they publicize the private experience of an entire community or "tribe," when their explicit motive is to testify to collective trauma. As unacceptable as the silence of the closet is for any AIDS memoirist, the alternatives, despite the Silence = Death slogan, do not promise an end to the trauma of AIDS, or even the closet. Instead, testimony functions like a map or key, a "how to" that can help the communities it fosters to negotiate the trauma of the epidemic. As a map or key, however, it may reach its optimum usefulness at some point in the unforeseeable future, seeing to it that "our stories" won't die with us anymore.

If AIDS testimony constructs a community, a "tribe," it does so with materials at hand—the community of gay men and lesbians which has been developing at least since Stonewall. AIDS has given new inflections to gay communities, and it has opened doors to non-gay, anti-homophobic people, but for better or worse, there is no widespread, public AIDS community which is not dominated by the presence of gay men. In his article "Testimony," Timothy Murphy notes that "there are precious few encomiums penned to poor, drug-using men and women who have died with AIDS. Gay men, either as authors or subjects, dominate the written word in the literature of the epidemic. Their publications and booksellers are the epicenters of writing about AIDS" (307). Not only our publications and booksellers but our doctors, our neighborhood hospitals, our community centers, our social workers, our gyms, our restaurants, our bars. Murphy has a point: Effective testimony constructs community. Our encomiums identify us and create social organizations around those of us at the epicenter of the epidemic. AIDS has been constructed in our cultural imaginations along axes of sexual orientation, class, and race, but it has been gay men who have responded most strikingly to AIDS, producing testimony, or speech acts, capable of forming communities well-organized enough to garner popular attention and widespread public support. Even Elizabeth Glaser, one of the United States' most famous "innocent victims" of AIDS, when she testified at the 1992 Democratic convention, declared herself "a strange spokesperson for such a group [an AIDS community]—a well-to-do white woman."[2] Glaser is astutely aware of the authority to signify that her "well-to-do white woman" status affords her. She is not an "AIDS Clone." A Paul Monette, a John Preston, a Hervé Guibert, a David Wojnarowicz, a David B. Feinberg does not make a politically marketable spokesperson. Glaser speaks in their place, a speech act in itself, which at once advances the causes of AIDS activism and partitions AIDS, marking it as other—"of color" and poor, yes, but mostly gay.

Monette's *Borrowed Time* is a portrait of two members of such a community:

> We were about to join a community of the stricken who would not lie down and die. All together, we beat down the doors of the system and made it take our count. Some have sat in medical libraries wading through the arcana of immunology. Others pass back and forth over the border, bringing vanloads of drugs the law hasn't got around to yet. This network has the feel of an underground railway. It could be argued that we're out there mainly for ourselves, of course, and the ones we cannot live without. But on the way we have also become traders and explorers, passing the word till hope is kindled in places so dark you can't see your hand in front of your eyes. (103)

Gay men, who have been the foundational members of AIDS communities, are "out for ourselves," but precisely because it is homophobia that has led to the widespread neglect of people with AIDS. The actions of such a community, or "underground railway," are nevertheless elusive to people unaccustomed to the terrain. Gay men whose HIV status is sero-negative are in a better position to negotiate AIDS discourse than many sero-positive, heterosexual men and women. Even AIDS memoirs, which hope to set such communities in motion, require a conversion to be read by "outsiders." They require readers to look at AIDS, and at the world in general, through a gay male lens. Those AIDS memoirs written by gay men, however, have the potential to alter relations between gay and lesbian communities and the world outside. Because AIDS has such a strong hold on all of our cultural imaginations, the testimony of gay men has begun to be heard, and perhaps understood, by a much wider audience than ever before, inviting "outsiders" to witness the experience of a community of AIDS clones, to hear the stories borne out of AIDS as well as the long-ignored stories we brought to AIDS.[3]

But if AIDS testimonies are speech acts, if they do in fact alter social relations, they do it at the expense of their own narratives. By the end, many AIDS testimonies close in upon themselves, re-evaluating the Silence = Death trope that had been the motivating force. When the community constituted through a memoir is fragile, the act of writing itself is precarious. When the body of the writer is losing strength, that person lacks the agency required to keep writing. AIDS memoirists often quit writing because they're too sick or because, as David Feinberg puts it, "I cannot write about being ill when I am ill":

> I could continue in this vein indefinitely. Future episodes could include: Davey gets a cane. Davey gets a Hickman catheter and matching bag and shoes. Davey goes blind. Davey loses all control of his limbs. Davey goes on total parenteral nutrition. Davey gets a walker. Davey gets his oxygen tube entangled with the telephone wire. Davey complains about not being able to wear a simple shift over the catheter and tubes. Davey develops Tourette's syndrome. Davey finds religion. Davey becomes even more bitter than before.
>
> But there comes a point when your sense of humor grows stale. It's time for a break. Writing these essays becomes too much of a strain. I've lost my taste for it. I can only mask so much bitterness and anger with humor. The subject ceases to be palatable. It all gets too ugly.
>
> I'm beginning to lose perspective. I need more distance. I cannot write about being ill when I am ill. (273)

Feinberg's use of the word "subject" (which "ceases to be palatable") suggests a double, overdetermined meaning. Ostensibly his "subject" is AIDS, but the "subject" of autobiography is always, of course, the self. What has ceased to be palatable may be the transformed subject of autobiography, the David Feinberg who has become a construction of his own testimony (and AIDS discourse in general). Silence may equal death, but writing, by the end of Feinberg's narrative, means tackling a subjectivity suffused with the virus the writing itself was designed to exorcize:

> Does writing actually help anything?
> People die everyday. Eventually I will die.
> I'm afraid of what the next year will bring.
> I'm exhausted.
> *I don't want to think about it anymore.* (274)

Writing himself with AIDS has "exhausted" Feinberg. Writing AIDS and living AIDS are incompatible. In part, the memoir has constructed Feinberg and AIDS as overlapping "subjects" which constitute each other. They exist only in relation to each other. Feinberg cannot escape the AIDS community that his narrative fosters, and as testimony, is intent on creating. The logical conclusion to a narrative in which "people die every day" is: "Eventually I will die." Silence = Death, and so does writing.

The danger of a relational model of subjectivity, when the impulse for its construction is collective trauma, is that the new, relational subject may not be able to sustain itself in writing. Repeatedly, AIDS memoirs which begin by shouting Silence = Death, in so many words, end in resignation. "More and more deaths," as Gregg Bordowitz pointed out (in Caruth and Keenan), give rise to a crisis of faith. The final essay in Paul Monette's last published testimony, *The Last Watch of the Night,* is another example:

> My own bark has grown softer of late, but that's because I've already scared off most of that class of intruders and trespassers who get too close. For all of that, my rage at my lost country is undiminished, but I choose my shouting matches carefully these days, husbanding my energy and adrenaline for the war going on inside me. Meanwhile, the dying continues unabated. Michael Callen gone three weeks ago—midsong as it were—after twelve years in the trenches. In yesterday's *Times* an obit for my friend Dan Bailey, one of the founding fathers of Gay Men's Health Crisis, the gentlest man imaginable, and there is no one I can call for details because all of our mutual acquaintance is dead.
>
> Three weeks, two dead—two more lost from the magic circle. Or, to put it another way, two more rocks flung at the vast glass house of the world's complacency—falling short as usual. (306)

Again "the magic circle," the community constructed by and through AIDS and its testimonies, diminishes, defying the hopes of the Silence = Death model, and so the writer's "bark has grown softer," and the alternatives to silence fall short "as usual." The subject of AIDS writing is not a comfortable thing to be. AIDS compels writing but does not accommodate it. The stories of AIDS break with convention; the characters in AIDS memoirs are not the self-reliant subjects of conventional autobiography. Nevertheless, Monette, who warned readers in the first sentence of *Borrowed Time,* his first AIDS memoir, that "I do not know if I will live to finish this book," lived to finish four books of AIDS testimony. Silence = Death, as a trope, fueled his life and his writing, but by the end of his writing, the end of his life, it gives way to resignation. Relational subjectivity, when "all of our mutual acquaintance is dead," when the realities of a community linked through risk are all too apparent, is faltering subjectivity. If the virus links us, providing us with the ability to fight it, it also kills us.

While the beginnings of AIDS memoirs foreground survival, their endings foreground death. With death comes, of course, the cessation of writing, or discourse, which calls to mind Paul de Man's declaration—that death, in autobiography, is primarily a "linguistic predicament" (930). De Man reminds readers and writers that autobiography is not an accurate representation but a collection of tropes performing a life. Death cannot be captured in writing, but AIDS memoirs make it clear that death cannot simply be reduced to just another trope. Death is, more precisely, a "linguistic predicament" involved in a complex set of social, political, and aesthetic relations. An AIDS memoir, like life with AIDS, is haunted by death at every turn, constructed by and through the likelihood of early death. So even though, strictly speaking, death is unrepresentable, these memoirs demonstrate very clearly the drive behind the will to represent the unrepresentable—in order to examine it more closely, to make sense of it. Death, as a literary convention, functions to open up the reading experience, to make reading an act of witnessing, creating a community of readers through the death of the author.

For example, in the very short final chapter of Hervé Guibert's *To the Friend Who Did Not Save My Life,* the foregrounding of death becomes a narrative predicament, but one linked to the corporeality of the writer: "My book is closing in on me. I'm in deep shit. Just how deep do you want me to sink? Fuck you, Bill! My muscles have melted away. At last my arms and legs are once again as slender as they were when I was a child" (100). Again, the subject becomes indistinguishable from his writing: "The book is closing in on me." Emily Apter's reading of the passage in relation to the rest of Guibert's narrative holds true for many AIDS memoirs: "The questionable asseveration, made at the end of the first section—'I was going to shake this, I was going to be, by some extraordinary chance, one of the world's first survivors of this inexorable illness'—is belied by Hervé's avowal, a mere page later, that the conditions of his book's closure are anchored in uncertainty, as wide open to imminently unforeseeable endings as the subject of the disease itself" (85). Again, Silence = Death compels the writing of the memoir, but along the way the writer and his narrative become "the subjects of the disease itself." Their project, the construction of an AIDS community, "belies" the normative subject of autobiography suggested by Silence = Death.

Guibert's explicit address to the audience, so necessary to transform writing into speech act, is telling here. By the end of the narrative, he is writing for the audience but at his own expense. Bill, who, within the narrative, is often the witness in whom Guibert sees himself constituted and with whom he has been linked via mutual infection, is now a source of anger. "Fuck you, Bill!" reflects what Feinberg calls the "shock and horror" that accompanies the recognition of oneself as the subject of an AIDS memoir, one whose very existence is constituted by the epidemic and the communities it fosters. Guibert is infantilized by the virus: "my arms and legs are once again as slender as they were when I was a child." His subjectivity, like his body, reflects that closeted, child self. It is ambivalent, split, simultaneously attracted to and repulsed by its difference from the normative subject of autobiography, the one who can write more than, in Paul Monette's words, "half a life story."

In AIDS memoirs, the book consistently "closes in on" the subject writing. The AIDS memoirist is not just another example of the famous, postmodern "death of the subject"—a casualty of historical shifts in the philosophy of the self. AIDS writers are, more concretely, members of a community whose ranks are periodically (and rapidly) diminishing, yet rallying to carve out space for itself in the culture. Nevertheless, alternatives to the Silence = Death trope, though they offer useful models for new understandings of the self in relation to a community, inevitably construct subjects of AIDS testimony who cannot survive the trauma they chronicle. However, the endings, or "deaths," of AIDS memoirs conclude lengthy, inventive, and moving narratives, texts that are a pleasure to read, stories that give shape to trauma, shape that defies readers to maintain "observer status." David Feinberg, Paul Monette, John Preston, Michael Callen, David Wojnarowicz, Reinaldo Arenas, and Hervé Guibert are all dead, but their memoirs are still here, bearing witness, despite the deaths of their authors.

NOTES

An earlier version of this essay appeared in *a/b: Auto/Biography Studies* 13.2 (Winter 1998): 235–56. Reprinted by permission of the editors of *a/b: Auto/Biography Studies*.

1. Both Austin and Searle agree that the effects of words depend upon a community's agreement to adhere to strict social conventions, like the marriage ceremony or a poker bet. Neither Austin nor Searle acknowledges literary utterances as speech acts, but Sandy Petrey makes a convincing case that the speech act theories in both Austin's *How to Do Things with Words* and Searle's *Speech Acts* have literary implications. According to Petrey, the highly conventional character of any literary utterance depends on a community of readers' willingness to subscribe to those conventions and make sense of the text.

2. Much AIDS testimony written by women, including Glaser's *In the Absence of Angels,* Califia's "Slipping," the essays in collections like *Positive Women* and

AIDS: The Women, and Sedgwick's premature memorial for Michael Lynch, "White Glasses," is very explicit in its demonstration of the inevitable confrontations with gay male norms, communities, writing, and general discourse anyone with (or writing about) AIDS must confront. While the construction of AIDS discourse *as gay* has been invaluable, even necessary, for gay men, it can have disastrous effects for women, whose doctors often fail to recognize their symptoms as HIV-related and whose communities cannot accommodate their illness or provide them with the psychological and medical support they need.

3. This is not to imply that all testimony concerning AIDS is written by HIV-positive gay men. There is also a great deal of AIDS "witness" literature, mostly written by friends and family members of PWAs and people who work in AIDS healthcare or social work. These include: Cox, Peabody, Schulman, and Corea.

WORKS CITED

Apter, Emily. "Fantom Images: Hervé Guibert and the Writing of sida in France." *Writing AIDS: Gay Literature, Language, and Analysis.* Ed. Timothy F. Murphy and Suzanne Poirier. New York: Columbia University Press, 1993. 83–97.

Arenas, Reinaldo. *Before Night Falls: A Memoir.* New York: Viking, 1993.

Austin, J.L. *How to Do Things with Words.* Cambridge, Mass.: Harvard University Press, 1962.

Califia, Pat. "Slipping." *Discontents: New Queer Writing.* Ed. Dennis Cooper. New York: Amethyst, 1992. 85–95.

Callen, Michael. *Surviving AIDS.* New York: Vintage, 1990.

Caruth, Cathy, and Thomas Keenan. "'The AIDS Crisis Is Not Over': A Conversation with Gregg Bordowitz, Douglas Crimp, and Laura Pinsky." *Trauma: Explorations in Memory.* Ed. Cathy Caruth. Baltimore: John Hopkins University Press, 1995. 61–75.

Chambers, Ross. "Reading, Mourning, and the Death of the Author." *Narrative* 5.1 (1997). 67–76.

Corea, Gena. *The Invisible Epidemic: The Story of Women and AIDS.* New York: Harper Collins, 1992.

Cox, Elizabeth. *Thanksgiving: An AIDS Journal.* New York: Harper and Row, 1990.

de Man, Paul. "Autobiography as De-facement." *MLN* 94 (1979): 919–30.

Edelman, Lee. "The Plague of Discourse: Politics, Literary Theory, and AIDS." *Displacing Homophobia: Gay Male Perspectives in Literature and Culture.* Ed. Ronald R. Butters, John M. Clum, and Michael Moon. Durham, N.C.: Duke University Press, 1989. 289–305.

Feinberg, David B. *Eighty-Sixed.* New York: Penguin, 1988.

———. *Queer and Loathing: Rants and Raves of a Raging AIDS Clone.* New York: Viking, 1994.

Felman, Shoshana, and Dori Laub. *Testimony: Crises of Witnessing in Literature, Psychoanalysis, and History.* New York: Routledge, 1992.

Glaser, Elizabeth. *In the Absence of Angels.* New York: Berkley Books, 1991.

Guibert, Hervé. *To the Friend Who Did Not Save My Life.* New York: High Risk, 1990.

Mason, Mary G. "The Other Voice: Autobiographies of Women Writers." Olney. *Autobiography.* 207–35.

Monette, Paul. *Becoming a Man.* San Francisco: Harper, 1992.

———. *Borrowed Time: An AIDS Memoir.* New York: Harcourt, 1988.

———. *The Last Watch of the Night.* New York: Harcourt, 1994.

———. *Love Alone.* New York: St. Martin's, 1988.

Murphy, Timothy F. "Testimony." *Writing AIDS: Gay Literature, Language, and Analysis.* Ed. Timothy F. Murphy and Suzanne Poirer. New York: Columbia University Press, 1993. 306–20.

Pastore, Judith Laurence "What Are the Responsibilities of Representing AIDS?" *Confronting AIDS through Literature: The Responsibilities of Representation.* Ed. Judith Laurence Pastore. Urbana: University of Illinois Press, 1993. 15–35.

Peabody, Barbara. *The Screaming Room: A Mother's Journal of Her Son's Struggle with AIDS: A True Story of Love, Dedication, and Courage.* 1986. New York: Avon, 1987.

Petrey, Sandy. *Speech Acts and Literary Theory.* New York: Routledge, 1990.

Preston, John. *Winter's Light: Reflections of a Yankee Queer.* Hanover, N.H.: University Press of New England, 1995.

Rieder, Ines, and Patricia Ruppelt. *AIDS: The Women.* San Francisco: Cleis, 1988.

Rudd, Andrea, and Darien Taylor. *Positive Women: Voices of Women Living with AIDS.* Toronto: Second Story Press, 1992.

Schulman, Sarah. *People in Trouble.* New York: E. P. Dutton, 1990.

———. *Rat Bohemia.* New York: E. P. Dutton, 1995.

Searle, John. *Speech Acts: An Essay in the Philosophy of Language.* Cambridge: Cambridge University Press, 1969.

Sedgwick, Eve. "White Glasses." *Tendencies.* Durham, N.C.: Duke University Press, 1993. 252–66.

Wojnarowicz, David. *Close to the Knives: A Memoir of Disintegration.* New York: Vintage, 1991.

———. *Memories That Smell Like Gasoline.* San Francisco: ArtSpace Books, 1992.

NINE

Off My Chest

Eve Kosofsky Sedgwick

FAT OR THIN? CAN'T WIN

What to Tell and How to Do It

Q. What on earth am I supposed to say to people who congratulate me on my successful diet? ("You've lost tons!" a suave guy assured me the other day.) I'm losing weight because I'm dealing with advanced cancer, but at the moment I apparently don't look sick, just thin. I really don't want to launch into the saga of my cancer with people I barely know, but you'd be amazed what a drag it is on a daily basis. Any ideas?

Q. Here's an unexpected problem for someone with metastatic cancer: I'm getting fatter and fatter. It started when I first had chemo, which apparently increased the setpoint of my weight by about 20%. (My oncologist told me—afterwards, of course—that this is a common side effect.) But on top of that I'm now taking Megace, which does the same thing again. At this point the people who know about my illness think the extra weight means I'm doing well, which I'm not particularly. People who don't know just think I'm letting myself go. My doctor says if I'm "distressed" about it she'll refer me to a nutritionist for advice on weight control. Am I "distressed"? No, I'm just sick and ugly and I sure don't want to be dieting too.

A. Holy double bind, Batgrrls! Do you ever suspect that when it comes to women and weight, we just can't win? And when it comes to women and weight and serious illness, forget about it. There is no cool way to handle this kind of thing—or if anybody's found one, will they let us know? What's striking to me is that both of you, whether fat or thin, have to suffer so much from the weird intricacies of what other people know and don't know—about you, about women, about cancer. Most of all, of course, from the things they wrongly assume they know. Like that the quest for slenderness is the single driving preoccupation in every woman's life. Or that the signs of illness are instantly legible to anyone with eyes. Bzzzzt—wrong and wrong again. Can you believe how rare the people are who know how to (a) ask a sensible question, and then (b) listen?

The practical issues both of you raise are about managing information and minimizing stress. At a time when the emotional and physical tasks that you're dealing with are so imposing, you probably need to give priority to minimizing stress. Now, ideally, that means remaining centered, buoyant, self-affirming, open to the flow of being, etc.—it's hard for stress to find its way into that kind of a personal space. But speaking from experience, I assume that the moments when we're able to access all that resilience are not the same moments when we're excruciatingly sensitive about what random onlookers think of our appearance. What's required at those maximally frazzled moments is an instant emergency application of your favorite spray-on nonstick surface. Keep this aerosol handy in your mental emergency kit, practice using it till it's automatic, and apply it whenever you need to. Its purpose is to slide you out of conversations without ruffling up any of the anger, vulnerability, tears, or general thin-skinnedness that suffering flesh is heir to. A non-warm smile, without eye contact, works for some people. The spray-on surface I like to use is a little shinier (or more aggressive?): at the first, routine "How are you?" from someone I'm not close to, I'll paste on a big bright smile and respond with great promptitude, "Oh, thanks, I'm doing really well—and how about you?" This ostentatious friendliness permits me to tune out the rest of the conversation, if any. And strangely, it works best of all at times when I look like something the cat dragged in. As far as managing information goes, you've probably gotten to know your own comfort levels, and understand which people you want to keep informed about your health. Just speaking for myself, it seems there are two good arguments for total candor. The first is that no one can ever successfully control the flow of information among other people, so it's exhausting and nerve-wracking, as well as futile, to try. And the second is that the more people understand about the actual experience of women with cancer, the fewer ignorant assumptions any of us will have to deal with. But it's slow work, and at any given moment any one of us may not feel up to doing it. Just be kind to yourselves, okay?

THE HAPPINESS TRAP

Sometimes You Just Got to Be Down

Q. I'm trying to get my act together psychologically after a bilateral mastectomy. It's harder than I expected. My prognosis seems good, and the decision to have the mastectomy wasn't difficult: I've never been into "femininity," whether of the ruffles-and-bows or earth-mother variety. In fact, butch has always been my style. And I hate all the tear-jerking prose about breasts in the cancer journalism I've read. Nevertheless, I keep having sad, terrifying, and upsetting feelings and dreams about breasts. I know I should be feeling other things instead: determination to beat the disease, or concern about my family, or Positive Thinking, or anger at the medical establishment, or . . . well, something else, anyway. What's the matter with me?

A. I wonder how much of the pain in your letter is attached to that killer phrase, I should be feeling. . . . What does should have to do with feeling? That's like saying blue is the wrong color for the sky to be, or Thursday is the wrong day for today to be. Should is for actions; what you feel, you feel. Sometimes you can make a mental note that if you did happen to be feeling x or y instead of z, you might be having an easier time of it. At most, this helps you recognize and appreciate the moments when you might spontaneously experience x or y—then, sometimes, the easier-to-take feeling will expand and take up more of your emotional landscape. But this strategy doesn't always work, and that's just as well. There's probably more to be gotten from respecting the feelings and dreams you are having, letting them take whatever time they take, walking right in at the front door of them and looking around with great interest—in short, having them. And don't let friends, family, or books tell you what your feelings ought to be doing, either. The good wishes of others are important, sure, but it's still worth being wary of amateur "experts" (or for that matter, professional ones) who are eager to prolong your life by micro-managing your mental hygiene. Just a few problems with this approach:

(1) Often people want you to "think positive" so they won't have to deal with their own feelings about your (or their own) vulnerability to grave illness. Lots of times, "Think positive" is polite-speak for "Shut up about it already."

(2) You already have an emotional style of your own, don't you? Individual feelings change, but the rhythm or idiom of your affective life is likely to have a long-term consistency—and even if it changes a lot over time, it certainly deserves respect right now.

(3) I always think there's something ass-backwards, anyway, when experts suggest that we should laugh, or have intimacies, or be truthful about our feelings and thoughts, or have pets, or enjoy happy moments, or explore our spirituality, or whatever, so that we can live longer. Like, excuse me, but aren't these things the point of living? If some multi-gazillion-dollar study were to demonstrate tomorrow that the key to surviving cancer lay in adopting a paranoid, envious, resentful, frightened, and unfunny mental posture, in avoiding other people and animals, and in lying to ourselves and those we love whenever possible, would we do that? The new work on mind-body connections is certainly long overdue, but sometimes it can turn into just another way of disavowing the present-day richness, variety, texture, and growth of our real emotional lives.

But listen, here's the bottom line. Whatever your prognosis, there will be time for you to have many, many different feelings about your breasts, about the disease, about your family, about the medical establishment and every related matter. The only certainties are that you will have feelings, and that over time even the strongest of them will change and change again. It's as inevitable for feelings to change as for the weather to—that's what being alive means. So don't try to boss your emotions around or second-guess yourself. Don't fear getting permanently stuck in a feeling that seems like the "wrong" one. Don't look for your feelings to be particularly consistent with your convictions, with your identity, with your politics, or with each other. As you grow more accepting of a wide range of feelings, you get to know yourself, your own surprises and mysteries, better and better and better. These are the weird but profound pay-offs that keep us survivors and sick folks interested—you don't want to miss them, do you?

THE PUNITIVE PHANTOM

Getting a Better Handle on Self Blame

Q. Doesn't it drive you crazy when cancer pundits try and blame the victim? If I see one more article, TV show, or book suggesting I could have prevented my cancer with a healthy lifestyle and a Positive Mental Outlook, I'll sue for slander. I'm a lifelong vegetarian! I'm thin! I run! I don't smoke! And up till my diagnosis, I was cheerful as a lark. Isn't there a way to put a stop to this nonsense? —R.G., Seattle

A. Blame—it's a blight, all right. For lots of people living with cancer, it seems as if the illness has been made even more nightmarish by the spectre of blame. There's probably more implicit blame that whirlpools around cancer than around any other disease except AIDS. And it's so damaging; it seems so unanswerable. Often, in fact, the most hurtful conversations are the phantom ones we have with ourselves. Most of those pundits aren't directly saying our cancer is our own fault; it's we ourselves, as patients struggling for comprehension and empowerment, who are connecting the dots in their rhetoric, whether rightly or wrongly. R.G., I hate to think of you seething in front of your television, feeling unfairly accused . . . and I can also picture how much worse it might make you feel if, like many of us, you'd smoked, *hadn't* exercised, *weren't* thin, or even hated veggies. The need to make treatment decisions can also be a potent trigger for these painful phantom scenes. Women often agonize about how much they "may" blame themselves "in the future" if they don't choose the most arduous treatment option now. "How will I feel IF—?" It's not only an excruciating question to ask; it's also, as psychological research shows, one to which people give consistently inaccurate answers. Yet it's hard to arrive at any decision we can live with until we have some handle on this issue of blame.

What are some of the mechanisms that make this dynamic so bad? One is that we live in a culture where blame seems like a crushing, all-or-nothing monolith. Maybe because American society is so legalistic, or because of a Puritan heritage, accusation and counter-accusation, suit and countersuit seem to exhaust the available models for thinking about responsibility. But if there's one thing we seem to know about cancer, it's that its causes are complex and multifactorial. Neither total villain nor total victim is a recognizable self-image for many people; and the more nuanced understanding of causality we have, the less we need to fear being overwhelmed by that huge, unrelieved sense of blame. (If your own or other people's implicit accusations still torment you, then read Sandra Steingraber's *Living Downstream: An Ecologist Looks at Cancer,* or some other powerful environmentalist book, and find some constructive ways to direct your blame!)

Another good thing to realize is that statistical studies can never be taken personally. The scientists doing these studies wouldn't so much as bat an eyelash if you contradicted them with your own experience, because the scale of one person's experience is so incommensurable with the wholesale scale of a study. And a statistic can't place blame on an individual, any more than a single person's experience can prove or disprove a statistic. It's easy, too, hearing advice on cancer prevention, to forget that we aren't the people it's "about." Sometimes when, like you, I feel personally accused by the prevention pundits, it occurs to me later that my indignation at them may be a way of refusing to grasp the fact that I'm already ill, that cancer prevention is just no longer very germane to me. I certainly want effective cancer prevention to become a possibility—for the sake of other people. And many folks without cancer may want or need an exaggerated sense of control over their health. But I'm in a different place by now, from which that strategy doesn't seem realistic or useful. Ultimately, society as a whole needs to think of illness in terms that aren't so tied up with blame. But that's bound to take awhile. Meanwhile, those of us living with serious illness can be clearer and more generous with ourselves if we get some distance from the phantom conversation of these punitive, blaming voices.

COMFORT CUSHION

Softening Pain with Perspective

Q. I've just had the most upsetting afternoon! It's only 10 days since my original diagnosis, so I've been dealing with plenty of upsetting things lately—and, as far as I could tell, doing pretty well, thanks. But all of a sudden I was bawling like a baby, unable to stop, just because some nurse was having trouble finding a vein in my arm. It caused a big fuss (all the nurses were trying to calm me down) and I was totally mortified. Now I hate the thought of ever going back there. I'm just about to begin 8 months of chemo, so I can't afford to lose it every time I experience a needle prick. I thought I was pretty brave, but now . . . help!

A. A sneaky thing about cancer, like other serious illness, is that it gets to you on so many levels at once. Challenges and pains that seem momentous arrive all mixed up with ones that seem trivial. It's hard to tell whether what you're really responding to at a given moment is your fear of death, your allergy to the adhesive on a bandage, your uncertainty over the right treatment strategy, or the fact that you cooled your heels in the waiting room so long you never got lunch. And of course, the "trivial" issues sometimes let you experience and express important feelings about the big ones: when you're dealing with cancer, there's no point second-guessing whether your emotional responses are proportional to their immediate cause. Pain, in particular, is the kind of intimate, immediate trigger that displays no sense of proportion at all. In the abstract, you'd think the pain of cancer itself, for example, must be bigger and more "serious" than the pain of a therapeutic needle-stick. Forget it—you'll learn to expect surprises here. Another thing you'll learn, I'm sure, is not to beat yourself up over crying or losing it occasionally. Fighting for health and life doesn't require mounting a pageant of stoicism for the medics. In fact, in my experience, they not only are very understanding but actually *do* treat me more carefully once they see that the stiff upper lip can easily fray.

But of course, you do want to avoid building up a wall of fear and aversion that will make your treatment experience worse than need be. I've heard meditation teachers say that a person's suffering in these situations is equal to the amount of physical pain multiplied by the amount of their resistance to the pain—or in simpler language, pain hurts a lot less if you don't freak out about it. But how to avoid that spiral where pain turns into fear of pain, which turns into fear of *fear,* which in turn sends you into some exhausting tailspin?

To begin with, it helps if you can unpack the one big, frightening concept "pain" into some smaller, more manageable gradations. When somebody's poking or squishing me in a medical context, I've learned to distinguish among four different things to say: "Feels okay," "That hurts," "That hurts a lot," and "That hurts too much." Easy enough? The first three remarks are aimed at keeping the nurse or tech informed along with me. After all, they can't read minds, and people register pain very differently. Number 4, "That hurts too much," on the other hand, means action: something concrete has to change before this continues. That could mean getting somebody else to complete the procedure; getting a (better) painkiller and/or tranquilizer into me; rescheduling to a time when I'll be less tired or stressed; or something as simple as boosting my blood sugar with a snack. (It's amazing how vulnerable we are to pain when we're hungry!) The point is, of course, that just having the four gradations—being able to recognize and articulate them—is reassuring, so an ordinary pain is less likely than before to plunge me into the depths of abjection. In seven years of living with cancer, I've only had to invoke #4 a couple of times, but it sure is calming to know it's there.

Remember, though, the very best thing to do with pain is prevent it—and you'll want to work actively with your doctors and nurses on this part of the strategy. It seems silly to say, but you have to make sure they know if minimizing pain is a priority for you. Like, duh, right? But maybe because the stakes are so high in dealing with cancer, the medical establishment can sometimes be cavalier about symptoms that aren't life-or-death. After all, the so-called side effects of many cancer treatments are severe enough that in another context they'd be considered major pathologies. In this context, "mere" pain can look pretty unimportant—from the outside. But of course we're not on the outside. It's a real plus when we can get well-enough acquainted with our own thresholds and priorities to make them clear to the professionals we're working with.

I GOT IT GOOD

. . . And That Ain't Bad

Q. Why do I sometimes get depressed by good test results? You'd think I'd be over the moon when my oncologist assures me that my aches aren't cancer related, or when a CAT scan comes out clean. But sometimes good news will throw me into a tailspin that's even worse than my initial fears. When I mention this to healthy friends, they think I'm crazy. Do you?

A. Oh, dear—will you feel even worse if I pronounce your psyche perfectly healthy? Few cancer patients discuss these paradoxical responses to good news. When you ask around, though, the phenomenon turns out to be as common as it is confusing. At the most superficial level, have you noticed that even the language of test results is emotionally ass-backwards. When a neurologist told me an MRI showed my brain to be "unremarkable," I almost punched him. Let's face it, it's hard to feel elated, rather than chagrined, at learning after a long chemo ordeal that your cancer shows "no progression." What, *no* progression? Ac-cen-tu-ate the negative, e-lim-i-nate the positive: That's the disorienting ditty that swirls through our heads when we're waiting for test results.

More substantively, these upsetting responses to good news often reflect how strongly we've defended ourselves against bad news. The an-

ticipation of a bad outcome sometimes seems like the best way to be prepared for any outcome: In our minds, we've already packed a bag for the
hospital, broken the sad news to our loved ones, even figured out who'll
adopt the beagle or cater the funeral. Most people with cancer have already had at least one devastating ambush, and our psyches are more than
ready to join the Boy Scouts and Be Prepared. As it happens, being mobilized for bad news can make it hard to process good news. Such defenses
can make hope feel more disruptive than fear. There's that anticlimactic,
all-dressed-up-in-chainmail-with-no-place-to-go feeling. One minute
we're ratcheted up for tragic melodrama; next minute, it's ordinary life
again with overdue work, ordinary worries, and that darn beagle waiting
to be walked. On top of that, it's still ordinary life *with cancer*. At some
points, many people with cancer diagnoses do manage to let go of this
form of defense. When I finished adjuvant chemo, I didn't even want to
have my port removed: I needed to be mobilized in expectation of a recurrence. Reassuring test results during that period confused and depressed me. But a couple of years down the line, when there was still no
evidence of disease, I found that I'd imperceptibly turned a corner. I was
approaching tests as a healthy person rather than as a sick one. Even
though I knew that a bad result was always a possibility, I was able to presume on my health even at the risk of being blindsided. And even when
my cancer did recur a few years later, I was grateful to have experienced
that period of presumptuous enjoyment of my well-functioning body.

What's most difficult though is knowing that the bullet we've dodged
today could hit us a year from now, or a decade; and what's worse is that
the same frayed emotional resources we've mobilized for each test will
have to get remobilized again and again. At least, that's how it can feel.
But the fact is that as time goes on, our strategies and resources for cop-
ing with information crises are able to change, replenish, and recycle. We
may struggle with one set of tests and yet sail through the next in the finest
of spirits. We get to explore the deep interest of surprising ourselves, along
with the unwelcome challenges that go with being surprised. And at best,
all this wrestling with hope and fear can make vivid to us what it means
to be able to live in the present.

NOTE

Earlier versions of these five "Off My Chest" selections appeared in *MAMM* magazine in Feb./Mar. 1998, Apr./May 1998, Oct./Nov. 1998, Dec./Jan. 1999, and June
1999. Reprinted by permission of *MAMM* magazine.

PART FOUR

Going Public

TEN

Memory Stains: Annie Ernaux's *Shame*

Nancy K. Miller

> The force which opposes scopophilia, but which may be overridden by it . . .
> is *shame*.
>
> —Freud, *Three Essays on Sexuality*

> "I" shames the reader.
>
> —Annie Ernaux, *Exteriors*

"My father tried to kill my mother one Sunday in June, in the early afternoon" (13).[1] That starkly simple sentence opens the slim volume of reminiscence called *Shame*. The sentence and the scene it introduces of a father's violence and a mother's terror come as a shock to the readers of Annie Ernaux's previous work. Why, many years after the memoirs devoted to her parents' lives, did Annie Ernaux decide to reveal this story to the public eye? "I have always wanted to write the sort of book that I find it impossible to talk about afterward," Ernaux declares on the back cover of the French edition of her memoir, "the sort of book that makes it impossible for me to withstand the gaze of others." If *Shame* is that book, we readers become those others, whose gaze its author cannot now bear. What is the nature of the experience that we in turn have been made to witness?

The scene. It was a Sunday. Annie had been to mass. Her parents, struggling owners of a small café/grocery store, had been bickering during lunch; her mother, in a bad mood, had picked a fight. Suddenly, beside himself with rage, her father grabs her mother and drags her into another room. The girl goes upstairs and throws herself on the bed, burying her head in the pillow. But she hears her mother's voice screaming from the cellar, calling for her daughter, calling for help. When the twelve-year-old reaches her parents, she sees her father holding her mother by the shoulders with one hand, and with the other threatening her life, wielding a bush axe used for cutting firewood. Despite the confident details of vivid recall, marks of doubt creep into the description: her father was grabbing her mother either by the shoulders *or* the neck. Then, abruptly, the images stop. In the girl's memory her mother puts an end to the drama she seems to have provoked: "Come on, it's over" (14). The three go for a bike ride in the countryside, as if nothing had happened, and by evening life has returned to normal. The event took place on June 15, 1952—the first precise date, Ernaux writes, of her childhood.

This is the defining moment of childhood memory that Ernaux now wants to recount for readers, after having already confessed it, she admits, to a few lovers, who seemed unable to respond. Something terrible, she thought, would happen once she put pen to paper. A punishment. A permanent writer's block. But no, the words continue to come; the words to describe how the effects of this trauma produced an inalterable sense of difference in the girl's idea of herself: "We stopped being decent people, the sort who don't drink or fight and who dress properly to go into town" (91). No matter what outer signs of belonging to the world of proper people she might display, inside the rupture was fatal. The sheer fact of having borne witness to the scene set in motion a free fall into abjection that cannot be halted.

Shame reshapes identity, becomes a way of life, becomes almost invisible, as though it had entered the body itself. The secret knowledge of shame that excludes you in your own eyes from decency operates *regardless* of whether others know about it. Does revealing the secret compound the effects of stigma? For Ernaux the question is almost rhetorical, as she wonders after throwing down the gauntlet, we've just seen, with Rousseauian defiance, read me if you can: "But what degree of shame could possibly be conveyed by the writing of a book which seeks to measure up to the events I experienced in my twelfth year?" (109). Over a decade ago, Ernaux described in *A Woman's Story* the details of her mother's descent into Alzheimer's disease. Ernaux remarked then that she was writing not only for herself—to make bearable for herself the drama of disintegration she witnessed daily—but others: "Now I am writing the same words, but for other people, so that they can understand" (80). For Ernaux, individual experience is always shareable—potentially collective, or at least social—and always passes through the mesh of class difference as the individual gathers cultural meaning in the world of others. And because of this belief that an event's meaning inevitably comes to be processed or understood through class relations, it makes a compelling kind of sense to put the writing of shame out into the world of so-called decent people against whom she defines herself—or did. But the shame of not belonging, of feeling excluded by a horrible secret is never wholly contained by class boundaries, and so the readers of *Shame* often join Ernaux where she might least expect to be met. I would argue further that the success of her work points to the complexity of class assignment, since readers both identify with (you tell my story) and disidentify (not my story) across unpredictable class lines. What I want to track here are the places in the memoir—the narrative that unfolds from this initial assault on the mother—where shame spreads, leaks into other domains for the writer, and also for the reader.[2]

• • •

If in doing memory-work we become detectives of our lives, as Annette Kuhn has suggested in her book *Family Secrets,* we often return to the scene of the crime, looking for clues to the mystery of how we became who we are. But despite the Freudian tones that we therapy-conscious American readers might hear in the repeated use of the word "scene," or the invocation of trauma, of perhaps a screen memory behind which stands an intolerable primal event, *Shame* is not, the author insists, turned toward psychoanalysis. Rather, you could say that the memoir is a complex *explication de texte* of a sentence, the phrase that Ernaux remembers having uttered as a response to her father's panic at his own behavior. He "kept on repeating, 'Why are you crying, I didn't do anything to you'" (14). The girl's hysterical reply is: "Tu vas me faire gagner malheur." In the French version the expression receives an explanation in a footnote (one of two in the narrative); in the English-language translation, the note drops out and moves into the text, but I keep it here: "In Norman dialect, you're going to make me 'catch' unhappiness [in the translation: 'You'll breathe disaster on me' (14)] means to become crazy and unhappy forever in the aftermath of a shock." It's the prolongation of the childhood panic that she will be driven crazy *even now* that has prevented Ernaux as an adult from putting the scene into the public domain. To write the scene might mean stripping those childhood words of their magical and terrifying meaning. In some sense the book reads as an apotropaic gesture, warding off further harm: to put the scene into words is to dislodge the memory from its sacred place as the origin of all that brought the woman to writing. But it also shows the desire by the writer, the adult in the present, to regain mastery over the child's terror. In this she is surprisingly successful: "In fact," Ernaux observes, "now that I have finally committed it to paper, I feel that it is an ordinary incident, far more common among families than I had originally thought" (16). Every memoirist measures her private, exclusive event against other people's memories and stories; in the process of putting the extreme into language, horror becomes banal.

Nonetheless, the retrospective account does not erase the shock. If trauma always means a blow to body or soul, trauma always also means its lived effects in memory. As Jean Améry memorably declared in another register of extremity, that of torture during the Holocaust, "Whoever was tortured, stays tortured" (34). Just as he writes of the "first blow" the victim in the camps receives: "At the first blow, however, this trust in the world breaks down. The other person *opposite* whom I exist physically in the world and *with* whom I can exist only as he does not touch my skin surface as border, forces his own corporeality on me with the first blow. He is on me and thereby destroys me. It is like a rape, a sexual act without the consent of one of the two partners" (28). I don't mean to compare the two experiences literally, of course, but there is an eerie overlap between the two descriptions of traumatic events even though one is by the physical victim and the other by the witness. Ernaux's account of the radical effects produced in her, in her body, from witnessing the scene, casts her as the victim of a blow that shattered her world, her view of her place in it, and her innocence, all through the threatened violence of the blow that doesn't land. Her (always ambivalent) identification with her mother's body and her more porous identification with her father make her a participant in the scene, however; the daughter feels the father's rage seeping into her mind and body. The gesture of the blow strikes fear into the daughter, a fear that lives on forty-three years later. Such is the afterlife of certain memories, memories that appear to function as indelible stains in the brain.[3]

Like most writers turned toward the past, Ernaux begins by opening the family album. She studies her past self through two photographs from the summer of 1952—before and after. The photographs will haunt the narrative. The first, an important placemarker of her Catholic childhood, was taken on the anniversary of her solemn communion. In this formal photograph, twelve-year-old Annie D. is kneeling on a prayer stool, holding her rosary beads and her missal. A studious-looking girl with glasses and a bad permanent, she seems to be just a face. "It seems there is no body underneath this small nun's habit because I cannot imagine it, let alone feel it in the way I have come to feel mine. Yet surprisingly it's exactly the same body as the one I have today" (20). Although the girl's face is detailed in the description, it's in fact the secrets (always veiled) of the body that preoccupy Ernaux in this narrative. The body's potential for shame and pleasure and its relation to writing emerge after the initial revelation as the driving subject of *Shame* (as it was also in the earlier book about her father's life and death, *A Man's Place*). The second photograph, and the one more important to Ernaux in the construction of her narrative, was taken almost three months after the disastrous day, at the end of the summer. The photograph is set in Biarritz, where the girl has gone with her father on an organized trip to Lourdes. Standing next to her father, the daughter is smiling. "In this outfit," Ernaux remarks, "I look like a little woman" (21).

Bent on retrieving the girl of that summer, the writer stares at the photographs, hoping, we might almost say, to reincarnate herself. But at the same time, the founding dilemma remains intact. If the writer had never seen these photographs before, would she even recognize herself? This is the autobiographer's torment: "Absolute certainty 'yes, that's me'; total disbelief—'no, that's not me'" (22). Ernaux worries how we can become historians of our past lives confronted with this degree of indeterminacy. Here she engages the paradox, defined by the theorist Philippe Lejeune, of the autobiographer who is condemned to write at the end of the twentieth century after the death of the author, not to say subject, as though she could coincide with her existence, her name, on paper. "We *indeed know* all this," Lejeune famously sighs, "we are not so dumb, but, once this precaution has been taken, we go on as if we did not know it" (131). There's something about the photograph that compels belief in a past if not present truth. "That was," says Barthes about the referent lurking in the photograph's aura.[4] That was, therefore I am? The riff on the cogito is seductive, difficult to resist, even for the hardheaded. Despite her skepticism, Ernaux reads the two photographs as evidence, as bookends that hold the closing days of childhood innocence: the one, the good little Catholic girl, the other, the girl who no longer coincides with the child posing in good faith. The second photograph marks the beginning of the time defined by shame, the time after which shame forever becomes her.

Ernaux's strategy as a memoirist—since solution there is not beyond the practice of writing—is to act, as she puts it, "in the manner of a historian" (22), collecting evidence. To locate her twelve-year-old self in history, Ernaux gathers the material traces of that fatal year: a black-and-white postcard of Elizabeth II, a sewing kit, a postcard from the trip to Lourdes, her missal, and the score for a song, "Voyage à Cuba" ("Miami Beach Rhumba") (23–24), the words to which she can still conjure up as she writes in 1995. And then, following the impulse to flesh out the time line that could recalibrate individual experience with the world historical record, Ernaux goes to the archives to examine the newspaper her parents read to see what really happened that day. That this research is not a neutral activity is confirmed by the return of the dread invoked earlier and summarized in the phrase from the scene punctuating her consciousness, as if just turning the pages of that month would bring the madness on, like the recurrence of a disease. Although some of the events and personalities in the newspaper are still familiar, they have lost their effect, or they signify only as historical markers, emptied of affective power in the present tense: "I found it strange to think that Stalin, Churchill and Eisenhower were once as real to me as Yeltsin, Clinton and Kohl are today" (28). Thus, despite moments of recognition—the comic strip, the title of some movies—in the end Ernaux concludes that these documents of a regional or national life, the thousands of little facts contained in the pages of the newspaper, cannot touch, do not coexist on the same plane as the traumatic vision of her parents in the cellar. "Only the scene I had witnessed was real to me" (31). She leaves the municipal archives suddenly aware that she had almost expected to find the scene reported in the local paper.

The signs of the public record, the surround of a collective life, can't in themselves explain what seemed an unspeakable reality; but in Ernaux's view, here and elsewhere, the crucial issue in any understanding of an individual or social life is the way the things of the world are divided up, not the things themselves. What matters is not the number of refrigerators, but who possesses them. These distinctions define the shape of a child's life by the power of social codes: what you don't have, what other little girls do. The writer's task is to find the words that mark out the boundary between what is normal (other people) and what crosses the line, between the ordinary and the extraordinary, the everyday and the extreme.[5] Finding the words to say it would not erase the problem of time and memory; impossible for the woman of 1995 to step back into the shoes of the girl of 1952 since that past has been reworked and transformed by the very memory of that scene and reshaped by the writer in the present tense. History and experience have already rescreened the event.

Ernaux here would seem to throw up her hands in face of the difficulty every autobiographer must grapple with: are you still what you once were? "We have no true memory of ourselves" (32). And since there is no true memory, she turns to another gamble of recovery. She will scrutinize the documents of her past life in preparation for the quest. "In other words, I will carry out an ethnological study of myself" (33). Object to her subjective gaze, and continuing to circle around the scene of the day (the day she thought she would go mad), Ernaux returns in memory to her village as a participant-observer committed to uncovering the protocols of archaic rituals and rites.

The bulk of the narrative that makes up *Shame* records and analyzes the codes and languages that contained the childhood world of her village. But over and over nothing in the traces of this provincial universe explains, Ernaux concludes, the scene of that Sunday in June, the day in Normandy after which nothing was—or ever could be—the same. The signifying status of this scene, Ernaux maintains, not only escapes psychoanalysis (not to mention the idea of "childhood trauma"—eliminated at the start [27]); it also ultimately seems to escape the class grids of social life that Ernaux typically relies on to make meaning. The scene remains an inexplicable but indelible stain in the fabric of memory.

Aftermath of the aftermath.

Much later in the reconstruction of the summer of 1952, we come to another scene of shame, which, in my reading, unsettles the foundational status of the first. This second scene (not literally the second in sequence since there are several others, minor, to be sure, that stud the narrative—shame, Ernaux remarks, "will only be followed by more shame" [95]) takes place three weeks after the domestic violence that opens the memoir. We move here from father to mother, from one extreme of bodily threat to another. It's a Sunday night and Annie returns home late after a school outing; with her are her teacher and some classmates. All is dark and shuttered in her parents' home. Finally, the lights go on and her mother, still half-asleep, comes down to open the door to the store. With the lights behind her, she appears as if on a stage to an audience of the teacher and a few pupils, wearing "a nightgown that was wrinkled and stained (we used to wipe ourselves with it, after urinating)" (92, TM). With a shock, the girl Annie D. sees her mother from the outside, through the gaze of the world of her private-school classmates.

Shame. I confess that as a reader, the description of the soiled night-gown, capped with the throwaway parenthesis of the ethnographic de-tail—we used to wipe ourselves with it, after urinating—brought me up short. Earlier Ernaux revealed that she slept in the same room as her par-ents, as was the custom of the country, and shared a chamber pot with them; so in a way, this further detail should not have been shocking. "It's as though," Ernaux writes, "through the sight of my mother's body, its hanging flesh, and her stained nightgown, that our true nature and way of life were exposed." Here the guidelines of social distinction give mean-ing to the epiphany: "It was the first time I had seen my mother through the eyes of the private school" (93, TM). Had it been customary in her par-ents' world to wear a bathrobe, Ernaux explains, neither the nightgown nor the mother's body would have been revealed to the teacher and the other girls, the memory of the episode forgotten in the wash of personal history. But since it was not, and since there was no bathrobe to cloak ma-ternal abjection, shame inevitably ensued. Suddenly, your parents are no longer your parents, in the way that parents tend to be for children until adolescent distance sets in; they have become other to you. Shame again here derives from an act of witness—seeing or being seen. Shame in this other sense is relational, not solitary; it depends on the gaze of another (here the teacher and the girls), which affects your own vision. And yet, Ernaux maintains, we feel we are alone in our shame. This is one of shame's paradoxes; shame is both what's most private and most revealed. Had her mother only worn a bathrobe, the nightgown would have re-mained indoors, unseen; but of course, the body will always confess its se-crets, no matter how much we try to cover it up.

If the traces of urine speak volumes about what makes the mother's body scary to a girl, especially a girl on the threshold of puberty, the night-gown talks, gives off messages, tells one kind of irremediable truth. I imag-ine myself in the daughter's place and share her shame, her embarrass-ment in front of her classmates, but am I with her or with the classmates whose distaste (stupefaction is her word) she imagines? My mother, my-self. How many times did I cringe at the very notion of being seen—say in junior high school—with my mother. But somehow, at the same time, the detail of the stained nightgown causes me to turn away, avert my eyes. I pull back and say no, not me, I don't want to be in this picture.

This moment of disidentification is central to the experience of read-ing autobiography. For every response of identification, there is a moment of distancing, where readers, however captivated, reconstitute themselves, replace themselves in their own stories, becoming the outsider—here, the decent person who remains at a judging distance. (No, not in my village, as dissenting anthropologists like to say.) But Ernaux's scene of exposure goes further into the dark zones of these familiar positions by attaching the shame to the body's soil. In my high anxiety about what's revealed, I think: she's gone too far, she's going to extremes. As soon as I make that judgment I realize something else: *My class is showing, as clearly as the stains on the nightgown.* And yet never in this memoir have I felt closer to what I take shame to mean, to the abjection that threatens even as it marks boundaries of identity. For me, the stained nightgown trumps the symbolic murder that itself stands in for the primal scene of parental sexuality.

Ernaux contends that this scene of maternal humiliation was incommensurate with the attempted murder, and yet in memory, she also states, the second appears to be an extension of the first. After the trauma, everything seemed shameful; shame inhabited every moment. As a reader of the two scenes, three weeks apart, that defined the summer of 1952, I reverse the measure. This one feels more personally upsetting, more traumatic. But this is perverse. What, on the face of it, could be more frightening than a murderous impulse captured in full swing. Maybe I'm feeling this because fear and terror (minus the bush axe, of course) are what I lived in my own family. Maybe because the father's act was a threat that remained incomplete—almost a symbolic gesture, the wrath of paternal authority—and the mother's associated with the abject domains of the murky, maternal body.

It's hard for a daughter to separate from the mother; this we know from the shores of feminist theory. In *A Woman's Story,* Ernaux clearly images the passion of attachment and resentment that inheres in the mother/daughter bond. In a dream she had about her dead mother as she was writing the book about her, she sees herself "lying in the middle of a stream, caught between two currents. From my genitals, smooth again like a young girl's, from between my thighs, long tapering plants floated limply. That place in my body was not only mine, it was also my mother's" (89–90, TM). But at the same time, Ernaux remembers in that book her adolescent desire to separate, to break from her mother's authority, in order to embark on her autonomous sexual life. When she hears her mother's discourse in her head, she is suddenly sixteen again: "Fleetingly, I confuse the woman who influenced me the most with an African mother pinning her daughter's arms behind her back while the village midwife slices off the girl's clitoris" (51). This mother/daughter boundary confusion underlines both scenes through the daughter's ambivalent connection. Perhaps this second scene feels closer to my readerly bone because it comes almost as an afterthought to the first, tormenting one that sets the entire narrative in motion. The scene carries less authorial freight, but it also portrays a vulnerable maternal body. What remained hidden by the traumatic assault upon the mother in the basement becomes disturbingly visible—like a wound open to the look of the outsider, the look Ernaux wishes as a writer to find unbearable.

That longing to share literature's extremes, which is excerpted on the book's cover, in fact appears at the memoir's close as Ernaux brings us up to the present. In the summer of 1996 bombs are falling in Sarajevo. In the pages of the newspaper, these episodes are called "the shame that grips us" (110, TM). A moral morass. In the face of this public sense of shame, Ernaux continues to dwell on the meaning of her personal, private—and now because of what she has written—exposed shame. If the Sarajevo bombing is forgotten by newspaper readers the next day, these intimate horrors remain embedded in memory. History with a capital H fades; personal history remains.

But wait, we have not come to the end of *Shame;* the book is not closed yet. In the very last paragraph of the memoir, Ernaux suddenly casts all she has written in a new light. She returns to the photograph, the photograph of a girl with her father. She thinks about the fact that her father has now been dead for twenty-nine years. And she marks her distance from the girl in the picture: "I no longer have anything in common with the girl of the photograph, except for the scene of that Sunday in June that she is carrying in her head and that made me write this book because it is still with me" (110–11, TM). Our past selves continue in us; our autobiography is the story of how we live that continuity in discontinuous time. The girl of twelve and the writer of fifty-six are joined by the scene. They are not, however, one and the same. Here, in the last sentence of the memoir, another radical break occurs. "It's only this scene that connects the two of us, that girl and myself, because orgasm, the moment when my sense of identity and coherence is at its highest, was something I was to experience only two years later" (111, TM). What separates the writer from her childhood self is an experience of sexuality she could only guess at as a maturing girl. If the self born out of extreme sexual pleasure—orgasm—is the source of permanent identity, sexuality seems to dislodge class as a defining, foundational knowledge.

Here follows the connection Ernaux implicitly makes between the scene in the cellar and the orgasm to come. What separates Ernaux the writer from "la petite D." is another intense experience that shatters categories: sexual bliss. Seen this way, Ernaux places the burgeoning of her own sexuality under the sign of an unconscious logic that exists in but also beyond class. Perhaps there is shame to come—or the refusal of it in sexual experience. In *A Man's Place,* a book also structured by the dynamics of class shame, Ernaux briefly describes her parents' affective relations, saying that her mother was "always ashamed of sex" (26). Her father would make remarks "alluding to sexual matters" (27) and hum tunes like "Parlez-moi d'amour" to convey his meaning; her mother would sing too, sometimes at the top of her lungs, *Voici mon corps pour vous aimer* (27). In *Shame,* Ernaux is demonstrably proud of her sexual curiosity—her lack of shame; she describes her fascination with the older girls in school, looking for signs of sanitary napkins; these are the ones she seeks out "to learn about sexual matters" (79). She doesn't ask her mother.

Shame closes, as Ernaux's work often does, on this always difficult question of what belongs to the past, what to the present; closes on the work that memory does keeping the world of childhood alive, work done always from another scene, from a geography removed from the scenes of childhood. But writers rarely resist the lure of the past.

Let me mention just briefly another piece of the family memoir that Ernaux published in 1997, *Je ne suis pas sortie de ma nuit* (I remain in darkness). This short work is a series of diary entries written during her mother's illness and disintegration, the subject of the 1988 memoir *A Woman's Story.* In the preface to the diary pages, Ernaux explains that she did not reread these pages during the time she was writing the memoir. She thought she would never publish the diary entries, wanting perhaps to leave the more distanced account of the later work as her final word on her mother's story, but then decides—at the time of publishing *Shame*— that the integrity and coherence of a work should be deliberately threatened ("mises en danger" [12])—whenever possible. Publishing what was not meant to meet the public eye is a way of courting that danger.[6]

In yet another publishing venue of this same literary season, in the 1996 winter number of Philippe Sollers's journal *L'Infini,* Ernaux published an autobiographical piece called "Fragments autour de Philippe V." (Philippe V. is also the dedicatee of *Shame.*) The frankly erotic character of the fragments, which describe Ernaux's first sexual encounter with a young man, a student, did not come as a complete surprise to Ernaux's readers, in particular to those of an earlier novel, *Passion simple* (Simple passion), a narrative that recounts the story of a French woman's passionate affair with a married man, "A.," who lives somewhere in Eastern Europe and that begins with the description of an X-rated movie. It's a porn flick that turned up on television one evening about the encounter between a man and a woman (represented by their genitalia) of which the crowning moment classically is the money shot, the sight of ejaculation that proves the sex is "real." The woman writes in the aftermath of the affair, in the first person. After providing the basic details of the movie shots, the narrator meditates on the surprising fact that "it's only now that it has become possible to see the genitals of two sexes join together, and sperm—something that one couldn't watch without almost dying, now as easy to witness as a handshake" (12). For Ernaux this spectacle has its importance for writing. "It seems to me," she concludes, "that writing should aim at this, the impression provoked by the scene of the sexual act, the anguish and stupefaction, a suspension of moral judgment" (12). (You may hear in these lines the elements of a connection to the representation of the second violent scene in *Shame*—in particular the sense of "stupefaction" produced by the sight of the private suddenly made public: the soiled traces of the mother's body and fluids. But in *Shame,* moral judgment is not suspended; the shock translates immediately into locatable class terms.) What's important here in *Passion simple* is the link established between the effects that writing can produce and the effects of witnessing a sexual act. Or more precisely, the desire for writing to enact a form of suspension: that in the time of reading you enter the scene. You see the sperm, you see the arm raised in violence. You catch your breath, but perhaps you don't suspend judgment.

"Fragments" narrates the early stages of another sexual passion. What's crucial here is the inaugural moment when Ernaux acts on her desire, makes the first move—or rather the first move that interrupts polite conversation, the physical act that sparks the explosion of sexual passion. The woman gets up and passes her hand through the young man's hair. It's a deliberate gesture. The next day (this text is largely though not entirely elliptical) Ernaux reviews the scenes of the previous night and reflects upon the importance of her gesture, of having started something: "It occurred to me that it was of the same nature as the act of writing the opening sentence of a book. For a woman, the freedom to write without shame is connected to that of being the first to touch a man's body with desire."[7] What would it mean for a woman to write freely? Without shame. (This desire for a kind of freedom also drives the writing of the narrative *Shame*, in which the repressed scene between the father and the mother is brought out of the shadow and into the domain of published words.) In the epigraph to *Passion simple* Ernaux asks, as did Sade, what is the relation between sex and writing? But, more specifically, what is this relation for a woman who wishes to express her desire for a man?

In a series of short paragraphs that come to embody that relation, Ernaux describes an experiment in which the couple makes love on a sheet of drawing paper to see what kind of painting would emerge from the mixture of his sperm and her menstrual blood. It was his idea; the two are pleased with the result. The man frames the first "drawing" and hangs it in his room. Over the next few months, they repeat the performance, which gave them the impression that sexual pleasure could have a kind of permanence, that "the orgasm was not the end of everything, that a trace of it would remain—we wrote the date and the time on the paper— something similar to a work of art." The fragments conclude with a statement that is also a poetics: "Writing and making love. I feel there is an essential link between the two. I can't explain it, I can only record those moments when this appears most clearly to me" (178). The paper written by the body, as Barthes might say, paper bodies—but also fleshy bodies that emit fluids, that leave indelible traces, like stains on the nightgown, or on the sheets. On sheets of paper, the writing of Ernaux's poetics bodies forth like a reenactment of the moment in which a sexual passion demands and requires expression. This writing produces the trace of pleasure, pleasure's document, the bodily signature, acts of presence marked in historical time: like the summer of 1952, or that moment in 1954 when Annie discovered orgasm.

In 1997, Philippe V. signs his name—Philippe Vilain—to a novel that tells the story whose beginning Ernaux evoked briefly in print in "Fragments." Published in Philippe Sollers's series called L'Infini, which is housed at Gallimard (Ernaux's publisher), *L'étreinte* (The embrace) is an "autofiction" that recounts the passion of a young man who has an affair with a woman, he does not fail to note, old enough to be his mother, a well-known writer named by her initials, A.E. The affair ends badly when the young man, a student, becomes insanely jealous of the lover, "A.," with whom Ernaux lived an intense affair revealed in *Passion simple*. Vilain's novel was well reviewed in *Le Monde* and excoriated in *Le Nouvel Observateur*.

In the novel, the details of the seduction mesh with those in "Fragments." The pronouns change, of course, and mark the difference in perspective that an encounter between a man and a woman—or any two people entering a relationship—necessarily entails. But there's an important difference in the young writer's point of departure. Part of his frame for that evening is Ernaux's first novel, *Les Armoires vides* (Cleaned out); reading that book brings Phillipe V. to make the move that in turn leads toward the sexual connection that now hangs between the two actors. He has read her novels; she has read his letters. He perceives, he writes in an early letter, in the heroine's difficulties with her parents, and the shame she sometimes felt about them, a deep connection to his own life. This identification is precisely the other side of the projected disgust of readers whose gaze she will not want to endure.

What ties these three texts together is the entwining of writing and danger, of a danger in turn bound to the exposure of uncontainable bodily acts and secretions. As you tell the secrets of others, and violate family codes, you separate yourself from their power over you, even as you return to them in memory. In French, as in English, there is a saying about what should remain private, in the family: "Il faut laver son linge sale en famille." In English we are exhorted not to wash our dirty laundry in public. The outed nightgown (part of the various meanings of "linge") is precisely the kind of dirty laundry meant to remain hidden from view, meant to remain indoors, protected by a bathrobe. Like many family memoirists, Ernaux knows this and yet daringly resists the maxim. It's as though you have to get your dirty little secrets out, out of your system and onto the page, into the public space, in order to integrate the past into present writing.

In autobiography, the acts—performed and witnessed—that might seem to beg not to be revealed are the very ones that produce writing. Thus the private, silent images of the scene in the basement are transformed into a shareable narrative when finally, with the logic of deferral always at the heart of trauma, they are put into words for others; secret knowledge becomes public shame, and shame becomes *Shame*. Ernaux's memoir project, in its deceptively simple language, gives voice to the scenes that never cease to haunt us, readers attracted in this fin de siècle, to the abyss of memory, the deep pool of reflection in which we furtively look to find our darker selves. "'I' shames the reader," Ernaux maintains in *Exteriors* (17). We might conclude that we enjoy being shamed.

What I've called memory stains are permanent traces of what we might hopelessly wish to forget: the screens of the primal scene, the abject forms of the maternal body, but also what we wish to preserve: the erotic performance of fluids (in a weird echo of maternal excretions) traced *in the place of words* on a sheet of paper. Publishing "Fragments" rescues the bodily acts that might otherwise vanish unless preserved on a page. Consigning to paper the scenes that threatened to obliterate you is to try as an adult to repair the irreparable in a child's past.

Can an auto/biographical writer go too far to get there? Rousseau didn't think so.

NOTES

An earlier version of this essay appeared in *a/b: Auto/Biography Studies* 14.1 (Summer 1999): 38–50. Reprinted by permission of the editors of *a/b: Auto/Biography Studies*.

1. In my quotations I will refer to Tanya Leslie's translation, which I will occasionally modify, indicating this as TM.

2. On this issue of reader response, I refer the reader to Lyn Thomas's illuminating study, *Annie Ernaux: An Introduction to the Writer and Her Audience.* Her chapters 4 and 7 are particularly relevant to this essay.

3. Ernaux's description of how this experience functioned for her, how it has nothing in common with the form other memories take, how it caused bodily fear, and so on, corresponds exactly to the discourse of scientists like Bessel van der Kolk. Ernaux: "That day is like an icon immured within me all these years" (26). Ruth Leys, who takes a dim view of van der Kolk's scientific evidence, challenges the "claim that trauma . . . leaves its mark on the brain in the form of a literal, 'eidetic,' or iconic 'imprint.' . . . Permanently 'etched' or 'engraved' in a way that is theorized as standing outside all ordinary cognition, traumatic memory on this hypothesis returns not in the form of recollected representations . . . but of literal icons and sensations" (*Trauma* 250). Leys's position notwithstanding, the similarity between Ernaux's language and that of psychiatric research is striking in the extreme. But perhaps the literary text mediates between the two theoretical positions. Leys rejects "the entire theory of trauma proposed by van der Kolk and Caruth as the failure of representation" (253); whereas *Shame* as a memory quest in words ultimately succeeds in transforming the icon into narrative, thus divesting it of its sacred status. For a more positive view of the relations between narratives of subjectivity, memory formation, and neurobiology, see Paul John Eakin's *How Our Lives Become Stories,* especially chapter 1, "Registers of Self."

4. On the complexity of the debates around the reading of photographs and reference, see Jay Prosser's and Marianne Hirsch's essays in this volume.

5. On the relation of the everyday to the extreme in a collective experience, see Michael Rothberg's essay in this volume.

6. The translations of *Je ne suis pas sortie de ma nuit* and *Passion simple* are my own; pages refer to French edition.

7. Lyn Thomas has translated "Fragments" and published the text as an appendix to her book *Annie Ernaux.* I quote from her translation.

WORKS CITED

Améry, Jean. "Torture." *At the Mind's Limits.* Trans. Sidney Rosenfeld and Stella P. Rosenfeld. New York: Schocken, 1986.

Eakin, John. *How Our Lives Become Stories: Making Selves.* Ithaca: Cornell University Press, 1999.

Ernaux, Annie. *Exteriors.* Trans. Tanya Leslie. New York: Seven Stories, 1996.

——. "Fragments." *L'infini* (Winter 1996): 25–26.

——. *I Remain in Darkness.* Trans. Tanya Leslie. New York: Seven Stories, 1999.

——. *Je ne suis pas sortie de ma nuit.* Paris: Gallimard, 1997.

——. *La honte.* Paris: Gallimard, 1997.

——. *La Place.* Paris: Gallimard, 1974.

——. *Le Journal du dehors.* Paris: Gallimard, 1993.

——. *Les Armoires vides.* Paris: Gallimard, 1974.

——. *A Man's Place.* Trans. Tanya Leslie. New York: Seven Stories, 1996.

——. *Passion simple.* Paris: Gallimard, 1992.

——. *Simple Passion.* Trans. Tanya Leslie. New York: Seven Stories, 1993.

——. *Une femme.* Paris: Gallimard, 1988.

——. *A Woman's Story.* Trans. Tanya Leslie. New York: Seven Stories, 1990.

Kuhn, Annette. *Family Secrets: Acts of Memory and Imagination.* London: Verso, 1995.

Lejeune, Philippe. *On Autobiography.* Ed. Paul John Eakin. Trans. Katherine Leary. Minneapolis: University of Minnesota Press, 1989.

Leys, Ruth. *Trauma: A Genealogy.* Chicago: University of Chicago Press, 2000.

Thomas, Lyn. *Annie Ernaux: An Introduction to the Writer and Her Audience.* Oxford: Berg, 1999

Vilain, Philippe. *L'étreinte.* Paris: Gallimard, 1997.

ELEVEN

After Lot's Daughters: Kathryn Harrison and the Making of Memory

Laura Frost

> The subject of incest belongs to the literature of extremity. . . . The language and genres for women's incest stories exist. What is lacking is critical interpretation and acceptance as literature, without questions about its truthfulness or the authors' autobiographical intentions.
>
> —Karen Jacobsen McLennan, *Nature's Ban*

Kathryn Harrison's memoir *The Kiss* appeared in 1997, at the peak of a publishing trend that has been called alternatively "the memoir craze" and "the memoir plague." *The Kiss* followed, and in some ways was the culmination of, memoirs of extremity such as Susanna Kaysen's *Girl, Interrupted,* Michael Ryan's *Secret Life,* and James Ellroy's *My Dark Places.* But Harrison's subject matter—the author's four-year affair with her father, beginning when she was twenty—topped them all. Even those reviewers who praised Harrison's writing were not entirely comfortable with her decision to publish such a book.[1] Negative reviewers vented their contempt for how Harrison lacked the moral fiber to resist her father, and yet now had the gall to publish an account of the affair. The coy titles of the reviews—"Daddy's Girl Cashes In," "Sex with Daddy," "Pants on Fire!"— demonstrate the moral valence coloring most of the criticism as well as the difficulty in discussing adult father-daughter incest in any terms other than puns, parody, or indictment. More than one reviewer enlisted a psychoanalyst to speculate about Harrison's unstated motivations for writing such an appalling book. And in April of 1997, a reporter for the *New York Observer* located Harrison's father and solicited his side of the story.[2]

These attempts to ferret out an extra-textual truth indicated a suspicion that Harrison was suffering from false memory syndrome or was, more damningly, an unreliable narrator. Clearly, something important was driving these responses. As Leigh Gilmore remarks, "When readers of autobiography become detectives or confessors, when they seek to verify the facts of an autobiography, when they are dubious of an eyewitness account, yet look to the eyewitness for truth, they indicate the extent of the confession's power" (110). Responses to *The Kiss* were most often put in terms of "truth" or "deception." Underlying the prurience of the "did she or didn't she?" query is a much more fundamental concern about agency and literary genre. In *The Kiss*, Harrison both blames her parents and admits her participation: she presents herself as a victim but also seems to reverse that position by publishing her story as a self-authorized memoir, the genre that most obviously raises questions of referentiality and authorial presence. Indeed, Harrison herself vigorously promoted *The Kiss*, making numerous appearances on television (*Charlie Rose, Dateline NBC*, etc.) and granting many print interviews.

Although critics were outraged at Harrison's violation of familial boundaries, this was further exacerbated by a largely unrecognized second violation of literary genre boundaries. The history of *The Kiss* shows how readerly pleasure is contingent upon an assurance of proper genre conventions. Harrison disrupts this traditional textual relationship in order to shape her reader's response to a transgressive sexual relationship. I will examine Harrison's deployment of various generic conventions—autobiography, memoir, and fiction—in order to tell her story. My interest here is not in putting Harrison "on the couch," so to speak, or in reading her extreme experience through a purely psychoanalytical model. Rather, I wish to examine both the internal logic of Harrison's narrative and its critical reception, which was profoundly determined by expectations about gender, genre, agency, and existing paradigms of extremity. I will try throughout this piece to maintain a distinction between Harrison the writer and the self-named narrators of Harrison's fiction and journalism, even as Harrison (the writer) conflates the two.

THE DAUGHTER'S SEDUCTION

Before exploring how Harrison's story is shaped by literary genre, it is important to understand the narrative precedents for this story of parent/ child incest. The first is the tale of Oedipus,[3] and the second is a more generalized story of a child victim and an adult perpetrator. Each involves a radically different configuration of agency, consent, and knowledge, and each exerts an influence over the generic properties and the reception of *The Kiss*.

The original conditions for the Oedipus story are farfetched indeed. In Sophocles' drama, Oedipus is desperate to avoid the prophecy that he will kill his father and marry his mother, and his hubris in thinking that he can control his fate leads to disaster. The essential tragedy of this Ur–incest narrative is its hero's ignorance of his lineage; the great *peripeteia* (reversal) on which the story turns is one of horrible *anagnorisis* (recognition) (Aristotle). Sophocles' Oedipus drama involves two consenting adults who are caught up in a force beyond them (Fate). That they do not know the nature of their relationship would seem to render them less culpable. However, once the truth outs, they are punished as severely as if they had entered into the situation knowingly. Freud transforms Sophocles' story of Oedipus into one of fulfilled (and universal) socially transgressive desire; in Sophocles, Oedipus is horrified by his inadvertent incest and, most crucially, recognizes and accepts responsibility for it. For Freud, agency is involved in the incest itself, and for Sophocles, Oedipus exerts agency only in recognizing and punishing himself for his terrible predicament after the fact. These two ways of reading the Oedipus story illustrate the slippages in knowledge and agency that also appear in *The Kiss*.

The more common incest paradigm involves an adult predator and a child innocent. In *Nature's Ban,* an anthology of women's incest literature, thirty out of the forty-one selections are about father-daughter incest, and each is about a young victim and an abusive father. Where there is ignorance in Oedipus, there is knowledge in these stories; where there is consent in Oedipus, here there is force. In every case, "incest means the expropriation of a child's body through transgression of the parental role" (McLennan 10). *Oedipus Ubiquitous,* a collection of world folk incest tales, finds a similar pattern: "Virtually all of our . . . tales depict father as the lustful one who rapes daughter or tricks her into incest against her will" (Johnson and Price-Williams 59–61). Otto Rank also notes "the daughter's purely passive role" in father-daughter incest narratives (300).

There are a few narrative precedents for a story where the daughter is an adult and initiates or willingly participates in the seduction. One is the story of Lot's daughters (Genesis 19:31–36), who live with their father in an isolated cave after their mother has died. Wanting to "keep the family alive through the father," Lot's daughters befuddle his mind with wine and seduce him. This incest is sanctioned by reproductive necessity; because it lacks consequences, this story is not a socially recognized narrative paradigm for incest. Among the tales of father-daughter incest in *Oedipus Ubiquitous,* only one features a daughter who deliberately commits incest with her father: Myrrha. Myrrha tricks her father, Cinyras, into sleeping with her. When he discovers it, he kills her. Dante places "the indecent Myrrha, she who loved / her father past the limits of just love," deep in his *Inferno. For Ovid, Myrrha's story is so horrifying that he cautions his audience that it might be better to "suppose that it never happened" (Metamorphoses* 233): a warning that is resonant with the criticism of *The Kiss.*

In the cases of both Lot's daughters and Myrrha, the daughter's seduction of the father has to be covert. While other incest configurations—mother-son, sibling—permit consensual agency, father-daughter incest does not; when the daughter displays transgressive sexual desire, the prohibitive father appears. If this sounds like certain dialogues within feminist theory (Gallop, for example, on "the daughter's seduction"), it still more strongly points out the difference between the theoretical and the literal. The Myrrha tale is a striking example of how, when grounded in a more literal (albeit fictional) set of referents, liberatory theoretical discourse loses much of its persuasive power. Seducing the father in order to wrest away or compromise his power appealingly combines female agency and desire in the forging of feminized power. In practice, as in Harrison's story, this theory is not quite so attractive.

Punishment is a crucial element of incest paradigms. Freud writes in *Interpretation of Dreams* that the legend of Oedipus "must include horror and self-punishment" (297–98). Plato proposes that playwrights should depict incest perpetrators as killing themselves (*Laws*). If Harrison's memoir prompted critics to dole out punishment, it was because in her version of a tale of ancient proportions things seemed to have worked out fine for the "incestress" herself. The author seemed to be feigning a victim status in order to capitalize on a publishing trend that was, in turn, presented as the moral high road of expiation. Harrison does try to have it both ways insofar as she attempts to assimilate her narrative to both of the dominant paradigms for incest, when it is in fact closer, in terms of agency and knowledge, to a repressed Myrrha story. Harrison's narrator acknowledges her initial attraction to her father, although this is superseded by a rhetoric of repulsion and resistance, and realizes that the affair satisfies a number of emotional needs for her.

The Kiss mediates between the Oedipus story (two ignorant but consenting adults) and the child/adult incest story (in which there is knowledge but no legitimate consent). Although Harrison's memoir restages the estrangement of Sophocles' drama (her narrator did not know her father growing up), there is no blindness to the nature of the bond, and Freud's idea of a primary incestuous attraction drives their relationship. The father is thrilled to see himself in his beautiful adult daughter, and the daughter is also narcissistically entranced with her father. Harrison's narrator's acceptance of her own complicity never quite measures up precisely because of basic discrepancies about agency and knowledge. Instead of gouging out her eyes and sending herself into exile, the proper etiquette for incest confession, Harrison chose to publish a story in which she casts her narrator more as a victim than as a desiring agent.

TWICE TOLD TALES

The incest taboo is conceived as universal, but incest stories are disturbingly common. Nevertheless, The Kiss appears to be that rare commodity: an original story. The configuration of the story (two consenting and knowing adults) is as unusual as its narrative perspective. For all its apparent singularity, when The Kiss appeared, it did not take long for critics to point out that the story had already been told by Harrison herself six years earlier in her widely praised debut novel, Thicker Than Water. That Harrison rewrote and in some cases repeated verbatim scenes from her novel, recasting them in an autobiographical light, is itself not grounds for condemnation. Many other writers have "double published" (Lessing, Roth, and Duras, for example). In Harrison's case, however, the act was seized upon as evidence of profiteering. The difference between the receptions of Harrison's novel and memoir demonstrates how most nonacademic audiences hold their authors to Lejeune's autobiographical pact and its assurance that the narrative "I" is the author. Nearly identical passages in Harrison's two texts were interpreted in radically different ways based on whether they were understood as fiction or as autobiography. In moving from fiction to memoir, Harrison moved to a genre for which audience sympathy is crucial. In The Kiss, Harrison writes, "My life is that of a fugitive. I'm always in an airline terminal, trudging after him over expanses of stained carpet and dull linoleum" (24). But "the fugitive" also admits her sexual power over her father, and in 1997 Harrison, a camera-ready author, seemed too much in control of her story. Telling this story of adult incest in a fictional guise was almost acceptable; telling and actively promoting it as an autobiography was taboo.

Both *The Kiss* and *Thicker Than Water* are told retrospectively by a female narrator: Isabel in the novel and Kathy in the memoir. Isabel and Kathy share a common history, with parents who were together for no more than two years and were married for less than one year. The narcissistic mother in both texts is obsessed with her ex-husband, a factor contributing to her emotional neglect of her daughter. The mother moves out of the house and leaves her young daughter to live with grandparents: a double abandonment. In both narratives, the narrator sees her father (a small-time politician in *Thicker;* a minister in *The Kiss*) a few times when she is a child and meets him again when she is twenty years old in *The Kiss,* and eighteen in *Thicker.* The father is amazed that he has such a beautiful daughter and lavishes her with attention. The narrator in both stories is overwhelmed to find her father wanting to know every detail about her, including what kind of toothpaste she uses. When she drops him off at the airport at the end of a visit, he kisses her, but it is the kiss of a lover, not a father. The kiss has a narcotic effect. Shocked by its inappropriateness but fascinated by its power—the narrator now possesses the object of her mother's affection—she begins an affair with her father that lasts until the day her mother is buried.

Both the memoir and the novel are told in a dazed, trance-like voice that the narrator of *The Kiss* identifies as post-traumatic. In fragmented, nonlinear narratives, the distant, self-involved mother and selfish, vindictive father are posited as the motivation for the narrator's participation in the affair. The most obvious difference between the two narratives is that the novel is much more elaborate, both in plot and in prose style. Almost all episodes in *The Kiss* can be found in the novel, and *Thicker* fleshes out all the events. The narrator of *The Kiss* appears more analytical and "therapized" than the narrator of the novel. In the first chapter of *Thicker Than Water,* Isabel calls her father "my tormentor, my Svengali, my ruin" (10), presenting herself as a passive victim. *The Kiss* begins with a different insight: "We meet at airports. We meet in cities where we've never been before. We meet where no one will recognize us. . . . One of us flies, the other brings a car, and in it we set out for some destination" (3).

The repeated pronoun "we" indicates collusion between the narrator and her father, a *folie à deux*. However, the father quickly becomes the initiator of the monstrous events. The most convincing and lucid interpretation of the events actually appears in the novel:

> Did it happen . . . because I enjoyed the power I had over my father? I had that power possessed by the sexually desirable, control over those who were not wanted for their bodies, those whose bodies were not wanted. My father used to weep sometimes when I said no.
>
> I know who he was. This is a story about desperate women and their unhappy destructiveness. My father was a man manipulated by women. His life was a long struggle to effect a shift in power, to disentangle himself from their terrible meddling. . . . [H]e needed to hurt my mother and so did I. (*Thicker* 193–95)

When the story is told the second time, in memoir form, it is done with apparently diminished understanding. Harrison's narrators are powerful storytellers, but as analytical presences, they are as puzzling to themselves as to their audience.

One scene stands out in particular in both texts and demonstrates how Harrison reworks her material. In *The Kiss,* when the narrator is eleven, her grandmother's Persian cat has a litter of kittens. The narrator impatiently waits for them to open their eyes. Finally, she can wait no longer:

> I laid one [kitten] in my lap and, with one thumb on the upper lid, the other on the lower, I carefully pulled its eyes open, separating one delicate membrane of flesh from the other. My heart was pounding and I was sweating with fear, but I accomplished the violation gently. The kitten made no sound, it did not struggle. What I did hadn't seemed to cause it any pain. . . .
>
> Within a day [the kittens'] eyes were swollen shut, tightly resealed under lids that showed red beneath the fine white fur. I picked one up and tried to brush away the yellow crust that had formed in the corner of one of its eyes. A worm of pus shot out, and, shocked, I dropped the kitten. (90)

The entire anecdote is told in fifteen sparse paragraphs. The same episode expands to five pages in *Thicker Than Water,* recounted in detail and including literary flourishes. The kittens "smelled sweet like butter, uncorrupted" (81), and whenever Isabel handles them, "The mother watched me anxiously," attending to her babies in a way Isabel's mother never does. The tearing open of the kittens' eyes is one sentence in *The Kiss;* in the novel, it is a paragraph long, replete with similes and metaphors. The narrator "applied pressure with the sides of each thumb, that place against which the boys next door would stretch a blade of grass to make a whistle"; the tearing of the membrane under the eye was done "neatly, like that of a perforated coupon carefully saved" (82). Although the two kitten scenes are nearly identical thematically, the criticism of the novel and memoir strikingly diverged. Michiko Kakutani breezes over the episode in her review of *Thicker Than Water:* "As a young girl, [Isabel] remembers helping her grandmother paste Blue Chip stamps in redemption books and watching their Persian cat's kittens grow up." Several reviews of *The Kiss* singled out the episode as "the single most emetic passage in all the book" (Eberstadt).

In both narratives, the kitten scene is a failed temptation and a failure to speak out. Had the narrator told her grandmother, the kittens might have been treated by a veterinarian; instead, their tear ducts are scarred. The episode resonates symbolically with the incest story in terms of guilt and violation, but there are significant differences. The kitten scene involves a complicated assignation of agency and generates a series of narrative possibilities that gestures to both the child/adult incest paradigm and the Oedipus paradigm (and to Sophocles' metaphors of sight: Oedipus is figuratively blind to his situation and responds to the revelation by blinding himself). Harrison's narrator can be read as both a victim and a violator: she acts out a violence upon the kittens that parallels her father's upon her. But the incest in *The Kiss* is between two adults: the narrator had already been sexually initiated, and her eyes were figuratively open. The kitten scene serves to alter this fact by imposing a retrospective trauma of premature awakening on the story. In this, it evokes the child/adult incest paradigm but is not fully assimilable to that polarized model. Harrison's narrator knows that what she did to the kittens was wrong and feels guilt; by positioning herself in the same place as her father, she comes close to admitting participation and complicity in the affair.[4]

"TOO TRUE FOR ITS OWN GOOD"

Harrison's difficulty in assimilating her story into either of the two dominant narrative paradigms for incest is reflected in her generic recasting of her story as a memoir. A number of critics declared that *The Kiss* was too much like fiction, either questionable in its veracity or too "self-consciously writerly" (Wolcott 34) or "unremittingly novelistic" (*Publishers*

Weekly), implying the same charge of fabrication. Mary Eberstadt insists that Harrison is an unreliable narrator ("no one has yet managed to explain . . . why we should believe that this story is true") (31), an accusation that uncannily resonates with the father's cruel prediction in *Thicker* that no one will ever believe the narrator (237). Eberstadt grounds this charge on a generic argument: "However coherent this tale may appear as fiction, it fails to convince as non-fiction on several counts" (31). The assumption here is that the appropriate prose style for writing about trauma, or other extreme experiences that demand a believable author, is one that is free of contrived literary devices. In her discussion of feminist confessions, Rita Felski observes that "the more obviously 'literary' the text—the most clearly it signals its fictional status through such textual features as irony, parody, and self-reflexivity, extended use of symbolic and 'poetic' language, or elaborated narrative structures—the less likely the reader is to respond to the text as the authentic self-expression of an authorial subject" (86). This is an argument that has been made about Holocaust testimonies and their struggle to establish authenticity in the face of unimaginably horrifying experiences that strain the powers of language.[5] In narratives of extremity, a stripped-down prose is demanded as proof of the author's sincerity, while narrative devices such as metaphor, which gesture away from the event at hand in order to evoke another frame of reference, are thought to call the story into question.

This conflict between the literary and the "factual" was exacerbated by Harrison's numerous public discussions of *The Kiss* as an accurate account of her life. Of course, Harrison calls her book a "memoir," not an autobiography. Memoir has generally been distinguished from autobiography on the grounds of its more collective, relational subject and its focus on a wider cast of characters. More recently, the term "memoir" has been used to describe texts that combine autobiography with more fantastic elements. As Diane Johnson notes, the memoir, as opposed to autobiography, is "a form which can neither be dismissed as fiction nor quarreled with as fact" (qtd. in Quinby, in Smith and Watson 298). These distinctions were collapsed in the reviews of *The Kiss* and by Harrison herself.

The first words of *Thicker Than Water* are "In truth," and many critics suspected that Harrison's book was an autobiography. Michiko Kakutani described it as "a story that possesses the harrowing immediacy—and visceral impact—of a memoir. Indeed, there is almost no authorial distance between Isabel and her creator, almost no indication that this is a novel we're reading" (C20). Scott Spencer speculated that he might have been "reading a harrowing, fully imagined work of nonfiction."

> Part of the power of the "I" in a novel is its power to convince us that the events described here have really occurred, quite as we are reading about them. Yet in Ms. Harrison's novel, this power is employed in such a way that the effect is as confusing as it is captivating.
>
> Perhaps if *Thicker Than Water* had more structural rigor, its fictional qualities would be more readily apparent and its pleasures would be unalloyed by morbid intrusions. . . . [A]re we witnessing the beginning of a brilliant career or a bleeding soul's attempt to bind itself in a tourniquet of words? A critical question presents itself: can a novel ring too true for its own good? (14)

Spencer asserts that the novelistic "I" should be believable, but only within an obviously fictional world. Novelistic pleasure is based on the assurance that the narrative "I" is not the "I" composing the novel. This is a corollary to the autobiographical pact, by which the reader's pleasure is secured and facilitated by a belief that the "I" is the author. Just as there is an objection to a memoir thought to be too literary and therefore imaginative, there is an equal discomfort with a novel that is not sufficiently fictional. The second-guessing about the author herself was aroused by generic indeterminacy and foreshadowed the debate about *The Kiss*. In both *Thicker Than Water* and *The Kiss*, Harrison encourages epistemological uncertainty by refusing to follow the rules of genre: thus denying the "readerly pleasures" of fiction and autobiography, respectively.

Many critics went further and argued that the story of *The Kiss* never should have been told at all. James Wolcott proclaimed that, "The truth is that some secrets have a healthy purpose. . . . For a writer, secrets are more than material; they are intellectual capital that accrues power and interest by being nursed in solitude" (35). Picking up on the economic analogy, Michael Shnayerson warns that: "Memoir[ists] who started as novelists—like Harrison—may find it harder than they realize to return to fiction with their psychic closets emptied, the 'capital' of experience spent" (61). In fact, Harrison neither "spends" all of her secrets nor exactly confesses, and this is precisely the source of the critical hostility. The logic goes like this. An incest story needs a victim—an innocent party (a young child) or an ignorant party (Sophocles' Oedipus)—and *The Kiss* had neither. The story of an affair between an adult daughter and her father had better be put in the guise of fiction. If that story is an autobiography, it had better be a confession. And the confession had better be in the proper form, with the conventional admission of guilt, catalogue of sins, and request for forgiveness. But Harrison does not answer these generic demands any more than she does those of fiction or memoir.

CONFESSION AND EVASION

The Catholic formula for confession is "Forgive me, Father, for I have sinned," followed by a reiteration of those transgressions. Given that Harrison's "father confessor" is himself blamed for the sin, and that the father in *The Kiss* is a minister, we should not be surprised that her narrator's confession is skewed. Still, Harrison grants confession a central place in all of her texts. For example, in Harrison's historical novel *Poison,* a woman has an affair with a Catholic priest during the time of the Spanish Inquisition (again, the "Father confessor" is deeply implicated in the "sin"). Most of the confessions, Harrison suggests, were fabricated to save the confessant's life. The confessions were lies—fictions. A similar paradox shapes Harrison's 1994 essay for *Harper's,* "Seeking Rapture," which describes her interest in confession and martyrdom. She compares caring for her mother, who is dying of breast cancer, to the story of Saint Catherine of Siena, who drank the pus of an older nun and "believed earthly suffering was the only way to correct the intrinsic baseness of mankind." Harrison manages both to flagellate herself for spoiling her mother's "attempts to make a separate life for herself—a life that did not seem possible to her unless motherhood were left behind" and to accuse her mother at the same time, demonstrating how confession comfortably accommodates both accusation and guilt. The language of martyrdom throughout *Thicker Than Water* and *The Kiss* similarly masks agency and the sadistic impulses that operate under the masochistic rhetoric.[6]

In an interview with Mary Gordon shortly after *The Kiss* appeared, Harrison remarks, "I believe in the form of confession. For long in my life—particularly with my mother, who never really wanted a child—I was an expert at shape-shifting, at being the person who the other person wanted. The pleasing one. . . . The challenge for me was to strip all that away. Good memoir writing is a kind of self-vivisection" (144). Harrison follows through on this declaration in *The Kiss* by not following the conventions of genre or confession, but the "self-vivisection" is not fully evident. Harrison leaves significant gaps in her story, most of which concern her narrator's agency. While the narrator admits the affair, this is surpassed by the greater accusations against her neglectful parents. Perhaps more important, the catalogue of sins that comprises the act of confession does not appear either.

Confession, in both Catholicism and Protestantism, pays particular attention to, and in turn shapes our understanding of experiences of sexuality. Secular literary confession does so as well, and for this reason, *The Kiss* was particularly susceptible to a "confessional" reading. Harrison implies the transgression, but the act that makes the relationship between the narrator and her father incest per se, the sex itself, is elided. In *Thicker Than Water,* Isabel recalls that her father used to bang her head against the floor when he "raped" her (246). The sex is never termed a rape in *The Kiss.* Briefly, and only in retrospect, the narrator contrasts the misery of sex in her father's church with the "heat" and "passion" that once characterized their contact (166). The only explicit sexual scene in *The Kiss* is a single sentence: "he opens my legs and puts his tongue between them" (128). It is an affectless and perfunctory description of an act that "feels neither good nor bad" (128).

Which brings us back to the kittens. Both *Thicker Than Water* and *The Kiss* present the kitten scene as one of failed confession. "I knew," the narrator of *The Kiss* states, "this was the worst thing I had ever done, too awful to confess" (91). In the novel, Isabel pronounces the kittens a cautionary tale of "the price of a confession withheld" (84), and this characterizes Harrison's memoir as a whole. Leigh Gilmore remarks that "the problem for many confessional subjects is profoundly narrative: How does one confess an experience and subjectivity that are not fully assimilated to the rhetoric of confession?" (164). Just as Harrison's incest story is not assimilable to dominant incest paradigms, it is also intransigent to confession. Without a full confession of the affair, the story is only incestuous by suggestion. Instead of sex scenes, Harrison provides a series of substitutes—a number of profoundly visceral anti-erotic episodes—that attempts to assimilate her narrative to the incest paradigm of child victimization.

A startling and memorable scene that appears in both *Thicker Than Water* and *The Kiss* describes the narrator's mother taking her to the gynecologist to be fitted for a diaphragm. This necessitates that her virgin daughter's hymen be manually broken, which the doctor does with a series of graduated plastic phalli, all under the mother's watchful eyes. This scene reproduces the child/adult incest configuration and the oedipal triangle, with the penetrating doctor standing in for the father, and the victim daughter quietly suffering impalement: another story of premature and forced sexual experience. In the kitten and doctor scenes, Harrison writes in an urgent voice that dwells on the most grisly details. Both episodes solicit a particular affect: revulsion and horror, sensations one might expect and want in a memoir about incest.[7] The expected affect of the absent sex scenes is transferred onto these childhood episodes in which the father is conspicuously absent. The kitten episode suggests a transformed sex scene: the tearing of the membrane of the eye of a cat and the phallic shot of pus. The defloration scene is still more obvious as a sexual analogue. Sex scenes would necessarily raise questions about the narrator's agency and complicity, while the kitten and defloration scenes extinguish any flickers of readerly pleasure and position the narrator as a sexual victim.

To where, then, is the agency and the investment in a four-year affair displaced? Harrison's 1996 *New Yorker* essay, "Tick," suggests an answer. "Tick," a "Personal History," begins with a description of Harrison brushing her daughter Sarah's hair. Out of the blue, Sarah asks her mother, "Did Daddy make a hole in you with his penis?" (32). "No!" Harrison replies (and the Daddy/Daddy confusion is off and running). Then Harrison finds a tick on Sarah's scalp, engorged with blood. Armed with tweezers, hydrogen peroxide, and cotton balls, Harrison yanks at the insect as Sarah struggles. Finally, the tick "comes free," and while Sarah weeps, Harrison writes, "I pursue my own drama" (34). She tortures the tick, beginning with a nutpick and moving on to a manicure set that is "a long-ago present from [her] mother" (34). A description of escalating mutilation and dismemberment with a knife blade follows, but "The tick, motionless, doesn't betray any suffering" (34), just as the kittens in *The Kiss* did not seem to feel any pain. The story circles back to Sarah's question about sex as a puncturing operation, except that in this case Harrison, not "Daddy," is the puncturer, a shifting of agency similar to the kitten scene. Finally, Harrison douses the insect with rum and the drama winds down. "I am waiting for Sarah's blood to drift into the rum, to waft pinkly over the tiny corpse. The reappearance of my daughter's stolen life will qualify as redemption. That's why I have performed this abomination. But . . . I have not drawn blood. . . . All of what the tick drank from my daughter is digested, evidently; Sarah's blood has turned to excrement before I could reclaim it. . . . The tick has won" (35). Harrison's description of mutilating the tick entails a fierce tunnel-vision purview and an intensely clear moment of violence—the same mode of writing in the kitten scenes. These moments center on the narrator's sadistic relationship to a body—

an animal, an insect—and they are evocative of bodily feelings of penetration and tearing. The notion of "redemption" resembles the masochistic martyrdom with which Harrison alludes to sex in *The Kiss*. Sexuality is converted into a story about dismemberment, destruction, and sadism: in this case, the author's sadism. When Harrison does acknowledge sexual agency, it is in an extreme, grotesque form: a girl who tears opens kittens' eyes, a woman who is entranced by the vivisection of a tick. As in the kitten scene, the narrator is both the child victim (the kitten/Sarah) and the sexually aggressive father.

The scenes that displace sex in *The Kiss* either establish the narrator's passivity or mask their agency; they also prevent the reader from perceiving pleasure in or deriving pleasure from the story.[8] *The Kiss* deploys parts of the Freudian reading of Oedipus but represses that story's implications of agency by emphasizing scenes that, like Sophocles' drama, are aimed to produce disgust and ultimately pity for her narrator. The contradiction is that in Sophocles, the audience feels pity because Oedipus accepts responsibility for his actions: he doesn't, for example, blame Jocasta. That many critics of *The Kiss* wondered about the welfare of Harrison's father demonstrates the ambiguity of Harrison's authorial presence.

OEDIPUS, THE TELOS OF ALL TALES

As "Seeking Rapture" indicates, Harrison's masochistic martyrdom carefully exposes her mother's narcissism and coldness. Her narrators are aware that the object of their rage and love is not so much the father as the mother. "Of course," Isabel observes in *Thicker Than Water*, "I could never have hated my mother so much, enough to allow her husband to fuck me, had I not loved her so desperately" (238). The father, the phallic cement of the oedipal triangle, is a pawn in a more urgent reunion—however vicious—with the mother. By this logic, *The Kiss* is a very conservative little tale. There's no Reichian reevaluation of the family, no rebellion against patriarchal figures. The incest story recedes as the story of the bad mother overshadows it. The not-good-enough mother is a more socially acceptable character than the seductive daughter.

And yet.

Harrison's work is a psychoanalytic textbook that brings us perhaps too directly to this daughter's victimization. The many declarations of personal hurt are not always consistent with the events recounted. After pages of explicit cataloguing of how Harrison tortures and mutilates an insect, "The tick has won" simply does not follow. By insisting on the oedipal triangle as the key to her story, Harrison assigns herself the role of the passive daughter and diverts attention away from the libidinally charged story of adult incest. The criticism of *The Kiss* suggested that no one could possibly have Harrison's experience and subsequently be competent or self-aware. Despite her rhetoric of masochism, Harrison speaks from a self-authorized position, which has not been historically available to women until quite recently. In just the past thirty years, there has been a proliferation of women's life writing about both sexual trauma and sexual liberation, and yet female agency and the responsibility that accompanies it is still vexed. In the mid- to late 1990s publishing climate, where nothing seemed to be too extreme to confess, Harrison's memoir makes evident what "going too far" means. Significantly, it is a story that threatens to redefine our understanding of incest and of female agency. *The Kiss* shows the frightening power of emotional deprivation and the desperate measures undertaken in the pursuit of love. An admission of the pleasures derived from such a situation would make of Harrison a Myrrha figure: a woman with perverse desires on which she dared to act. Even after years of feminism, this is a frightening prospect. Like a well-trained penitent, *The Kiss* produces only those "truths" that reinforce the incest taboo, and its most disturbing implications are unspoken. Nevertheless, despite Harrison's narrator's claims to passivity, the silences in *The Kiss* point to the very investments they are designed to conceal. Agency and sexual pleasure are two empowerments for which women have fought hard in the last forty years, but *The Kiss* represents a kind of female agency that no one wants to claim.

NOTES

An expanded version of this essay appeared in *a/b: Auto/Biography Studies* 14.1 (Summer 1999): 51–70. Reprinted by permission of the editors of *a/b: Auto/Biography Studies*.

1. Compare, for example, Mary Gordon's glowing book jacket blurb for *The Kiss* to her ambivalent interview with Harrison in *Harper's Bazaar*. Robert Cole retracted his book jacket blurb for *The Kiss* when he heard that Harrison had children (Begley).
2. The unnamed retired minister neither confirmed nor quite denied Harrison's story. See St. John.
3. Electra is another possible paradigm and is susceptible to the same double readings as Sophocles' and Freud's versions of the Oedipus legend. Although a

Freudian Electra is libidinally driven, a literal reading of the drama suggests that loyalty is her motivation. I focus here on the Oedipus story because Oedipus does commit incest, and this is a closer parallel to Harrison's story.

4. In an interview, Harrison says that *Thicker Than Water* was "inherently dishonest" because it did not indicate the narrator's complicity: "I betrayed my own story" (Bruning).

5. See, for example, James E. Young's *Writing and Rewriting the Holocaust: Narrative and the Consequences of Interpretation* (Bloomington: Indiana University Press, 1988).

6. In *The Kiss,* the narrator lives in her father's home for a period, and they have sex in his church office: "Following his lead in imposing a religious context on the act, I concentrate on mortification of the flesh. I tell myself that if I give myself over to him to be sullied, then by the topsy-turvy Christian logic that exalts the reviled, I'll be made clean" (165).

7. Jeff Giles remarks of *The Kiss,* "What you might want more of, actually, is rage or insight" ("A Father"); the interviewer on *Dateline NBC* demanded of Harrison, "Where is your anger? I'm angry for you!"

8. This raises parallels between the critic/reader and the confessor/analyst (see Leigh Gilmore's chapter on "Policing Truth" in *Autobiographics*). In *Trauma and Recovery,* Judith Herman remarks that the testimony of sexually abused patients may arouse the analyst. Harrison's narrator encourages her critic to assume the position of an analyst, and in this respect, the evasion of sexual scenes in *The Kiss* may be an attempt to forestall voyeurism.

WORKS CITED

Aristotle. *On Poetry and Style.* Trans. G. M. A. Grube. New York: Bobbs-Merrill, 1958.

Begley, Adam. "When a Kiss Ain't Just a Kiss: Robert Coles, Blurbist, Repents." *New York Observer* Apr. 7, 1997: 31.

Bruning, Fred. "How Far Is Too Far?" *Newsweek* May 20, 1997: B04.

Dante. *Inferno.* Trans. Allen Mandelbaum. New York: Bantam Books, 1982.

Eakin, Paul John. "The Referential Aesthetic of Autobiography." *Studies in the Literary Imagination* 23.2 (Fall 1990): 165–76.

Eberstadt, Mary. "Pants on Fire! Who Really Believes Kathryn Harrison's Incest Tale?" *Weekly Standard* May 24, 1997: 31+.

Felski, Rita. "On Confession." Smith and Watson, 83–95.

Freud, Sigmund. *The Interpretation of Dreams.* Trans. James Strachey. New York: Avon, 1965.

Gallop, Jane. *The Daughter's Seduction: Feminism and Psychoanalysis.* Ithaca: Cornell University Press, 1982.

Giles, Jeff. "A Father. A Daughter. A Kiss Wasn't Just a Kiss." *Newsweek* Feb. 17, 1997: 62.

———. "The Father Won't 'Kiss' and Tell." *Newsweek* Apr. 28, 1997: 81.

Gilmore, Leigh. *Autobiographics: A Feminist Theory of Women's Self-Representation.* Ithaca: Cornell University Press, 1994.

Gordon, Mary. "Sex with Daddy." *Harper's Bazaar* Apr. 1997: 136+.

Harrison, Kathryn. *The Kiss.* New York: Random House, 1997.

———. *Poison.* New York: Random House, 1995.

———. "Seeking Rapture." *Harper's* Sept. 1994: 64–72.

———. *Thicker Than Water.* New York: Random House, 1991.

———. "Tick." *New Yorker* July 29, 1996: 32–35.

Herman, Judith Lewis. *Trauma and Recovery.* New York: Basic Books, 1992.

Johnson, Allen, and Douglass Price-Williams. *Oedipus Ubiquitous: The Family Complex in World Folk Literature.* Stanford: Stanford University Press, 1996.

Kakutani, Michiko. "Yearning to Be Normal beneath a 'Normal' Veneer." *New York Times* Apr. 26, 1991: C20.

Lejeune, Philippe. *On Autobiography.* Ed. Paul John Eakin. Trans. Katherine Leary. Minneapolis: University of Minnesota Press, 1989.

McLennan, Karen Jacobsen. *Nature's Ban: Women's Incest Literature.* Boston: Northeastern University Press, 1996.

Ovid. *Metamorphoses.* Trans. Mary M. Innes. London: Penguin Books, 1955.

Publishers Weekly. Unsigned review of *The Kiss.* Feb. 10, 1997: 71.

Rank, Otto. *The Incest Theme in Literature and Legend: Fundamentals of a Psychology of Literary Creation.* Baltimore: Johns Hopkins University Press, 1992.

Shnayerson, Michael. "Women Behaving Badly." *Vanity Fair* Feb. 1997: 54–61.

Smith, Sidonie, and Julia Watson, eds. *De/colonizing the Subject: The Politics of Gender in Women's Autobiography.* Minneapolis: University of Minnesota Press, 1992.

Spencer, Scott. Review of *Thicker Than Water. New York Times,* Apr. 21, 1991: 13–14.

St. John, Warren. "Kathryn Harrison's Dad Responds to Her Memoir." *New York Observer* Apr. 21, 1997: 1+.

Wolcott, James. "Dating Your Dad." *New Republic* Mar. 31, 1997: 32–36.

Yardley, Jonathan. "Daddy's Girl Cashes In: Kathryn Harrison Writes a Shameful Memoir of Incest." *Washington Post* Mar. 5, 1997: D2.

———. "'The Kiss' of Death for Literature?" *Washington Post* Mar. 10, 1997: B2.

———. "Thanks for the Memoirists." *Washington Post* Apr. 14, 1997: D2.

TWELVE

The Aryan Boy

Wayne Koestenbaum

STORY

At some overnight nature retreat, long ago, outside of Berlin, my father woke to discover someone pissing on his head. It was the Aryan boy in the upper bunk. While my father told me this story, I was bathing, under his supervision; a plastic cup floated beside me in the soapy water.

I've often thought of this Aryan boy, circa 1936, pissing on my father's head, and of my position, naked in the tub, while he told me the story—one of the few anecdotes he passed on to me about his childhood in Nazi Germany.

Another story: Hitler paraded through the streets, and my father saluted him because everyone else was saluting. It was the thing to do.

Otherwise I heard little about tyranny.

Who knows if the boy in the story was really Aryan, or if I'm misremembering the story?

CUP

In the bathtub, I pissed in the plastic cup. Pissing in the cup produced a hard-on, but once the penis grew hard, pissflow paradoxically stopped. I liked to use the cup as a ladle, gathering bathwater to rinse shampoo suds out of my hair.

Enjoyable, to place the cup over one's newly emergent penis in the bathtub.

GALICIA

On my mother's side, there were some shadowy relatives—I don't know their names—in Galicia. My mother remembers conversations in the early 1940s, late at night, at the Brooklyn kitchen table. Letters from Galicia. Nothing could be done to save these relations. I guess I'm Galician.

The window of my great-grandfather Wolf's jewelry shop in New York was smashed. Did that hate-filled atmosphere shape his son's character? At my grandfather's death, his unfinished project was a book about the Jew in American literature. "When did you stop being an observant Jew?" I asked him, and he said, "What are you talking about? I never stopped."

THE REPRODUCTION STORY

My older brother had a new book, *The Reproduction Story,* about vagina and penis, secrets of mating, special feelings you develop for members of the opposite sex. I was taking a bath. My mother threw the book into the bathroom, saying "Your brother isn't old enough for this book." She was furious at him for some misdeed, sass, or subversion. He was in the doghouse. "Your brother's not mature enough for this book," she said, meaning, *The bastard's lost his right to learn the reproduction story.* Good. Now the story was my property. Naked in the tub, I read about gonads. I lost track of plot. I pissed into the plastic cup.

MORE ON THE ARYAN BOY

A miracle, that piss stops once you want to come, that "come" and "piss" functions are dialectical, mutually exclusive.

Did my father consider the boy an Aryan? Was that the term? Or did my father simply call him Gentile? I should ask my father about that incident, but our rapport has diminished. The times of bathing, of pissing into the cup after he left the bathroom, are over. Just as well. But I should figure out whether his aunt's middle name was really Sarah or whether that was just the name the Germans put on her visa to signify her race.

MORE ON THE ARYAN BOY PISSING

"How are babies conceived?" I asked my older brother, and he told me, "Daddy pisses in Mommy." Therefore from the beginning of time I knew that such relations were degrading.

MORE ON PISSING

Is urine a home remedy? Two scholars—women—were swimming in the ocean. A jellyfish stung one. So the other pissed on her colleague's sting: a proven antidote.

When you piss in the ocean you are not ejecting fluid; rather, you are accepting fluid's absence. You are deciding that you don't want to hold in those muscles, that your liquids sympathize with the saline surround; you want intimacy with coral, crabs, jellyfish, and wrack. That's probably why the little girl in *The Exorcist* pissed on her parents' fancy rug during their dinner party. She wanted to make a big Satanic statement. She wanted to show exactly what she thought of their Georgetown regime. My next step in life is to identify with the possessed girl in *The Exorcist*.

KEITH WRITES:

"This is how my lover and I met, at a sleaze bar (now closed), getting our fill in the restroom. . . . We both like to give as well as receive golden showers. Meeting others into this 'sport' is becoming impossible. We display our yellow hankies proudly—and sometimes our wet crotches!—only to receive puzzled looks and outright stares. This is in leatherbars! Can you put us in touch with groups, organizations?" (*Honcho,* April 1994)

ORGASM

I was naked in the tub. My father said, "And I woke to discover I was all wet." Or he said, "I wondered where the liquid was coming from." Or he said, "And I looked up and there was the Aryan bully, pissing on my head." Meanwhile I was ensconced in Mr. Bubble.

There is a time in life when one's own penis—if one has a penis—is a negligible article of faith.

This is what passed through my mind as my very first hand-manipulated orgasm approached: "There's no way I'm going to mess up this clean bathtub with my spermy stuff." So I stopped. For weeks afterward I thought I'd irreparably damaged my potential to come, because I'd interrupted that originary burst.

SHE DIDN'T SAY A WORD

My grandfather said, of his mother, "She never once raised her voice." This was a compliment. She never raised her voice to her husband, Wolf, who translated the Bible into Yiddish at night: during the day he was a jeweler with a broken shopwindow. Wayne stands for Wolf; shared W, meager memorial.

MORE ON THE CUP

My fundamentalist friend lay naked on his bathroom throw rug. I said, "I've discovered a neat trick. Look." And I put the bathroom cup over my hard penis. I wanted to teach him secrets of the cup. But he had other plans. He said, "Lie on top of me." My fundamentalist friend wanted me to fuck him. I said, "No way." Then he decided we should stay up past midnight playing World War II strategy games.

Perhaps I misremember the story. I might have wanted to fuck the fundamentalist; he might have said, "No way." Or perhaps no mention of intercourse was made. Perhaps he simply said, "Let me lie on top of you."

In my own fashion I, too, am a fundamentalist. I believe in the fundament and I believe in these fundamentals.

PROSTHETIC MATH

I believed the math teacher's penis was prosthetic because I'd seen it hang loose and inanimate like a stale *bûche de Noël* out of his pants at the urinal.

The squirt named Wasserman who sent a thank-you card to the math teacher: was Wasserman Jewish, too, and did that explain his safari shirt and his friendship with the math teacher with prosthetic penis and recipe for Waldorf salad tucked between algorithmic pages? Even then I thought of Wasserman as Water Man.

SHAKE IT OUT

Shake it out afterward, my father wisely said. Smart man. I'm sure he showed me how to shake it out, but there's always more dribble than science can account for. At what exact moment in sexual arousal is the flow of urine stopped? Do you have to wash your hands after pissing? Rumor has it, urine is hygienic. I suppose humiliation has nothing to do with masculinity, my father and I have nothing to do with masculinity, and shaking the penis out after pissing to make sure there are no leftover dribble drops has nothing to do with masculinity.

TYRANNY

Kobena Mercer wrote that we have plenty of discussions about desire and pleasure but not enough about "pain and hatred as everyday structures of feeling." I agree. To "pain and hatred," I would add "tyranny." Tyranny is an everyday structure of feeling. We do not have enough discussions of tyranny's mundanity; everyone who analyzes tyranny pretends not to be friends with it, but what if finally we narrated our tyrannic urges?

MY FATHER SALUTING HITLER

It was a parade; my father didn't know better. My father, little Jewish boy, saluted Hitler. Someone must have found it cute, someone else must have found it not cute. Up went my father's hand in mimic salute.

ONE PROBLEM WITH THIS DISCOURSE

is that it sounds like a victim's, or like the discourse of someone who considers himself a victim. I must find a way not to sound the victim note. I must find a way to speak as tyrant, not because I want to be a tyrant or become more tyrannical but because there is little about my desire or my death that does not fall under the heading *tyranny*.

CALL MASCULINITY TYRANNY AND SEE WHAT HAPPENS

My mother did the disciplinary work—for example, when she threw *The Reproduction Story* like dog food into the bathroom while I lay in the tub.

I always wondered about the difference between breasts in men and breasts in women, and I prayed I would not grow up to become a man with breasts, though now in retrospect I realize that the male chests I feared (men at the beach, men in my family) were just fatty muscles, good pectorals gone to seed. I looked down at my chest to make sure that it did not protrude. I longed for absolute flatness, but also at other moments was eagerly stuffing crumpled paper towels in my shirt to simulate *La Dolce Vita*'s Anita Ekberg.

"VISIT THE RABBI WHILE YOU'RE IN VENICE,"

my grandfather said, and I wondered why I should waste time in Venice visiting the rabbi. Why squander an afternoon visiting the ghetto, I thought, when there are so many more uplifting tourist sites? My grandfather wanted to prove that Robert Browning was a Jew; I wondered why anyone would bother.

I tell my imaginary son, "Visit the sleaze bars while you're in Venice." I'm sure I feel the same wash of sentiment, anger, pride, self-righteousness, and victimization about queerness that my grandfather felt about Jewishness.

ICE CUBE

Ice cube my grandfather sucked as he died: so my mother told me. Hard to take in moisture while you're dying, I suppose, so he sucked an ice cube—or, rather, my grandmother brought the ice cube to his lips. My mother has his features, and I have my mother's: slim mean face, hysteric brown button eyes that will not see the other side of the equation.

Someone must bring ice to the dying man's lips, quenching tyrannic thirst, like the thirst of Prometheus, tied to the rock, liver eaten by vultures. Find the rock we're tied to, find the source of the rivets.

WHERE PROMETHEUS PISSED

Right on the rock. Tied to rock eternally he pissed right where he was tied. That was part of the Promethean picture. I suppose the rock was in the middle of the ocean, so the piss just washed off the sides of the rock and blended with the wandering sea. You piss where you are bound. When Prometheus was thirsty, my grandmother was not there to give him a taste of ice cube wrapped in handkerchief.

NUN JEW

My mother said "Nun Jew" to refer to non-Jews. "Nun," as in *The Flying Nun*. Does it matter what words you use? It matters what words you use.

NUN JEW CUM

The first time I swallowed cum I didn't care what I was swallowing. The second time I swallowed cum I gargled afterward with Listerine. The first two times were Nun Jew Cum. I don't remember the third time I swallowed cum. That's how it is with origins.

AGORAPHOBIA

I once knew a therapist who treated agoraphobics in their own houses. She'd visit them, help them overcome their fear of agoras. My father voted for Nixon because of the Israel question. My father usually based his votes on the Israel question. Long ago as part of a Sunday-school project I gave money to plant a tree in Israel. I didn't know what Israel was. I thought Israel was a country that needed shade. The space of this discourse—these words, here—is agoraphobic. I am visiting my own discourse in its house to see if I can help it overcome its fear of the agora. If you never leave your house can you do damage? You can do damage inside your house, but can you do damage outside your house if you never leave it?

I IMAGINE

that the Aryan boy was once my father's friend but then the boy turned Aryan in ideology and pissed on my father's head, but the pain of the incident lies in the Aryan boy's betrayal, his flight from peaceful boyhood into Aryan identification, his movement from friend-of-my-father into Aryan thug. It is not possible today to say something absolute about history or hatred, but it is possible to say I was naked in the tub and that a story infiltrated my constitution; it is possible to speak about the bathwater and my waterlogged skin; it is possible to say I remember my father laughing as he told me this story. Have I misconstrued it? Maybe the boy who pissed on his head was actually a Jew. In 1936 (or a few years earlier) could my father have shared a bunk bed with an Aryan? In any case, I remember my father chuckling as he told me the story.

TRANSFERRED TO A JEWISH SCHOOL

My father liked to eat mashed carrots, sweetened, in a bowl.
    Before long, he transferred to a Jewish school.

Idyllic black-and-white photo of my father at five years old in Berlin, naked, in the yard of his house, unselfconsciously urinating on the flowers or the ferns with a small and not yet interesting penis: if I were merely imagining this picture, I would tell you, but I am not merely imagining it.

WHY DIDN'T SOMEONE JUST SHOOT HITLER

In *Triumph of the Will*, Hitler moves along a row of soldiers, shaking their hands. Leni Riefenstahl films it so that he stares directly into the viewer's eyes, as if to shake the viewer's hand. I stare right into his eyes when he reaches his hand out to clasp mine. That is how Riefenstahl planned it. I have no other place to look.

I find many propagandistic manipulations seductive, including Wagner, but I draw the line at *Triumph of the Will:* I do not find its panoramas seductive. I expected I would find the near-naked Nazi boys attractive, showering in preparation for the rally. I'm relieved to find them scrawny. I'm relieved to know that I might not have found the Aryan boy attractive as he leaned over and let pour onto my head his golden arc.

NOTE

An earlier version of "Aryan Boy" appeared in *Cleavage* (New York: Ballantine Books, 2000), 55–63. Reprinted by permission of Random House, Inc.

THIRTEEN

A Palinode on Photography and the Transsexual Real

Jay Prosser

> "I was wrong but I was right to be wrong!" Undoubtedly self-criticism, like autobiography, is an impossible undertaking.
>
> —Philippe Lejeune, "The Autobiographical Pact (bis)"

What happens when we recognize the limits of our previous formulations, when as critics we turn our criticism in on ourselves? How do we return to our work, already in print, to consider its shortcomings and its failings—describe what we would do differently now? The palinode is not a defensive turn in which the author accuses the other of misreading and goes on to restate imperiously or painstakingly the argument. Nor is it a full-scale retraction, an exercise in self-abnegation (I take it all back). The palinode is rather a recantation (palin-ode: literally singing back or again); it is a counterbalancing of one's primary ode in which what one could not see before, one brings to light. The origin of the form, known to us for its citation in Plato's *Phaedrus,* is the *palinoidia* Stesichorus of Himera sings to Helen as reparation for his insults to her which had caused him to be struck blind; after his palinode his sight is restored (Phillippy 14). The palinode discovers some crucial insight which, one realizes in the return, only one's oversight made possible. The text's outside, the palinode returns the text's extremities. This figure of return, as Hal Foster suggests in the different context of his history of avant-garde art, *The Return of the Real,* may be a way of disrupting a relentlessly evolutionary model of intellectual history in which one must abandon projects to begin new ones, always and fully break with the old. Indeed the palinode may be the true nature of scholarship since one learns by recognizing one's mistakes, one's blindnesses, in the never-ending desire to see more and to see more accurately.

The palinode is a form not uncommon in poetry and can certainly be practiced in criticism. In the precedents of this form what returns is an awareness that throws into question that first theoretical model; invariably this is of the author's own position. The palinode is autobiographical criticism at its most literal: literally one takes oneself as the subject of one's criticism. In Philippe Lejeune's "The Autobiographical Pact (bis)," the "autobiographical pact" which Lejeune had conceived in order to distinguish between autobiography and fiction is muddied, indeed broken, by Lejeune's awareness that he had generalized *his* desires as a formalist for all readers. In his return to his work on Robert Mapplethorpe's photographs, Kobena Mercer remembers (after the death of the photographer from AIDS) how his own identity as a black gay man draws him into the same "fantasy of power and mastery which I said was the projection of the white male subject" (320). In "Afterthoughts on 'Visual Pleasure and Narrative Cinema' Inspired by *Duel in the Sun,*" Laura Mulvey similarly recognizes how her own "love of Hollywood melodrama" as a woman was "shelved as an issue in 'Visual Pleasure'" in the insistent focus on the male gaze (69). Finally, at the end of his career Roland Barthes returns to rethink the conception of photography from early on in his career. As with these other palinodes but more transparent and poignant here, what returns in *Camera Lucida* is doubt in a previous theoretical system, doubt, through autobiography, that theoretical systematization is possible. The palinode's return (and the loss of certainty that goes with it) is symbolized in the most autobiographical scene in *Camera Lucida*— possibly in the whole of Barthes's oeuvre—of Barthes looking for the essence of his mother, who had just died, by going through photographs of her life in reverse, this process of "gradually moving back in time with her, looking for the truth of the face I had loved" itself an irresistible desire to go back (*Camera Lucida* 67). "Palinodic discourse," writes Patricia Berrahou Phillippy in her study of this form in Renaissance poetry, "is language about loss, error, and belatedness" (199). As a mode that returns in the attempt to get back what has passed, the palinode is intrinsically caught up with grief, loss, and retrospect.

Though I was unconscious of the form then, these palinodes (excepting Mulvey's) appear cited in my book, *Second Skins: The Body Narratives of Transsexuality,* ode to my palinode here, mostly toward the end of the book where I sought to clinch my theoretical system. My book had argued that theories and representations of performativity current in gender studies had left out the matter of sex and with it the matter of transsexuality. I proposed that transsexuality in its "body narrative" brought back the referent of sex, and thus I effectively equated transsexuality with the real of sex. My mistake was to conflate the referent and the real, and to believe that in transsexuality I could represent the real. The terms are mostly interchangeable in my book, yet in Lacan the real lies outside representation, is "what resists symbolization absolutely" (*Seminar* Book 1 66). I sought to drive home my equation in my epilogue in photographs of transsexuals because I thought that photography was a form distinctively connected with the real, a medium that seems to show its referent unmediated. Key to this conclusion of my argument was my reading of Barthes, my belief that in *Camera Lucida* was a legitimation of the theoretical turn to the real through photography, and moreover that this was a turn in crucial friction with poststructuralist theory and its emphasis on the signifier and the performative. Through Barthes I wanted to give my claims about transsexuality theoretical clout; I wanted transsexuality to *have* theoretical clout, for it to mark a larger turn against poststructuralist gender performativity. Yet the language with which I sought to enlist Barthes for transsexuality should itself have told me something about the problems in my argument, did in fact tell me something, but *faute de mieux,* I used the vocabulary and hurried on: "From structuralism to poststructuralism to this signing off with the referent, the personal, and the search for his mother's presence (mater, matter): is there not something of an *allegory* in the final trajectory of Barthes's writing, a story for our specific theoretical time?" (211; emphasis added). I just couldn't get beyond that word "allegory," even though I knew that it took me away from the ontological direction in which I sought to go, toward the figurative and further signification. I was even conscious at the time that Judith Butler, against whom I had most directed my critique of gender performativity, had used the base of this word, in "allegorization," as a way to describe the performative relation of drag to heterosexual gender (237). In the very sentence in which I sought to urge the importance of our doing so, I couldn't get *underneath* language.

Nevertheless, believing that I could reveal the real of transsexuality in photography I showed *that* photograph, the penultimate one in my book, the incredible close-up of a female-to-male transsexual's genitals before surgery but after hormone treatment (the shot was retroactively named "Transcock" by the photographer, Del LaGrace) (233). This photograph shows, I argued, neither a genetic penis nor a clitoris but the referent of transsexuality because it captures this body as literally different in the actual process of somatic transition. Adamantine, huge, and irreducible, particularly when I projected it in slide shows at talks publicizing my book, "Transcock" was the star in my showcase: it had the effect at least initially of shocking my audience to see a substance beyond refutation—to see the substance of my argument. Yet to think now that I thought I could reveal the real, even through that photograph! Barthes of course does *not* show the most referential photograph in *Camera Lucida,* the photograph of his mother in the winter garden that he finally finds embodying her essence, who she was for him. This was a crucial and telling detail which like the word "allegory" troubled me but which I didn't deal with. The reason why Barthes does not publish this photograph has generated much discussion—indeed a volume that works as a memorial for Barthes (Rabaté). Yet only the critic Paul John Eakin gets it absolutely right when he states that for Barthes the photograph is unspeakable. Pointing out that the Winter Garden Photograph is "truly . . . the most memorable photograph in the book"—and indeed it is surely its absence that makes it memorable—Eakin writes that it is "in order to illustrate what he has shown and what he cannot show [that] Barthes deliberately omits the 'Winter Garden Photograph'" (20). "(I cannot reproduce the Winter Garden Photograph," Barthes writes. "It exists only for me. For you, it would be nothing but an indifferent picture, one of the thousand manifestations of the 'ordinary'; it cannot in any way constitute the visible object of a science; it cannot establish an objectivity, in the positive sense of the term; at most it would interest your *studium:* period, clothes, photogeny; but in it, for you, no wound.)" (73). What Barthes wants the photograph to show is precisely absence, loss, a gap in language. And this is what its absence does show. The photograph's omission is evidence not of any *thing*—analysis, description, familial gazes, looks, or even the subjectivity of experience—but of the failure of language in the face of loss. The fact that Barthes's explanation for the photograph's absence appears in parentheses emphasizes that it is inarticulable within conventional representation. Bracketed off from the text, a discursive extremity, the absent photograph articulates only the final failure of expression, of speaking the ineffable.

This ineffable is the real, trauma—the "wound"—which in Barthes's case is his mother's death: life's extremity. In believing I could represent the real I failed to "see" Barthes's absent photograph. Further I equated both the real and the referent with the body. Naïve, yes, but I was totally enthralled by my theoretical system as one is in one's primary ode, working against a queer elision of the sexed body to bring this body back through transsexuality. As that which had not been represented in gendered signification, transsexual flesh came to stand *by default* for the referent/real. My grasping of the referent as real was itself an unconscious (and failed) attempt to make the real speakable. Now I see that "Transcock"—the photograph of my friend Zachary Nataf's penis—is not the referent of transsexuality or its real. For without the brilliant enlarging techniques of LaGrace's photography and without the tape measure next to the genitals which *encode* the image with size as a penis, the genitals would, I admit, probably not be seen as a penis. They neither reference nor realize transsexuality. In attempting to reveal the real, to symbolize it, I made it something else—part of the symbolic—and hence the real *qua* real escaped me.

At the time of writing my book I hadn't read a lot of the critics on *Camera Lucida*. Of this I'm slightly ashamed although it must be said that many of these critics apparently hadn't read each other before writing their essays. Eakin is the exception in both cases here: I'd read him; he'd read the others. Of the wealth of material on *Camera Lucida*—and in the profundity of its thought and the poignancy of its writing this really is a very rich body of work—very little of it is cross-referenced. It is as if the commentary has been shaped by a kind of traumatic blindness (in repetition of Barthes's own trauma), with each critic beginning only to repeat or echo very closely the observations of those who have gone before, so that reading it one has the sense that something—something unresolved in Barthes —keeps returning.

I had also not explored the history of photography or thought about Barthes's work in relation to this. But not realizing the complexity of the history of photography is an easy mistake. Even Paul de Man, in the very same essay that he famously defers the referent of autobiography, in the very same sentence in fact, assumes the photograph as unproblematically referential: "But are we so certain that autobiography depends on reference, as a photograph depends on its subject?" (69). Anyway the problem with most discussions of photography as I realized is that conventionally they are too discursive. Even when ostensibly following Barthes, they analyze photographic "codes" and "signifiers" and "construction"; they approach photography as a technology of representation. And I knew that *Camera Lucida* was certainly a quite different engagement from all this, a work that sought through photography to cut through "theory." (Barthes: "What did I care about the rules of composition of the photographic landscape, or, at the other end, about the Photograph as family rite?" [7]; "The photograph touches me if I withdraw it from its usual blah-blah" [55]; I wanted to explore [photography] not as a question (a theme) but as a wound" [21]). Having read something of the history of photography now, I realize that photography has always constituted a battle over the status of the referent: whether the photograph's representation is constructed or referential, real or figurative; whether the medium is "documentary" or "pictorial" (Trachtenberg; Sontag). The techniques and practices of photographic illusionism, which were developed with the invention of photography, mean that from the beginning nothing has been given or referential as I thought. As Susan Sontag writes of the very early recognition that photography is a form of representation, "as people quickly discovered that nobody takes the same picture of the same thing, the supposition that cameras furnish an impersonal objective image yielded to the fact that photographs are evidence not only of what's there but of what an individual sees, not just a record but an evaluation of the world" (88). Photographs don't record reality: they change the very nature of reality—by representing it.

In spite of the fact that in my theory of photography I missed half of this history and equated photography with the real, nevertheless in the critical approach to photographs in my book I read —yes, read, even as I sought to get beyond code—what Barthes calls the *studium* and not the *punctum,* the code and not the wound or the real. I read connotation and not denotation, which Barthes first theorizes in the ode to *Camera Lucida*'s palinode, the essay "The Photographic Message." In 1961 in "The Photographic Message," Barthes had said that the photograph is a "structural paradox" (19). On the one hand the photograph is like any other form of representation for structuralists, made up of codes and signifiers; it is connotative and connotation is "culture" (22). On the other hand the photograph is denotative and this is what makes it exceptional among all forms of representation. That is, it "transmit[s] . . . literal reality," it is a "perfect *analogon*" of reality and to this extent "*it is a message without a code,*" not a form of representation at all (17; all emphases from Barthes in originals). However (and here's the second level of paradox), although Barthes writes that connotation is "not strictly speaking part of the photographic structure" (20), looking at the photograph we cannot get beyond or underneath this level of connotation because "From this point of view, the image—grasped by an inner metalanguage itself—in actual fact has no denoted state, is immersed for its very social existence in at least an initial layer of connotation, that of the categories of language" (29). In my approach to photographs in my epilogue, then, I did not make contact with the real but "read" the *studium* or connotation, in keeping with the message the photograph sought to connote. This is especially obvious when I was guided by the captions of photographs, as I most often was. As Barthes had made quite clear in "The Photographic Message," captions are a key mechanism of connotation. In my reading of many of the photographs, what I say about the images is wholly determined by the written text that appears in or outside of the photograph. Indeed that I pointed to the verbal frame of the photograph in my discussion of the self-portrait of Loren Cameron, that I cited it ("You're so exotic! May I take your photograph? . . . Do you have a penis?") as "literally fram[ing] the viewer's gaze, reflecting back . . . that look of fascination, objectification and desire s/he may cast," makes transparent how much of a textual reading, a reading of and in language, this is (230). Even in the case of photographs where my discussion is not explicitly determined by the written text, I am still reading according to connotation. In response to an opening image of a female-to-male transsexual at his desk with a pipe and a pen I dutifully develop a reading from the props of the pipe and the pen. In relation to four photographs appearing on a single page I discuss how this arrangement produces a narrative of transsexual transition. Even the putatively most referential photograph for me, "Transcock," needed the prop of the measuring tape for my reading, as many in my audiences tripped over each other in their haste to point out to me once they had recovered from the initial shock of the image. All of these features—text, photographic composition, and layout—are part of what Barthes calls the "connotation procedures" through which the photograph seeks to control its reading. As Barthes says of the caption in "The Photographic Message," in the world of the press photograph and advertising in which photography can no longer be thought innocent (but was it ever?), "the text loads the image, burdening it with a culture, a moral, and imagination" (26). It is this culture, this moral, this imagination—this *studium*—that I read.

And yet whose *studium* did I read, and for whom? For if I read the image according to how the photographer or the subject represented want-

ed me to see it (and this is what constitutes connotation: it is whoever is
behind the production of the photograph who "connotes"), this surely
had everything to do with where I was reading from. The return of the real,
which is a reaction against the postmodern "inflation of text and image"
that Foster traces in his history of avant-garde art, comes in two forms: first
of all through the body, "through the violated body and/or the traumatic
subject"; and second through autobiographical or ethnographic work in
which the artist becomes representative of a community, "a turn to the referent as grounded in a given identity and/or a sited community" (xviii).
My approach combined both of these turns, for this is surely where I was
writing from: as a transsexual; from and for a violated body; from that "as
a" position Nancy K. Miller has called "representativity"—though she
urges that we seek to avoid it in part by foregrounding the autobiographical (xiii). But how to avoid representativity when there is no (authentic)
representation of oneself—representation in the entwined imagistic and
political senses of the word? Or more to the point, how to avoid reading
oneself into the other when what one sees represented *is* oneself, when
there is no real identity difference between who's represented and who's
reading? In response to transsexual narratives but especially in relation to
the photographs of transsexuals, I succumbed to a process of what I later
discovered Susan Rubin Suleiman had just called "autobiographical reading": that is "the autobiographical imperative [that] applies not only to
writing about one's life but to reading about it; reading *for* it; reading, perhaps, *in order to* write about it" (200). Autobiographical reading, Suleiman
writes of her own experience of reading memoirs of concentration camp
survivors, "independently of any appreciation for the author's style or
depth of vision, is shameless, unsophisticatedly, *referential*" (205; emphasis added). Crying not only on first but second reading of these memoirs
Suleiman realizes that what she's reading for is herself: "What exactly am
I looking for, and finding in these works? . . . I recognize the stories all too
well. They could have been my own" (207). And although she doesn't theorize it as such Suleiman seems to suggest that autobiographical reading,
or at least the kind of autobiography that she reads and writes, is, like photography, caught up with the real (okay, also the referential: perhaps in the
attempt to speak of the real that slide is inevitable). One reads autobiographically because what one reads, what one wants to write autobiographically, is ultimately unrepresentable: "the only kind of autobiography I find truly essential to read *or* write . . . is the kind that tries to recover,
through writing, an irrecoverable absence" (214). Reading and writing for

transsexuality's absence, reading in the struggle to make it present, not surprisingly I got caught up in the connotation codes of transsexual photographs. Reading only with and for transsexuals, I read for my life.

Barthes makes a crucial point about the connotation and coding of the photograph at the end of his essay "The Photographic Message." He suggests a way in which the layer of connotation can be shattered off the structure of the photograph leaving only denotation. This shattering is in effect what happens in *Camera Lucida,* as Barthes is no longer interested here in decoding connotation/*studium* but in pointing to the photographic *punctum* or denotation, in the photograph as a wound. And indeed in *Camera Lucida* the *punctum* is described as that which breaks or punctures the *studium,* that which wounds connotation. Here is what Barthes writes at the end of "The Photographic Message" in a passage that is extraordinarily prophetic of what will motivate his *Camera Lucida,* palinode to his ode, some forty years later: "These few remarks sketch a kind of differential table of photographic connotations, showing, if nothing else, that connotation extends a long way. Is this to say that a pure denotation, a *this-side-of-language,* is impossible? If such a denotation exists, it is perhaps not at the level of what ordinary language calls the insignificant, the neutral, the objective, but on the contrary, at the level of absolutely traumatic images. The trauma is a suspension of language, a blocking of meaning" (30). Although conventionally we cannot grasp the photograph in its denotative state, at a time of trauma, as an effect of trauma, the photograph is revealed as denotative, underneath language. It is only trauma that can return the photograph to us as real, *punctum*—a stopping of language. If this is *Camera Lucida*'s conception of the photograph in palinodic recursion of "The Photographic Message," if the photograph now becomes referential on the this-side-of-language (and this is one of the most reiterated tenets of *Camera Lucida:* "every photograph is somehow co-natural with its referent . . . I call the 'photographic referent' not the *optionally* real thing to which an image or a sign refers but the *necessarily* real thing. . . . it is Reference, which is the founding order of Photography" [76–77]), it is because of the trauma in Barthes's own life that interrupts his theory and his work: the death of his mother, the loss he says of the one he loved the most. Trauma sparks this return to photography and this return *of* photography as traumatically this side of language.

In this way the palinodic return of *Camera Lucida* enfleshes the tension between connotation and denotation that was already present in the earlier essay but enfleshes it into a tension between theory and the real. His desire to write on photography sparked by the trauma of his mother's death, Barthes writes, lays bare "a discomfort I had always suffered from: the uneasiness of being a subject torn between two languages, one expressive, the other critical; and at the heart of this critical language, between several discourses, those of sociology, of semiology, and of psychoanalysis—but that, by ultimate dissatisfaction with all of them, I was bearing witness to the only sure thing that was in me (however naïve it might be): a desperate resistance to any reductive system" (8). This ultimate dissatisfaction with all of the theoretical languages that had made up Barthes's career, this (re)turn to the naïve and only sure thing at the end of it, the resistance to any reductive system which, surely, is theory, is reproduced in the palinode within *Camera Lucida*. For *Camera Lucida* contains a palinode. Part 2 of the book begins by revealing the personal trauma that has made necessary this return to *untheorize* photography and drop connotation: "Now, one November evening shortly after my mother's death . . ." (63). It is this loss of Barthes's real in the essence of his mother that makes this return—in the book and of this book in the context of Barthes's entire oeuvre—necessary: "I would have to descend deeper into myself to find the evidence of Photography. . . . I would have to make my recantation, my palinode," he writes at the end of part 1, which has not elucidated the personal, which has remained therefore in theory (60). No wonder then that I eagerly seized on Barthes—and photography—as a way to show what happens when a theoretical system is brought down by the experiential, its system ripped open by a lived belief in the referential. Barthes's commentators pick up on the same tension, describing it remarkably *un*variously as that between theory and subjective experience (Kennedy); theory and expression (Gratton); and theory and autobiographical reference (Eakin). All of us over and over again find a tension not only obviously between the structuralist and poststructuralist Barthes but much later and much more shockingly between the poststructuralist and—what? post-theoretical? *living? dying?*—Barthes. Most commentators speak of this book (and sometimes the autobiography that just preceded it, *Roland Barthes by Roland Barthes*) in terms of a "turn" (Kennedy 387) or a "discursive shift . . . 'recessive' movement" (Gratton 58) in Barthes's work; and indeed in an essay that emphasizes *Camera Lucida* as the final work of Barthes and thus quite literally the end of his writing, Kennedy in his own moment of prophesying even sees it as a crucial turn out of poststructuralism: "Insofar as [Barthes's] career has provided an accurate barometer of French intellectual trends, the book may some day mark a general turn from structuralist and post-structuralist abstraction toward a more pragmatic and humane discourse" (397). With Barthes's last utterance and the death that was so absurdly and yet so uncannily to coincide with it (*Camera Lucida,* as *La Chambre Claire,* was published on January 28, 1980; Barthes was knocked down by a laundry van on February 25, 1980, and died on March 26, 1980), the form of the palinode acquires a remarkable and epic folding of theory back into itself.

If trauma in this palinode returns Barthes to photography as a point before language and before theory (or beyond it) it is because of the melancholy he experiences in the face of his mother's death. All of these things, trauma, the palinode, photography, and melancholy, layered so heartrendingly onto *Camera Lucida,* work according to the figure of return. In trauma one only realizes what's traumatic in the repetition of the event; it is this deferred realization that *is* traumatic. The palinode is a return as should be obvious by now. And photography may work according to this same dynamic, itself contains something of the palinode. Indeed return is the essence of Barthes's "ça-a-été" which he says is the "noeme" of photography, its defining unit: the thing *was* there. Finally what is melancholy except a looking back, to draw on Freud's distinction between melancholy and mourning, a failure unlike mourning to look forward? In front of the Winter Garden Photograph Barthes cannot work through the loss: "I am alone with it, in front of it. The circle is closed, there is no escape. I suffer, motionless. Cruel, sterile deficiency: I cannot *transform* my grief, I cannot let my gaze drift; no culture will help me utter this suffering which I experience entirely on the level of the image's finitude (this is why, despite its codes, I cannot *read* a photograph): the Photograph—my Photograph—is without culture: when it is painful, nothing in it can transform grief into mourning" (90). Thus it is a mistake to read *Camera Lucida* as a work of mourning (Hirsch; Kuhn), or even as a work that is somewhere in between melancholia and mourning (Woodward). *Camera Lucida* is a work of melancholy in that classic sense of inarticulability, distinct from mourning. Barthes doesn't use photography to work through his grief. Rather photography is returned through grief, through melancholy, as *itself* inarticulable, this side of language. Photography is a "melancholy object," to recall Sontag's formula for the way in which photography relentlessly represents what's no longer there. Barthes's melancholy puts photography in the ineffable place of his mother's death. Photography is "asymbolic Death" or *"flat death"* (92); "the Photograph always carries its referent with itself . . . like the condemned man and the corpse" (5–6), photography is the "return of the dead" (9). In his trauma, photography is Barthes's mirror. Melancholy, Freud says, "behaves like an open wound" (262)—like photography for Barthes then. The loss in melancholy cannot be stanched with a binding of language. Barthes's Latinate term for what matters in photography performs this overlaying of melancholy and photography. "*Punctum*" is derived from the Latin "to prick" ("this wound, this prick," Barthes writes [26]), in echo of "trauma," from the Greek for "wound." Early on in *Camera Lucida,* photography's *punctum* is defined in terms of the Lacanian real: "In the Photograph, the event is never transcended for the sake of something else: the Photograph always leads the corpus I need back to the body I see; it is the absolute Particular, the sovereign Contingency, matte and somehow stupid, the *This* (this photograph and not Photography), in short what Lacan calls the *Tuché,* the Occasion, the Encounter, the Real, in its indefatigable expression" (4). Like trauma, photography and melancholy fail to transcend their object, cannot get symbolic distance on the real. The loss, the absence, keeps returning, insuperable, inconvertible. In writing a book that overlays his loss with photography—that *photographs* his trauma we might say—Barthes certainly does not keep his pain secret; but what he speaks is that he has nothing to say: "I have no other resource than this *irony:* to speak of the 'nothing to say.'" (93). The melancholy of death sends him spinning palinodically back to photography as traumatically real, that which blocks meaning: exactly in the manner Barthes predicted trauma made possible at the end of "The Photographic Message."

In his *Return of the Real*—which itself may be read as a palinode since the author criticizes the semiotic turn in postmodern art theory for which he confesses he is in no small part responsible—Foster follows Lacan's theory to suggest that postmodernism has left us with a very different conception of the real. There has been a shift "from reality as an effect of representation to the real as a thing of trauma" (146). Foster's real, conceived as "traumatic realism" in avant-garde art, disrupts the conventional—both realistic and postmodern—polarized conceptions of reality: that reality is either referential, or it is simulacral. Returned by trauma, in Foster's formulation the real is neither before the representation nor produced by it but absolutely confused with it, in a way that crucially upsets or traumatizes representation. Illustrating this notion of the real as traumatic with a reading of car crashes in Warhol photographs, Foster writes: "repetition in Warhol is not reproduction in the sense of representation (of a referent) or simulation (of a pure image, a detached signifier). Rather repetition serves to *screen* the real understood as traumatic. But this very need also *points* to the real, and at this point the real *ruptures* the screen of repetition" (132). The involuted trajectory of the real (like the palinode it turns in on itself) may perhaps best be understood by that word "screen," which seems here to have a double sense. In the first sense Warhol's attempt to represent the real in his photographs of car crashes actually *veils* it. But the real then returns with unexpected force (traumatically) to rupture the screen in that second sense, which is on the contrary the cinematic *display* of the object; the real traumatically returned disrupts representation itself. And it does so perhaps by dropping that "re-" and becoming sheer presentation—or at least apparently doing so: for the point is (and here's the trauma) that we can't tell the difference between screen and referent, what's there and what is added in the "re-." Foster makes this very point. Drawing out the confusion in Barthes's description of the *punctum* ("it is what I add to the photograph and *what is nonetheless already there*" [*Camera Lucida* 55]), Foster writes that "it may be this confusion [of 'subject and world, inside and outside'] that *is* traumatic" (134). Slavoj Zizek, who has made this shift from reality to the real a key theme of his work, has also identified this same confusion between the image and the real in postmodernism as traumatic. Both Foster and Zizek moreover describe this confusion—but particularly our quest for the real in representation—as *melancholic.* Foster suggests that "In recent intimations of postmodernism . . . the *melancholic* structure of feeling dominates" and this reveals a "symbolic order in crisis"; this melancholy is associated with the desire for the real—"later postmodernisms want to possess the real thing" (165). And in a moving image Zizek suggests that "the inherently painful dimension of our contact with reality"—our desire for the real but surely our inability to catch it—renders our archetype Tim Burton's cinematic protagonist Edward Scissorhands. Edward Scissorhands "epitomizes the postmodern subject: a melancholic subject," since everything he touches he cuts up and causes unbearable pain (and we might add causes himself unbearable pain in the attempt to make contact with the real) (59). If our moment in late postmodernism is melancholic then it is because of our refusal to accept the loss of the real. Like the melancholic, we fail to transcend the object. We want not to render the real symbolic, but to join with it, literally to take it in. It is surely not incidental that the real becomes a fundamental psychoanalytic category at the very moment (1953) that structuralism was being taken up in most disciplines. The split between the signifier and signified was a trauma that made of the referent the real. The referent became that which could *only* traumatically and ineffably return. No wonder we (it's not just me) keep mistaking the referent for the real.

For Lacan what is traumatic about the real, what makes it a category able to return, is that it is split off from our contact with it. "The function of the *tuché,* of the real as encounter—the encounter in so far as it may be missed, in so far as it is essentially the missed encounter—first presented itself in the history of psychoanalysis in a form . . . of trauma" (*Four Fundamental Concepts* 55). Although the real is all presence ("there is no absence in the real" [*Seminar* Book 2 313]; "the real is absolutely without fissure" [*Seminar* Book 2 97]) we are not there where the real is. We not only miss its encounter; we are products of this missed encounter. To return then, to my palinode, to think about what I missed. Fundamentally I think that in reading transsexuality *as* the referent (and taking that for the real) I missed the real *of* transsexuality. This real—most ineffable, most impossible—may be the ultimate failure of the transsexual (*all* transsexuals) to be real, that is to be real-ly sexed. If, overwhelmingly, I read the *studium* in photographs of transsexuals, the *punctum*—which Barthes describes as that which ruptures the *studium,* the partial "detail" which interrupts and refuses the "unary" in the image (31)—is surely the transsexual's missed encounter with the real. These partial details in the transsexual image are literally traumatic: the wounds of transsexuality, the scars from surgery or the physical traces in this body that sustain this as a different body. These scars or traces—for me it is an absence of parts—won't allow a prereassignment history to disappear into the apparent reality of reassigned sex. Perhaps transsexuality resonates for our moment because the process of surgical reassignment seems to offer a literalization of the traumatic loss of the real and our attempt to regain the real *through* trauma. Like Edward Scissorhands we cut *ourselves* up in the attempt to touch the real. The hope is that surgery will provide us immediate access to the real—like photography.

Indeed the two procedures of surgery and photography have been compared. For Walter Benjamin, writing in an essay that sees in photography a demotic approximation of the real (photography is emblematic of "the desire of contemporary masses to bring things 'closer'" [217]), photography is like surgery because it "diminishes distance . . . and penetrat[es] into the patient's body" (227). For Barthes also having one's photograph taken is like being subject to a surgery: "to become an object made one suffer as much as a surgical operation" (*Camera Lucida* 13). What's painful about photography and gender reassignment surgery both is that, in spite of how close they come to reproducing the real, to making contact with it (and I emphasize that they are our best means for approximating the real), they ultimately fail. Surgery fails most obviously in the case of female-to-male transsexual reassignment, which has found no way, half a century after its invention, of reproducing a functioning penis. It is almost impossible to develop a penis one can piss through without it developing disabling fistulas or complications. It *is* impossible to develop a penis with which one can have penetrative sex without having first to "pump it up" or insert a stiffening rod into the head (which may well shoot out during intercourse). And still one must choose between these "options," between *either* pissing *or* having sex—as if life could be decided between urinary or sexual function. And one makes this decision knowing (a) that *neither* will be fully successful and (b) that the end result will anyway leave severe scarring, the loss of flesh in the donor body part sometimes so shockingly large as to leave that part dysfunctioning. Literally, to have a penis, one must give an arm and a leg. And then—sorry: but the trauma goes on—years after the surgery, the penis (often misshapen and ugly and looking nothing like a penis) can still fall off. Believe me, it happens. For male-to-female transsexuals, although by no means to the same degree, there is also some trace, some remnant, something that returns that can't be realigned or reassigned: a voice, height, hands, or as was made traumatically evident in the recent experience of a dear friend of mine who was sure that at least in this way she passed perfectly, even postreassignment genitals. This failure to be real *is* the transsexual real.

This transsexual real is there in some of the photographs I showed in my book although it's often not immediately, nor even completely apparent (the *punctum* is the partial detail that ruptures the unary). In the Loren Cameron self-portrait, for instance, the real is the scar that runs across the wall of the chest. One can barely make it out (one of the reasons I chose this image) but in other photographs in *Body Alchemy* where Cameron is straightened up the scars are evident, indeed unavoidable. And what these scars make evident is the constructedness of transsexuality. For surely even if it does become possible to reproduce a perfectly reassigned sex in the future (tissue engineering is perhaps the way as I suggested in my book, although what government health service or private insurance is going to fund this for transsexuals?), the irony will always remain that this real was achieved only through the latest forms of technological construction. Here's the paradox of the real: transsexuals can only approximate the real of their identity through reconstruction—a truth that transsexual scars make evident. As reconstruction, transsexuality, like the palinode and photography, is an attempt to return, to get back the lost referent— the ça-a-été of sex, the gender that was really there. And the scars on the body are, like the photographs that don't hide them, that terrible thing, the return of the dead; they show the gender that was not really there—not as sex anyway, which is (still) surely what matters for transsexuals. In fact Cameron leaves this trace of construction/reconstruction in the form of the shutter-release bulb that he quite visibly holds in many of his self-portraits. This bulb reveals the process of photographic construction. Emblematic of the brave facing up to the absence of the real that *is* Cameron's photography, the bulb means that the photograph does not try to pass itself off as real, but makes evident that it is a representation. Cameron himself reads the trace of the bulb as a metaphor for his self-construction as a transsexual: "People have asked me, however, why I don't try to conceal the bulb in my photographs. . . . I am creating my own image alone, an act that reflects the transsexual experience as well" (11).

The palinode returns the real as ineffable. Flying to Brazil where I first presented this palinode as part of a seminar series I was giving on photography and autobiography (my Brazilian colleagues, bless them, afterwards *congratulated* me on my transsexuality), I was reminded by a friend and my traveling companion of a footnote that had appeared in an early draft of my dissertation but which had not made it through the revisions into the book. This footnote, the existence of which I had completely forgotten, consisted of a discussion of a self-portrait by Cameron which had appeared two years before publication of *Body Alchemy* in a female-to-male transsexual support journal, *FTM Newsletter*. Checking the journal to make sure I discuss the right image, I am startled to discover as true something that I realize in retrospect I had already unconsciously known: this photograph did not make it into Cameron's final version of *Body Alchemy;* like my footnote, it proved unreproducible, both discarded extremities. Here's my footnote on Cameron's photograph, finally found on a computer disk of discarded writings, and written in 1994 as I began my transition. It discusses the difficulty in representing transsexuality:

> Many of Cameron's shots are nudes. When the inscription of transsexuality on his body is occulted, that is, when he passes (i.e. as not transsexual), he appears as an integrally gendered subject. But when he represents his transsexuality, when he makes it visible, a splitting of the subject (and for me as viewer the split takes place in looking and looked at subject) seems to occur as a matter of course. The look/my look is drawn and fixed to what might be thought of as the transsexual markings on his body, as it tries to reconcile these markings with the remainder of the body. The splitting in viewed and viewer takes place precisely because of a (my?) fail-

ure at reconciliation of these parts/past. Cameron's stylized (*passing*) masculinity—his muscular chest and shoulders and the beautiful tattoos spread across them—only makes more visible what is excessive or absent from this picture: what doesn't pass. My girlfriend's immediate reaction to these photographs voiced what I thought but couldn't say: "But he has no penis!" While Cameron's photographs are brave and brilliant testimony to the fact that transsexuality is certainly not unrepresentable, they do suggest that transsexuality exceeds the limits of (gendered) representation and, for me (at least for now), remains profoundly unreadable, irreconcilable within these limits.

One reason why I must have cut this footnote is that for a footnote it is ridiculously long (and I've even winnowed it down here). Following the precedents of my betters, I've been moving toward writing without footnotes: they strike me as a tangential kind of writing that distracts from the main flow of reading. (Although as exemplified here perhaps excluding the textual extremity of the footnote only serves to create the preconditions for a longer one: for what is the palinode if not an article-length footnote?) But there were many embarrassingly long and unnecessary footnotes that made it into my book. What really proved so elidable, so necessary to eliminate, about this footnote for me (as perhaps Cameron's photograph for him)?

Obvious to me now is that this is a footnote precisely about the unspeakability of transsexuality. Although I couldn't name the nature of the splitting that took place for me both in the photograph and in the viewing subject—I am conspicuously vague here: "*that* splitting . . . *that same* splitting"—it seems clear to me now that the splitting that I tried to describe was between what was representable and what was not. This division of speakability/unspeakability corresponded absolutely to the sexed splitting of the photograph. Simply, maleness, what can be represented in the image of Cameron's passing as a man, proved speakable. What can't be reconciled with the apparently male subject in the photograph proved unspeakable. Or rather I should quickly particularize this and say speakable/unspeakable *for me*, since this is patently an autobiographical footnote. Surely for my then girlfriend (then)—and I made this point absolutely clear at the time—what *I* found unspeakable *she* spoke in her very first response to the photograph: "My girlfriend's immediate reaction to these photographs *voiced what I thought but couldn't say: 'But he has no penis!'*" Was this failure of Cameron's body to be genetically male-ly real (and I emphasize this failure as not just his but as universally inevitable)

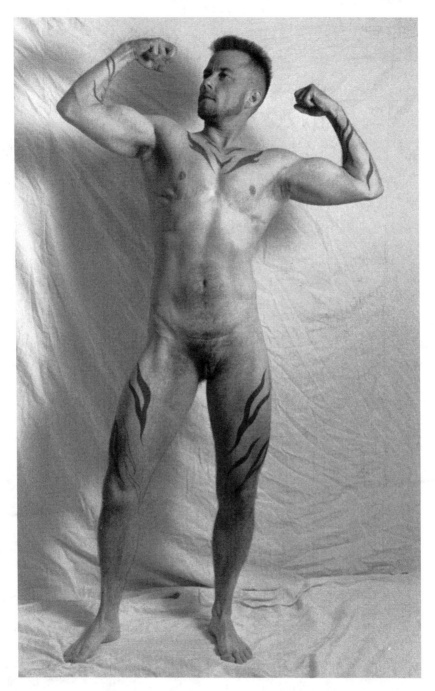

Loren Cameron, *Self-Portrait*, 1993, from *Our Vision, Our Voices* (copyright © Loren Cameron; reprinted by permission)

speakable for my girlfriend because she was not transsexual? But I was doubtful even at that time (evident from that undecided "my?" in parentheses) that the lines of the speakability/unspeakability of the transsexual real were firmly pasted onto the division between nontranssexuals and transsexuals. In retrospect, as my girlfriend found *my* transsexuality increasingly unspeakable (literally: she couldn't speak about it for three years after we split, and is only starting to be able to discuss it and its role in our split now that she is with a genetic male, a man with a penis), I am certain that that division is not so correspondingly neat. As my final sentence in the note suggests, perhaps something about transsexuality remains not only unspeakable for me but for us all, irreconcilable within the limits of gendered representation per se.

What this unspeakable is, I am trying to suggest (although of course this is an impossible paradox), is precisely the failure of transsexuality to be real, the failure of us all to achieve the real however much we desire to. It's important, I think, that in this photograph Cameron does not show the shutter-release bulb of the camera. It is one of the few self-portraits of Cameron I've seen, and certainly the only full-length nude of him, that does not foreground, make visible as trace, the processes of technological (photographic/medical) construction. *For why the need to do so when the full frontal makes these processes of construction irrefutably evident themselves?* What do we *not* see in this image except a genetic male? (And my difficult placing of "not" is advised here because I think quite possibly we see everything in this photograph *but* a genetic male. We see a transsexual, a transsexual male, a self-constructed man, a body that is no longer woman but once was; we see the trace of a woman . . .). The photograph itself—and surely this is where the eye is drawn: to what's not there, that absent ultimate male bodily extremity—makes evident the missing penis. This then finally is the transsexual real, what's not there, what can't be represented because indeed it's not achievable. I can hardly speak it.

And yet I don't want to leave us here. The palinode, though tied up with the language of loss, grief, error, and belatedness—ultimately like transsexuality an attempt to return to get it *right this time*—goes back only to move forward. It leaves us not with our blindness but restores our sight; indeed its purpose, like transsexuality, is restorative, healing. What strikes me now about the real—and it's so obvious that I'm dumbfounded I couldn't see it before—is that it is precisely our failure to achieve the real that makes us desire it. If we *were* real of course, always already there where the real was, we would not only not strive for the real, we wouldn't even know what it was. It is only our distance from the real that allows us to prize it, recognize it—indeed perhaps in proportion to our distance from it. Our desire for the real is not only not the same as our capacity to achieve it; these two things are antithetical. And this is true of the unspeakability of the real. If we could state the real that would truly be the end of writing and of representation. Good old Lacanian conceit which I've only really understood for myself just now: it is the loss of the real that engenders our desire for it, that engenders desire—movement, writing, transition.

Lejeune also captures something of this paradox. In his palinode, when he realizes that autobiography is no longer sustainable as an absolute structural category, a genre that can be defended through theory as distinct from fiction, he nevertheless goes on believing in the real—the nonconstructedness, the referentiality, the absolute truthful existence—of autobiography. Citing from *Roland Barthes by Roland Barthes* the famous question which encapsulates the poststructuralist wavering around the existence of the referent—"Do I not know that, *in the field of the subject, there is no referent?*" (56)—but transforming it in his citation into a statement as if to have something certain to oppose—"In the field of the subject, there is no referent" (131)—Lejeune acknowledges the truth of this, and thus the impossibility of autobiography. Yet, he says, in a wonderful moment of fetishistic defiance upon which his very self seems to depend: "We *indeed know* all this; we are not so dumb, but once the precaution has been taken, we go on as if we did not know it. Telling the truth about the self, constituting the self as a complete subject—it is a fantasy. In spite of the fact that autobiography is impossible, this in no way prevents it from existing" (131–32).

In spite of the fact that transsexuality is impossible this in no way prevents it from existing. Indeed as with self-criticism, a similarly "impossible undertaking," I would do it over again.

NOTES

An earlier version of this essay appeared in *a/b: Auto/Biography Studies* 14.1 (Summer 1999): 71–92. Reprinted by permission of the editors of *a/b: Auto/Biography Studies*. Thanks to those who refused to believe me in the first place. Also to Shohini Chaudhuri for her thoughts on the real and "presentation"; to Clare Hemmings for reminding me of the lost footnote; to Liliane Phan at Éditions Gallimard and Isabelle Creusot at Éditions du Seuil for their correspondence on La Chambre Claire; to Loren Cameron for permitting me to reproduce his photograph (again); but especially to Nancy K. Miller for the idea of a return and suggestions for a reading list.

258 • JAY PROSSER

WORKS CITED

Barthes, Roland. *Camera Lucida: Reflections on Photography.* Trans. Richard Howard. London: Vintage, 1993.

———. "The Photographic Message." *Image Music Text.* Ed. and trans. Stephen Heath. London: Fontana, 1977. 15–31.

Benjamin, Walter. "The Work of Art in the Age of Mechanical Reproduction." *Illuminations.* Ed. Hannah Arendt. Trans. Harry Zohn. London: Fontana, 1992. 211–44.

Butler, Judith. *Bodies That Matter: On the Discursive Limits of "Sex."* New York: Routledge, 1993.

Cameron, Loren. *Body Alchemy: Transsexual Portraits.* Pittsburgh: Cleis, 1996.

de Man, Paul. "Autobiography as De-Facement." *The Rhetoric of Romanticism.* New York: Columbia University Press, 1984. 67–81.

Eakin, Paul John. *Touching the World: Reference in Autobiography.* Princeton: Princeton University Press, 1992.

Foster, Hal. *The Return of the Real: Avant-Garde Art at the End of the Century.* Cambridge, Mass.: MIT Press, 1996

Freud, Sigmund. "Mourning and Melancholia." *The Penguin Freud Library.* Original trans. and ed. James Strachey. Present ed. Angela Richards. Vol. 11, *On Metapsychology.* London: Penguin, 1991. 245–68.

FTM Newsletter 27 (Apr. 1994).

Gratton, J. "*Roland Barthes Par Roland Barthes:* Autobiography and the Notion of Expression." *Romance Studies* 8 (1986): 57–65.

Hirsch, Marianne. *Family Frames: Photography, Narrative, and Postmemory.* Cambridge, Mass.: Harvard University Press, 1997.

Kennedy, J. Gerald. "Roland Barthes, Autobiography, and the End of Writing." *Georgia Review* 35 (1981): 381–98.

Kuhn, Annette. *Family Secrets: Acts of Memory and Imagination.* London: Verso, 1995.

Lacan, Jacques. *The Four Fundamental Concepts of Psycho-Analysis.* Ed. Jacques-Alain Miller. Trans. Alan Sheridan. New York: Norton, 1981.

———. *The Seminar of Jacques Lacan.* Book 1. *Freud's Papers on Technique. 1953–1954.* Ed. Jacques-Alain Miller. Trans. John Forrester. New York: Norton, 1991.

———. *The Seminar of Jacques Lacan.* Book 2. *The Ego in Freud's Theory and in the Technique of Psychoanalysis. 1954–55.* Trans. Sylvana Tomaselli. New York: Norton, 1988.

Lejeune, Philippe. *On Autobiography.* Ed. Paul John Eakin. Trans. Katherine Leary. Minneapolis: University of Minnesota Press, 1989.

Mercer, Kobena. "Reading Racial Fetishism: The Photographs of Robert Mapplethorpe." *Fetishism as Cultural Discourse.* Ed. Emily Apter and William Pietz. Ithaca: Cornell University Press, 1993. 307–30.

Miller, Nancy K. *Getting Personal: Feminist Occasions and Other Autobiographical Acts.* New York: Routledge, 1991.

Mulvey, Laura. "Afterthoughts on 'Visual Pleasure and Narrative Cinema' Inspired by *Duel in the Sun.*" *Feminism and Film Theory.* Ed. Constance Penley. New York: Routledge, 1988. 69–79.

Phillippy, Patricia Berrahou. *Love's Remedies: Recantation and Renaissance Lyric Poetry*. London: Associated University Presses, 1995.

Prosser, Jay. *Second Skins: The Body Narratives of Transsexuality*. New York: Columbia University Press, 1998.

Rabaté, Jean-Michel, ed. *Writing the Image after Roland Barthes*. Philadelphia: University of Pennsylvania Press, 1997.

Sontag, Susan. *On Photography*. London: Penguin, 1977.

Suleiman, Susan Rubin. *Risking Who One Is: Encounters with Contemporary Art and Literature*. Cambridge, Mass: Harvard University Press, 1994.

Trachtenberg, Alan, ed. *Classic Essays on Photography*. New Haven: Leete's Island Books, 1980.

Woodward, Kathleen. "Freud and Barthes: Theorizing Mourning, Sustaining Grief." *Discourse* 13.1 (1990–91): 93–110.

Zizek, Slavoj. "Grimaces of the Real, or When the Phallus Appears." *October* 58 (1991): 44–68.

FOURTEEN

Writing Wrong

Sandra M. Gilbert

> I am still at the same subject—
> Shredding facts—
> As old women nervously
> Pull apart
> Whatever is put in their fingers;
> Undoing all the years
> Of mending, putting together.
>
> —Ruth Stone, "Something Deeper"

It is now seven years, ten months, and eighteen days since the sunny February morning when two orderlies arrived to wheel my husband of thirty-three years into the operating theater where he had a routine prostatectomy from which he never recovered. Though he was in robust health apart from the tumor for which he was being treated, Elliot died some six hours after my children and I were told that his surgeon had successfully removed the malignancy. But to this day, no one from the hospital has explained to us how or why he died. And as Ruth Stone puts it about the mysterious death of *her* husband nearly a quarter of a century ago, "I am still at the same subject— / Shredding facts."

"Dad's had a heart attack." That was the explanation my husband's doctor offered us as he strode grimly into the hospital lobby on the night of February 11, 1991. But the next day the medical center released a different story, alleging that the cause of death was "heart failure." And two weeks later, a death certificate signed by the chief resident who worked with my husband's physician gave still another account, asserting that death resulted from "liver failure."

Through painful investigation—first with the help of a close friend who is a pathologist, then with the aid of an attorney—we discovered that my husband had suffered a massive post-operative internal hemorrhage. In fact, he evidently bled to death because someone in the recovery room failed to get the results of a hematocrit, a simple test that would have detected the problem.

Eventually, we filed suit for negligence—and our lawyer won a settlement just two days after he deposed the attending surgeon. Although, as in most settlements, the hospital admits no guilt, my husband had clearly been the victim of what researchers call a "negligent adverse event": an event defined by one writer on the subject as "an injury caused by the failure to meet standards reasonably expected of the average physician, other provider, or institution."

Eventually, too, I wrote a book entitled *Wrongful Death* along with a collection of poems entitled *Ghost Volcano,* each focusing in its own way on the painful story I've just told. In doing so, I understood that I was writing (recording) as well as seeking to right (to rectify) wrong, and now, as I retell the tale, I realize that "I am still at the same subject," still engaged in the same fearful and fierce activity: writing and seeking to right a terrible wrong.

That the effort to write (record) and right (rectify) wrong involves both fear and ferocity is at the heart of my argument here today, but in unfolding this line of thought I'll offer five linked propositions about the problems implicit in the very process of writing wrong, an activity that is, of course, as much a process of remembering, testifying, and reorganizing as it is of reiterating and striving to repair or *readjust.* As I'll try to show, such processes generate a range of fears and awaken a host of angers all of which must perhaps evoke in the would-be writer some kind of ferocity—ferocious defiance, fierce stubbornness—in order for her to persist in her efforts to transcribe and transform the wrong on which she meditates.

1. Perhaps most draconian: writing wrong is, or ultimately *becomes,* wrong—at the least problematic—because it's a hopeless effort at a performative act that can never, in fact, be truly performed. You can't, in other words, right wrong by writing wrong, even though you are engaged in the writing because consciously or unconsciously you believe that your testimony will reverse, repair, or undo the wrong you're reporting.

It may be significant, then, that I began writing *Wrongful Death* on July 23, 1991, precisely the day—five months after my husband's death—when my children and I had our first meeting with the attorney who represented us in the lawsuit we brought against the medical center where he died. Although I wasn't aware of feeling this, I must have secretly believed that in some sense the "performance" of the narrative my children and I had just outlined to our lawyer would somehow reverse or at the least revise or repair the script in which we were trapped. Did I feel that if I could *tell* the whole story, the "true" story, it might end differently, be replaced by another plot? Or did I suppose that if I got *that* story out of the way it might be replaced by another?

I certainly don't indulge in such speculations in the book itself. On the contrary, I offer a fairly conventional expository paragraph in which I introduce my plans to write the book that the reader is now reading: "that night . . . or more accurately, at three in the morning, when as usual I couldn't sleep—I went into the kitchen with a notebook, and began, weeping as I wrote, to try to write. Began to try to remember what happened to Elliot and me and the kids so people who get angry at supposedly greedy plaintiffs, and so maybe even doctors who self-righteously deplore the escalating costs of malpractice insurance, might understand the impact of medical negligence on one 'real-life' family" (239).

Earlier in the book, though, I wondered, speculatively, "Do I still believe that the lawsuit will, if only temporarily, resurrect my husband?" Did I, I'd now add, believe that by recounting the story of both the negligent, adverse event and the lawsuit to which it led I could subtly, furtively, change its ending? Such a sense of authorial potency may be akin to the feeling some people have (I'm one of them) when watching films of great catastrophes— the assassination of JFK, for instance—that if it were only possible to run the film backward or freeze a crucial frame, the inexorable plot of what-has-been might magically modulate into what-didn't-happen: the motorcade would take a different route, the grassy knoll would turn out to be just *grassy,* the rifle wouldn't fire, the young president and his pink-suited wife would return triumphantly to Washington the next day.

By the time I was ending the book, I have to admit, I was more moderate. "I know you, Mom," I report my son saying with a curious combination of weariness and trust. "You're going to write a book." "And my daughters agreed," I add. "Yes, I was going to write a book, and yes, that was what I should do. Because, sad as it is, there isn't and wasn't and never was anything else to do."

Nothing to do, I seem to be saying, but testify, bear witness, swear to the truth of this account I hereby proffer to you, the reader. A sentence later, though, I can see that I must have been thinking in some part of myself of something different. If I couldn't inscribe a spell that would heal, that would repair and resurrect, then I wanted to spell out words that would curse, that would blast, damn, and destroy those guilty of the crime that left my husband bleeding to death in the recovery room of a university medical center at this super high-tech end of the twentieth century. Thus, and with deep passion, I quoted Elizabeth Barrett Browning's scathingly ritualized diatribe against slavery "A Curse for a Nation": "Weep and write. / A curse from the depths of womanhood / Is very salt, and bitter, and good." Then, not insignificantly (as I'll try to explain), I withdrew from my own rage. "I didn't want to curse. I don't," I insisted in an open letter to all the doctors who seemed to me to be responsible for my husband's death. I just "want to *talk* to you. I want you to hear me. . . . And I guess this is the only way."

What did I have in mind, though, when I ended this meditation with the following sentence: "Says Barrett Browning, at the end of her poem, 'THIS is the curse. Write'" (341)?

2. Writing wrong is wrong, or at least problematic, because it's not only painful but *writing* pain—pain that, as I've just claimed, can't really be righted, healed, soothed, sedated. On the contrary, to write wrong is to tunnel into darkness, to drive oneself into the heart of fear, pain, rage. Barrett Browning's sentence to slave-holding America was also a sentencing *of* slave-holding America. "THIS is the curse. Write": consider the ambiguity of this phrase, which can surely be taken to imply that *the act of writing is itself a curse* inflicted as much on the accuser as on the accused, as much on the writer as on the target of the writing.

Of course, even to bring a lawsuit—that would-be performative motion of accusation always hurling itself toward the judicial words "I now *pronounce* this or that culprit guilty"—even to bring such a suit is to suffer the inscription of pain. You, the witness and accuser, do testify before the clerkly attorney-at-law who records your statements. "BE IT REMEMBERED," begins one of the depositions I quote in *Wrongful Death,* "that on Friday, the 27th day of December, 1991, at the hour of 1:23 P.M., of said day, at the Law Offices of Walkup, Shelby [et al.] before me, Julie A. Carroll, a Notary Public, personally appeared Sandra Gilbert, who was examined as a witness in said cause." The ancient formula has hardly changed: "Comes now before me so-and-so and *deposes*"—which is to say *puts down her word*—"and *says.*"

Maybe I shouldn't have been surprised, then, at the number of people who wondered how I could stand to bring a lawsuit (*how can you keep on reliving it again and again,* they said) and worse, how I could stand to write a book about such loss and grief—and such anger. How could I bear, they seemed to be asking, to bear witness over and over again, both before the law and on the page? How could I bear to see it again and to say it again?

My answer—always affirmed by my children—was always the same, both to questions about the lawsuit and about the book: we're bringing the suit because we have to, he'd want us to; I'm writing the book because I have to, he'd want me to. He'd want! How could we possibly know what or how he'd "want," a man so shockingly dead in what is called the "prime" of life? Yet we were haunted by the remorselessness of a subjunctive we ourselves—I in particular—created. And perhaps such a subjunctive was a way of keeping the dead one alive: "he'd want," after all, was only a grammatical step away from "he *wants.*" Somewhere, in another dimension, another shape, there he is, *wanting* you to go to this lawyer, write this book. Surely such visionary confidence helped us—*me,* anyway—to relieve the pain of reliving the pain.

At the same time, I was and am troubled by the no doubt well-meant comments of people who assume either the lawsuit or the writing were "cathartic," "therapeutic." Am I deceiving myself when I insist that in fact I undertook what I believed to be actions that would have consequences *outside* myself—and that I didn't believe I was doing this primarily *for* myself? To be sure, I understood that one always engages in acts one considers moral for the sake of one's own conscience as well as for the effect such actions will have on what Emerson called the "not-me." But even the concept "my own conscience" wouldn't really altogether define the *consciousness* I was trying, darkly, to assuage.

Yet what of the fear not just enacted but elicited by the writing of this wrong? I'd be dissembling, or at least deceiving myself and others, if I denied the pain that surrounded the very process of transcribing what I knew to have happened and, worse, *what I didn't know about what had happened.*

"That which you fear the most, that you must do." I said this sentence to myself over and over again, like a mantra, for several months in the spring of 1992. "That which you fear the most, that you must do." At this point, I was trying to imagine the contours of the story I have still never been told, the story of the moments at the heart of what I *have* told: the moments of my husband's death. In order to imagine something of that darkness I had to quell my fear of the hospital records I'd been given and struggle to reconstruct at least an approximation of the event. That which I feared the most, as I bleakly put it to myself, was what I had to confront; and I had to confront it precisely because in order to stand the pain of my loss I had to strive to stand *up* to the pain and loss, strive to *with*stand them by looking at them.

Of course I realized—and still realize—that this aspect of my procedure for grieving might be disconcerting, if not intensely disturbing, to those who wanted to shield themselves as well as me from suffering. We live in a culture where grief is frequently experienced as at the least an embarrassment; at memorial services for the dead, many would prefer to "celebrate" the completed life rather than lament the irreparable loss. In daily life, mourners are often greeted either by silence or by circumlocutions like "I hear you've had some troubles lately." All too often grief is seen as an illness or a disorder from which one "recovers," as from alcoholism. The surgeon who came to tell us of my husband's death was accompanied by a woman wearing a badge that said "Carolyn, Office of Decedent Services"; she carried a large folder labeled "Bereavement Packet." Lacking traditional religious strategies for solace, we're so dumbfounded by death that we'd rather leave the pain to professionals.

Thus I know that in the three years since *Wrongful Death* and *Ghost Volcano* were published I've probably embarrassed or distressed listeners at a number of readings from these books. To be frank, I myself am sometimes troubled by the words I have to say out loud when I tell the story that I tell. By the time I say the words I'm saying now, I suspect I'll have been through a kind of performance anxiety very different from the nervousness ordinarily associated with public speaking. Have I required too much—too much indulgence, too much sympathy—from my audience as I reiterated my script? In describing my writing of a wrong, as well as in the very act of writing this wrong, have I done something *socially* wrong—turned myself into a "loser," a "whiner," a "complainer"?

Without attributing such thoughts to those who are hearing me today, I can certainly testify that these judgments have been made by some readers. One, the well-known physician-author of bestselling books about medicine, praised the book privately but refused to make a public statement because he felt passionately that I was wrong to write the name of the real hospital where my husband died along with the name of the real surgeon who operated on him. And some people associated with that hospital have conveyed to me, via various colleagues, their view that I was somehow a "bad sport" [sic] to continue writing the wrong after their attorneys had settled our wrongful death suit.

Such remarks lead to proposition 3 about writing wrong: writing wrong may be wrong or at least problematic because you, the writer, might actually be the one who is wrong either in your perception of events or in your response to them. Perhaps people are embarrassed or distressed by your assertion that you've been wronged because you're asking them to judge the merits of a case they can't evaluate. Perhaps you, the writer, are a wrongdoer who has leveled your "*j'accuse*" against an innocent person. What if writing wrong is really a confession of guilt on the writer's part, in any case an evasion of responsibility?

Or, perhaps just as bad, what if writing wrong is an effort to exploit (and thus intensify) a wrong? This last notion, of course, is at the heart of public scorn for those so-called "ambulance-chasing lawyers" and greedy plaintiffs who are together held responsible for the escalating costs of malpractice insurance and thus (so some commentators would have it) the rising cost of medical care. But it's probably also at the center of the distaste some people seem to feel for so-called "confessional" poetry and indeed the disgust many express for any kind of tell-all memoir writing that can be characterized as sensational and hence exploitative.

Grace under pressure, we're taught, is "cool." Writing wrong, then, may be *un*cool as well as uncouth. "Revenge is *mine*," saith the Lord—not Job's or yours or any mere *writer's*. In the face of pain, one should be stoic, unflinching, *courteous*.

A few months after *Wrongful Death* appeared, my husband's surgeon was named director of a cancer research clinic at the medical center where he works, and I imagine that it was in connection with this promotion that he gave an extended interview to a local reporter, who produced an article that featured a prominent sidebar entitled "When a Patient Dies," recounting the doctor's comments on what was clearly my husband's case.

Here's what the reporter recorded.

> Dr. X [that's right, at the moment I'm feeling too anxious to spell out the man's name] recently lost a patient for the first time in his career. "How do you deal with it?" reflects Dr. X. "You're there to look after people. You practice the best medicine that you possibly can. I don't think there's anything else that you can do. If you're talking in an abstract way about how you deal with the fact you may be sued, you thank God that most of the people you treat, and their families, *are marvelous people*." (emphasis added)

There it is. "Marvelous people" don't sue. Marvelous people don't write wrong: they don't seek to rectify wrong nor do they try to record the wrong. Perhaps, indeed, because they are marvelous people *wrong does not befall them!*

My husband, a Victorianist, was always especially fond of the skewed logic manifested by the eponymous speaker of Robert Browning's "Childe Roland to the Dark Tower Came." Catching sight of a "stiff blind horse, his every bone a-stare," Browning's "Childe Roland" comments that the creature "must be wicked to deserve such pain."

How many woeful mourners, wailing grievers, sufferers of injustice or absurd mischance haven't at one time or another considered this possibility? *I think I have been wronged but I must be wicked to deserve such pain.* How write wrong, then—how inscribe pain—if the pain and wrong are themselves stigmata of *guilt?*

4. Writing wrong is wrong or anyway problematic because after all, as contemporary theory would tell us, if you can write it you've written it wrong.

This proposition, to be sure, can be applied to the writing of any memoir. Haven't I already confessed that what I feared the most was that I had to *imagine* (which is to say, I had in some sense to write *wrongly*) the for-me crucial moments of my husband's death, the moments whose truth I never had a chance to witness? "Art is a lie one tells in order to tell the truth," declared Picasso, who was, in fact, not just serene but seraphic about rearranging faces, bodies, curves and angles. But Defoe said—and his comment is darker, scarier—"Supplying a story by invention . . . is a sort of Lying that makes a great Hole in the Heart."

There's a hole in my heart where I had to supply the story of my husband's wrongful death by lying—that is, by imagining what I hadn't seen and thence by writing wrong.

And what of the "true"—supposedly real-life—episodes to which I declare I *have* borne witness? Have I transcribed them rightly or wrongly, wrong*fully?*

Even when and if I think I have gotten the story somehow *right,* surely it's wrong, surely I haven't said all there is to say. The story itself, as any memoirist knows but perhaps as the traumatized writers of wrong particularly know, continually recedes into an infinite, untellable distance. That's the point of "Something Deeper," the Ruth Stone poem I've offered as an epigraph here. And the something deeper, as Stone observes, seems always to have been there, like a question behind or beyond appearances:

I am still at the same subject—
Shredding facts—
As old women nervously
Pull apart
Whatever is put in their fingers;
Undoing all the years
Of mending, putting together;
Taking it apart now
In a stubborn reversal;
Tearing the milky curtain,
After something deeper
That did not occur
In all the time of making
And preparing. (*Second-Hand Coat* 85)

"Something deeper" always there but untellable: it isn't surprising that my sense of such a deeper, unreachable story gives me a feeling of affinity with other poets—rememberers and questioners—that's often powerfully confirmed. But maybe it's surprising, even in some bizarre way fortunate for me that others have corroborated the practical as well as theoretical conundrum proffered by my husband's death. Robert Pinsky's beautiful "Impossible To Tell" was in part written in memory of Elliot and includes the same kind of effort at writing the wrong of his unspeakable death that I myself have made both in prose and verse. Pinsky writes that often a joke he liked "was Elliot's," then, about a particular joke he'd heard at one point, he notes that "The doctors made the blunder / That killed him some time later that same year," adding, further on in the poem, that

It was a routine
Procedure. When it was finished the physicians
. . . .
Told Sandra and the kids it had succeeded,
But Elliot wouldn't wake up for maybe an hour,
They should go eat. . . .
. . . .
When she got back from dinner with their children
The doctors had to tell them about the mistake. (*Figured Wheel* 34, 36)

Yet still, admits Pinsky, though he has told this story, like so many other "true stories" it is ultimately "impossible to tell" because, yes, there's some other story one is always trying to tell in telling this tale or any other tale of wrong and woe.

5. Isn't that "other" story the story of storylessness, the story of death, loss, grief—the story we don't want to tell because we can't tell it? Writing wrong is wrong—difficult, problematic, painful, guilt-inducing, or all of these—because it is *writing death,* writing *the* absence that can't be written. In the center of his poem, Pinsky tells a joke about a dead man that he says my husband told to *him,* then bursts into the words hidden behind the joke, the protest behind the writing of any wrong:

> O mortal
> Powers and princes of earth, and you immortal
> Lords of the underground and afterlife,
> Jehovah, Raa, Bol-Morah, Hecate, Pluto,
> What has a brilliant living soul to do with
> Your harps and fires and boats, your bric-a-brac
> And troughs of smoking blood? Provincial stinkers,
> Our languages don't touch you.

Nor will our languages ever touch that wrong. Our languages, all of them, lie and leave a hole in the heart. I've been turning here, in my effort at a conclusion, to the words of others who've written wrong rather than to my own words, yet each passage on which I've meditated is in one way or another a good instance of the concept of testimony as it has been defined by Shoshana Felman and Dori Laub in their absorbing collection of essays on the subject, subtitled *Crises of Witnessing in Literature, Psychoanalysis, and History.* To the extent that it is an historical study, their book focuses primarily on the European Holocaust of World War II, but its theorizing of the relationship between trauma and acts of witnessing has considerable relevance for any theoretical overview of what I've described as "writing wrong." For in fact, as Felman defines testimony it is the fragmentary product of a mind "overwhelmed by occurrences that have not settled into understanding or remembrance . . . events in excess of our frames of reference" (5) not unlike those I've been reporting.

Holocaust survivors have obviously had to confront a trauma of such magnitude that it dwarfs almost any other, becoming in a sense a paradigm of collective as well as personal nightmare for the era in which we live. Yet anyone who has suffered the shock of what is experienced as a wrongful death has had to engage with what is impossible to tell yet somehow essential to speak, if only stammeringly. Sylvia Plath was another poet who repeatedly made such halting, breathless efforts at rendering an account of the unspeakable, especially as she struggled to define the grief for her father that had made a hole in the heart of her childhood. Toward the end of her cryptic "Little Fugue" she struggles to evoke the lost "daddy," even while confessing "I am lame in the memory": "I remember a blue eye, / A briefcase of tangerines. / This was a man, then!" she notes, and then adds:

> Death opened, like a black tree, blackly.
> I survive the while,
> Arranging my morning. (*Ariel* 72)

"I survive the while, / *Arranging my morning*": these two lines define what is perhaps the only thing that I'm sure is deeply right about writing wrong. Facing the inevitable chaos of loss, the continual undoing that opens "like a black tree" behind what Ruth Stone saw as the "milky curtain" of the quotidian, I have to join other artists in believing that the process of writing wrong is a special way of arranging not just the beginning of each of my days but my *mourning*—the untellable grief out of which I strive to bring some order, some meaning.

NOTES

An earlier version of this essay appeared in *a/b: Auto/Biography Studies* 14.1 (Summer 1999): 108–17. Reprinted by permission of the editors of *a/b: Auto/Biography Studies*.

WORKS CITED

Barrett Browning, Elizabeth. "A Curse for a Nation." *The Complete Works of Elizabeth Barrett Browning.* Vol. 3. New York: Thomas Y. Crowell, 1900.
Browning, Robert. "Childe Roland to the Dark Tower Came." *The Poetical Works of Robert Browning, 1833–64.* Oxford: Oxford University Press, 1970.
Felman, Shoshana, and Dori Laub. *Testimony: Crises of Witnessing in Literature, Psychoanalysis, and History.* New York: Routledge, 1992.
Gilbert, Sandra M. *Ghost Volcano: Poems.* New York: Norton, 1995.
———. *Wrongful Death: A Medical Tragedy.* New York: Norton, 1995.
Pinsky, Robert. *The Figured Wheel: New and Collected Poems, 1966–1996,* New York: Farrar, 1996.
Plath, Sylvia. *The Collected Poems.* Ed. Ted Hughes. New York: Harper, 1983.
Stone, Ruth. *Second-Hand Coat: Poems New and Selected.* Boston: Godine, 1987.

Contributors

Ross Chambers is the Marvin Felheim Distinguished University Professor of French and Comparative Literature at the University of Michigan, Ann Arbor. Under the working title of "Untimely Interventions," he is currently investigating the rhetorical character of testimonial writing.

Wendy Hui Kyong Chun is Assistant Professor of Digital Media in the Department of Modern Culture and Media at Brown University. She has studied both systems design engineering and English literature, which she combines and mutates in her research on and teaching in media theory. She is completing a manuscript on the crisis of disciplinary and regulatory power brought about by high-speed telecommunications networks, entitled "Sexuality in the Age of Fiber Optics," and is editing a collection of essays on the relationship between "old" and "new media," entitled "The Archaeology of Multi-Media Project." Her writings have appeared in *differences* and *New Formations,* among other places.

Laura Frost is Assistant Professor of English at Yale University, where she teaches twentieth-century British and comparative literature and gender studies. *Sex Drives: Fantasies of Fascism in Literary Modernism* (Cornell University Press, 2002) is her first book.

Sandra M. Gilbert, Professor of English at the University of California, Davis, is the author of six volumes of poetry, most recently *Kissing the Bread: New and Selected Poems, 1969–1999* (Norton, 2000), and a memoir, *Wrongful Death* (Norton, 1995). With Susan Gubar, she has coedited numerous books of literary criticism, including *The Madwoman in the Attic: The Woman Writer and the Nineteenth-Century Literary Imagination* and the three-volume *No Man's Land: The Place of the Woman Writer in the Twentieth Century* (Yale University Press). In addition, among other works, she has edited *Inventions of Farewell: A Book of Elegies* (Norton, 2001) and, with Gubar, coedited *The Norton Anthology of Literature by Women* (1996).

Susan Gubar is Distinguished Professor of English at Indiana University. Her most recent books are *Racechanges: White Skin, Black Face in American Culture* and *Critical Condition: Feminism at the Turn of the Century.* With Sandra M. Gilbert, Susan

Gubar has coauthored and coedited a number of books including *The Madwoman in the Attic,* the *Norton Anthology of Literature by Women,* and the three-volume *No Man's Land: The Place of the Woman Writer in the Twentieth Century.* She is currently at work on a manuscript entitled "Poetry after Auschwitz: Remember What One Never Knew."

Marianne Hirsch is Professor of French and Comparative Literature at Dartmouth College. Her recent books are *The Mother/Daughter Plot: Narrative, Psychoanalysis, Feminism* (1989) and *Family Frames: Photography, Narrative, and Postmemory* (1997). She is also the editor of *The Familial Gaze* (1998) and coeditor of *Conflicts in Feminism* (1991). She is currently writing a book with Leo Spitzer entitled "Czernowitz Album: Four Jewish Families and the Idea of a City before, during, and after the Holocaust."

Wayne Koestenbaum is the author of four books of prose, most recently *Cleavage: Essays on Sex, Stars, and Aesthetics* (Ballantine, 2000), and three books of poetry, most recently *The Milk of Inquiry* (Persea, 1999). His second book of prose, *The Queen's Throat: Opera, Homosexuality, and the Mystery of Desire,* nominated for a National Book Critics Circle Award in 1993, was reissued in 2001 by Da Capo Press. He is Professor of English at the CUNY Graduate Center.

Orly Lubin is Associate Professor in the Department of Poetics and Comparative Literature and the head of the Gender and Women's Studies Program at the School of the Humanities at Tel Aviv University. She publishes on feminist theories, theories of reading, and on feminist issues in literature, cinema, and visual culture. Her book *Women Reading Women* (in Hebrew) is forthcoming from Haifa University Press, and she is now working on a book on "Testimonial Autobiographies" in the context of nationalism and post-Zionist critique.

Nancy K. Miller is Distinguished Professor of English and Comparative Literature at the CUNY Graduate Center. Her books include *Subject to Change: Reading Feminist Writing; Getting Personal: Feminist Occasions and Other Autobiographical Acts;* and *Bequest and Betrayal: Memoirs of a Parent's Death.* She is the editor of *The Poetics of Gender.* Her book *But Enough about Me: Why We Read Other People's Lives* is forthcoming from Columbia University Press.

Jay Prosser is Lecturer in American Literature at the University of Leeds. He is author of *Second Skins: The Body Narratives of Transsexuality* (Columbia University Press, 1998).

Michael Rothberg is Associate Professor of English at the University of Illinois, Urbana-Champaign. He is the author of *Traumatic Realism: The Demands of Holo-*

caust Representation (University of Minnesota Press, 2000), as well as articles in journals such as *Cultural Critique, New German Critique,* and the *Yale Journal of Criticism.* He is currently working on the relationship between the postcolonial and the post-Holocaust.

Eve Kosofsky Sedgwick teaches in the Ph.D. program in English at CUNY Graduate Center. Her books include *Between Men: English Literature and Male Homosocial Desire; Epistemology of the Closet; Tendencies;* a book of poems, *Fat Art/Thin Art;* and a memoir, *A Dialogue on Love.* She is a contributing editor of *MAMM,* a magazine about "women, cancer, and community." Initially diagnosed in 1991, she has been living with metastatic breast cancer since 1996.

Jason Tougaw is Lecturer in the Writing Program at Princeton University. His writing has appeared in *a/b: Autobiography Studies; Journal of the History of Sexuality;* and *Journal of Medical Humanities.* He is currently completing a book entitled "Strange Cases: The Medical Case History and the British Novel."

Patricia Yaeger is a professor of English and Women's Studies at the University of Michigan. Her books include *Dirt and Desire: Reconstructing Southern Women's Writing, 1930–1990; The Geography of Identity* (ed.); *Nationalisms and Sexualities* (co-edited with Andrew Parker, Mary Russo, and Doris Sommer); and *Honey-Mad Women: Emancipatory Strategies in Women's Writing.*

Index

absence: of agency, 26–27; of documentation, 123–25; of mourning, 44–46; photograph's showing of, 241–42, 249; of real, 67; of witnesses, 114, 123–25; writing wrong as writing the, 269–70. *See also* death; loss

academics and academy: commodification of loss and, 46–49; Jones's death and, 29–33; status of griefwork in, 40; stories reproduced by, 28–29; textualization by, 43–45

Act Up (organization): Silence = Death metaphor, 166–74; speech act and, 167, 168

Adelson, Leslie, 68n. 4

Adorno, Theodor W., 36–37, 112

aesthetics: in creating identification, 86–87; empathic type of (feminist inflection), 9; ethics and, 15–17; in postmemory, 77–78

affect: community based in, 12; theory's flattening of, 41. *See also* emotions

After the Montreal Massacre (film), 153, 160–61

Agamben, Giorgio, 8, 11

agency: absence of, 26–27; in AIDS testimonials, 174; in daughters' transmission of trauma, 88–90; of dead, 31–32; female, 227; *Fragments* and, 99–101, 108; generational differences in, 82; in incest account, 215, 216–17, 220, 223–26; in jail hangings, 45–46; in literary conventions, 214; martyrdom and, 223; in massacre testimony, 154–56. *See also* individuals

AIDS community: exegesis of risk and, 172–73; writers as subjects in, 173–75; writing in construction of, 170–71, 175–83

AIDS testimonial writing/memoirs: ambivalence of, 176–77; asyndeton in, 11, 107–8; community of readers created through, 13–14; death foregrounded in, 180–83; discourse produced by, 168–69; extreme suffering and, 2; goals in, 169–70; instructional aspect of, 167–68, 177–78; subjectivity in, 170–75, 180–83; trauma exacerbated by, 175–77; types of, 166–67; "witness" literature as component of, 184n. 3

allegory: of death and survival, 109–10; difficulties with, 240–41; Warsaw Ghetto uprising as, 135

allo-identification, concept of, 76, 77, 80, 81, 86

Altman, Tossia, 131–32, 139

Alzheimer's disease, 198–99, 207

Amazon.com, 4

Améry, Jean, 68n. 9, 120, 200

anagnorisis, in reading, 108, 215

Anderson, Benedict, 46–47, 132

anthropology, 40–46; anthropography concept and, 41–42, 50n. 3. *See also* cultural studies

Apter, Emily, 182

Arenas, Reinaldo, 166, 167, 183

Arendt, Hannah, 8

Arias, Arturo, 141n. 6

asyndeton: concept of, 10–11; in *Fragments*, 103, 105, 107–8

atrocities: age of extremes and, 1; "reading" of, 41; thick descriptions of, 43–45. *See also* extremities; trauma

Au-delà du six décembre (film), 152–53, 154–55

audience: as community, 12–14; continuity supplied by, 107–8; disorientation of, 7; location of, 8; as secondary witness, 5–6; shame exposed to, 203–5; testimony adapted for, 133–40, 141n. 7. *See also* listening; readers; witnesses

Auerbach, Erich, 66

Auschwitz-Birkenau (concentration camp): children of survivors of, 75–76;

Schocken Books, 95
Schulman, Sarah, 169, 170
Searle, John, 183n. 1
secondary witness, audience as, 5–6
self: childhood vs. present, 206–7; constituted yet submerged, 135–40; illness
and, 180–83; true memory of, 203; writing for, 198–99
Seltzer, Mark, 68n. 8
sense memories: bodily experience of, 75–
76; language of, 72; visuality as figure
and vehicle for, 80–83
separation: phantom pain of, 101–5, 107–9;
as theme in Holocaust writing, 100, 110
Sexton, Anne, 117
sexuality: confession and, 224; in disjoint-
ed memories, 231–37; Ernaux's writings
on, 207–10; father-daughter incest and,
216, 224–26; identity constructed in,
206–7; women's writing on, 227. See also
gay men; gender
Shakespeare, William (Hamlet), 92
shame: identification through, 210; identity shaped by, 198–99, 206; personal and
private meanings of, 206; as relational,
203–5; sexual experiences and, 207;
writing without, 208–10. See also Shame
(Ernaux)
Shame (Ernaux): danger of writing, 210–11;
desire to break silence in, 15, 16; events
in, 197–98; on memory and shame, 5,
197–99, 203–4, 211n. 3; memory-work
in, 199–211; photographs in, 200–201,
206; strategies of, 202–3
Shnayerson, Michael, 222
Shoah (film), 6, 141n. 8
silence: breaking of, 2–3, 15–16; call for
(Montreal Massacre), 149–51; of dead,
39–40; as death, 166–74, 179–80; of Hunger Strike, 27–28; imposed on knowledge, 114; politics of listening to, 161;
publication vs., 215–17, 222; respect for,
80, 83; stakes of violating, 4, 14–15; textualization of, 45–46
Silverman, Kaja, 90n. 5, 90n. 7, 117
Simic, Charles, 114, 116–17
skin. See body; tattoos and marks
slavery: claiming mark of, 71–73; filling
space in memory of, 89–90; question
about, 49; women's lives in, 34
Sollers, Philippe, 207–8, 209
Sontag, Susan, 243, 248
Sophocles, 215–17, 220, 226

South Africa. See Biko, Steven
speech act: balanced with politics of lis-
tening, 161–63; difficulties of, 79; literary
implications of, 183n. 1; political intent
of, 167, 168; testimony as, 11; transfor-
mation via, 170–83
Spencer, Scott, 222
Spiegelman, Anja, 88
Spiegelman, Art, 3, 8, 87
Spiegelman, Vladek, 88
Spillers, Hortense, 34
Spitzer, Leo, 141n. 8
Spivak, Gayatri, 72, 77
Sri Lanka, nationalist violence in, 40–41,
47–48
Steiner, George, 112
Steingraber, Sandra, 191
Stevens, Wallace, 25
Stewart, Kathleen, 41–42
Stone, Ruth, 260, 267–68, 270
studium (connotation): Barthes's use of,
241, 243, 244–47; in images of transsexuality, 251
stutterance, concept of, 42, 46, 96
Styron, William, 95
subjectivity: in AIDS testimonials, 170–75,
180–83; postfeminism's construction of,
156–57
suffering: extreme, 2; fetishization of, 122;
Holocaust as exemplar of, 3–4, 19; marketing of, 2–3; martyrdom and, 223;
reduced to instrumentality, 115; specific
vs. universalized, 6; vicarious, 2
Suhrkamp (publisher), 95
suicides: Fragments and, 120–21; Plath's
poetry and, 119–20; writing about possible, 29–30, 31–33, 45–46
Suleiman, Susan Rubin, 10, 90n. 6, 245–46
surgery, photography compared to, 251–
52. See also cancer; transsexuality
survival: allegories of, 109–10; conditions
for, 101, 109; fostered type of, 100–101
survivor guilt: absence of exoneration for,
113; concept of, 98; narrative of absolv-
ing, 132; rejection of, 150
survivors: borrowing identity of, 92–93,
94–95; dilemmas of communicability
and, 58–60, 63–64, 98; others as witnesses for, 8–10; photographs of, 83–87. See
also cancer; generations; testimony;
victims
Switzerland, post-Holocaust unreality in,
93–94

violence: absence of prevention of, 155–56; assumptions of, 145–46; dehumanization of, 43–45; ethnography vs. pornography of, 41

violence against women: denial of, 154–56; feminist vs. postfeminist perspectives on, 152–57; linkages among events of, 158, 160–61, 163; patriarchalism's role in, 147–49; rape, 150–51, 200, 224; testimony and, 137. *See also* father-daughter incest; Montreal Massacre; *Shame* (Ernaux)

visual discourse of trauma: aesthetics in postmemory and, 77; concept of, 72–73; Kellner's use of, 78–83; nonappropriative kind of, 88–90; transmission of trauma and, 77–78; Wolin's use of, 83–87

Vogel, Miso, 86

Walker, Alice, 14–15
Wangrover, Yehuda, 139
The War After (Karpf), 75–76
Warhol, Andy, 60, 249–50
Warsaw Ghetto: Du Bois's trip to, 5; escape from, 83–84; fire in, 136, 139
Warsaw Ghetto uprising: as allegory, 135; memorials to, 131–32, 133; personal vs. collective testimonies on, 12–13, 132–40
Weir, John, 172
Whitman, Walt, 116
Wiesel, Elie, 112, 113
Wilkomirski, Binjamin: allegories of death and, 109–10; approach to, 92–93; ethical questions about, 9, 10; Ganzfried on, 120–21, hauntedness and, 93–94, 95, 103; impersonation of, 94–95; implausibilities of, 110n. 1; orphanages and, 100–101; orphaned memories and, 98–109; response to, 15–16, 95, 96–98
Williams, Patricia, 89–90
witnesses: absence of, 114, 123–25; AIDS testimony by, 184n. 3; artists as, 86–87; attaining consciousness of, 141n. 5; definition of, 149–52; poet as, 5–6; secondary type of, 5–6; to shame, 203–4.

See also audience; bearing witness; testimony
Wojnarowicz, David, 166, 167, 176–77, 183
Wolcott, James, 222
Wolin, Jeffrey: aesthetic strategies of, 86–87; feminist postmemory and, 88, 89; works: *Written in Memory*, 83–87
Women Workers' Council (Israel), 135, 136
World Trade Center catastrophe, 20
writing: as act of commodification, 48–49; as agent of relay, 101–3, 105–10; as alternative to silence, 166–74, 179–80; as anthropography, 41–43, 50n. 3; as bearing witness, 4; creating communities through, 13–14, 19, 170–71, 175–83; danger of, 210–11; as getting it all down, 169; as obligation to dead, 28–29; problems of thinking subject and, 36–37; proper/improper styles of, 30–33, 221–23; for self and others, 198–99; as ventriloquism, 45–46; without shame, 208–10; as written-in memory, 86–87. *See also* tattoos and marks
writing wrong: as arranging mourning, 270; concept of, 14–15; as having written it wrong, 267–68; as hopeless effort at performative act, 261–63; writer as wrong in, 266–67; as writing death, 269–70; as writing pain, 263–66
wrongful death: effects of, 262; expected response to, 266–67; explanations for, 260–61. *See also* writing wrong

Ya'ari, Mair, 131
Yeats, William Butler, 116
Yildiz, Yasemin, 68n. 9
Young, James, 87

Zionist cause: narratives in, 132–40, 140n. 2; Palestinian as other to, 139; parental interest in, 236; symbols in, 131–32; testimony focused on, 12–13
Zizek, Slavoj, 68n. 6, 68n. 10, 250
Z Magazine, 38–39
Zuckerman, Antek, 132, 139

The University of Illinois Press
is a founding member of the
Association of American University Presses.

University of Illinois Press
1325 South Oak Street
Champaign, IL 61820-6903
www.press.uillinois.edu